THE SOCIAL STRUCTURE
OF RIGHT AND WRONG

THE SOCIAL STRUCTURE
OF RIGHT AND WRONG

REVISED EDITION

Donald Black

University Professor of the Social Sciences
University of Virginia
Charlottesville, Virginia

ACADEMIC PRESS

San Diego   London   Boston   New York   Sydney   Tokyo   Toronto

Academic Press
An Imprint of Elsevier Science
525 B Street, Suite 1900, San Diego, California 92101-4495, USA
http://www.academicpress.com

Academic Press
Harcourt Place, 32 Jamestown Road, London NW1 7BY, UK
http://www.academicpress.com

Library of Congress Catalog Card Number: 97-80734

International Standard Book Number: 0-12-102803-8

PRINTED IN THE UNITED STATES OF AMERICA
02   03   04   05   06   PC   9   8   7   6   5   4   3

To
Malachi

Contents

1

Social Control as a Dependent Variable   1

2

Crime as Social Control   27

3

Compensation and the Social Structure of Misfortune 47

4

Social Control of the Self 65

5

The Elementary Forms of Conflict Management 74

6

Toward a Theory of the Third Party 95

with M. P. Baumgartner

7

Taking Sides 125

8

Making Enemies   **144**

Appendix:

A Strategy of Pure Sociology   **158**

Prologue
to the Revised Edition*

This volume introduces a new field of sociology and applies a new paradigm for the understanding of human behavior. The field is conflict, and the paradigm is pure sociology. Each deserves a few words of elaboration.

CONFLICT

Here conflict does not refer to a clash of interests, such as economic or political interests—its usual meaning in sociology (see, e.g., Dahrendorf 1959; Collins 1975). Instead it refers to a clash of right and wrong: a matter of morality. Justice. Conflict occurs whenever anyone provokes or expresses a grievance. It occurs whenever someone engages in conduct that someone else defines as deviant or whenever someone subjects someone else to social control. Conflict in this sense is ubiquitous. It is not merely crime and punishment. It is not merely disobedience, disagreement, or a demand for damages. It is not merely the topics covered in fields of social science such as criminology, the sociology of law, the anthropology of dispute settlement, conflict resolution, and mental health. It is vastly more.

The handling of conflict includes such diverse phenomena as aggression, avoidance, negotiation, reconciliation, restitution, retribution, gossip, apology, and confession (see "The Elementary Forms of Conflict Management" in the present volume). It includes crying and arguing, lying and conspiring, firing and quitting, helping and hindering, berating and beating, giving and taking, begging and stealing, cursing and praying. It may be unilateral (such as discipline in a school or workplace), bilateral (such as a feud or fight), or trilateral (such as adjudication or mediation). It may attract partisans—people who take sides —or it may not (see "Taking Sides" in the present volume; see also Cooney 1994). It may be moralistic or supportive (see "Making Enemies" in the present volume; Horwitz 1982). It may be direct or indirect, active or passive, overt or covert, explicit or implicit, immediate or deferred, discrete or continuous, individual or collective, human or supernatural. The handling of conflict, moreover, may itself be conflictful. Social control from one standpoint may be deviant behavior from another. Conflict begets conflict. It is endemic. Endless. The clash of right and wrong pervades the social universe and dominates history.

Even so, conflict is commonly unseen and unrecognized, shrouded in darkness. It is often mistaken for something else, misclassified and misunderstood by experts who know little about it. Why?

Conflict is not yet established as a separate field of sociology. Although pervasive, it is not recognized as a subject matter in its own right. It is scattered across diverse fields such as criminology, race and ethnic relations, international relations, labor and industrial relations, collective behavior, social movements, politics, organizations, stratification, the family, law, and religion. If studied at all, it is typically by experts unschooled in its behavior and unfamiliar with the larger family to which it belongs. Consider, for example, violence.

Violence is the use of force, such as the infliction of personal injury, the attempt to inflict personal injury, or the threat of personal injury. It thus embraces an extremely broad range of human behavior, from the spanking of a child to the beating of a wife, the burning of a witch, the assassination of a political leader, the lynching of a thief, blood vengeance, feuding, fighting, rioting, terrorism, torture, revolution, genocide, and war. It includes law as well—insofar as force is employed. It includes supernatural force, such as sorcery against an enemy, sickness inflicted by a witch or god, and suffering in the afterlife. It even includes self-inflicted force, such as fasting and suicide (see "Social Control of the Self" in the present volume). All these forms of violence normally occur in the name of justice, and they may themselves attract violence in the name of justice. Yet violence presently belongs to the jurisdiction of diverse fields and is studied by diverse specialists who do not recognize it as part of a single field: conflict.

Some violence is studied as crime by criminologists. This makes sense when violence accompanies predatory behavior such as robbery or rape. But most does not. Most homicide or assault, for example, is not predatory at all. It is social control: It defines and responds to conduct as deviant. It is moralistic. It is punishment. The one called the victim by the criminologist is called the offender by the killer or assailant. And vice versa (see "Crime as Social Control" in the present volume). Violent crime of this kind resembles law (such as criminal justice) more than other crime (such as theft or vice). What does moralistic homicide or assault share with shoplifting, prostitution, public nudity, or the sale of illegal drugs? Almost nothing. They are drastically different forms of human behavior. All they share is their legal status as crime. In short, the surest way to obscure the understanding of most violence is to call it crime.

Another example of social control is collective violence such as lynching, rioting, and terrorism (Senechal de la Roche 1996; see also Sciulli 1996). Lynchings are close relatives of legal trials and executions: In the typical case, someone is accused of a particular offense (such as a homicide or rape) before being punished (see Senechal de la Roche 1997). Rioting and terrorism normally express grievances as well, only now the liable party is collective (such as members of a race, religion, or nationality). Collective violence has nevertheless been studied primarily by specialists in collective behavior, politics, labor relations, and race and ethnic relations—as though it belongs only with subjects such as fads and fashions, voting behavior, economic competition, or racial inequality. And just as those subjected to personal violence are called victims by criminologists, so those subjected to collective violence are called victims by experts in collective behavior, political sociology, and race and ethnic relations—a practice again guaranteed to obscure socio-logical reality. The reality is that most collective violence is punishment. But it has fallen into the hands of experts who know little about punish-ment or any other form of social control. So has other violence: Family violence is the property of marriage and gender specialists, assassination and revolution the property of political specialists, vengeance and feud-ing the property of specialists in tribal and peasant societies, criminal punishment the property of legal specialists, supernatural punishment the property of religious specialists, suicide the property of mental health specialists, and so on. Most violence resembles law more than crime or other subjects studied by other fields. Most defends right against wrong, though others (including those subjected to it) may disagree, and though it may attract law or other social control (including more violence) as well. But where are the violence specialists who address all of this? And where are the conflict specialists who recognize that violence belongs to a larger family frequently not violent at all?

Consider another member of the family: avoidance. Avoidance is the curtailment of interaction. Reduction of contact. A parting of the ways. It may be the most unrecognized form of conflict in the social universe. It may also be the most common. Often it involves doing nothing—giving up and going elsewhere (see generally Hirschman 1970; Baumgartner 1988; Horwitz 1990:Chapter 6). It may be passive. It may be silent. It may be secret. It may even deny what it is: "No, I'm not avoiding you. I've just been very busy." But it may also be explicit and include a degree of violence. Avoidance thus appears in various forms on a continuum from the voluntary and covert to the coercive and overt: exit (voluntary departure), exclusion (denial of access), expulsion (denial of membership), and exile (isolation). When collective, it may become an exodus. When violent, it may become extermination. Avoidance constantly operates as an invisible hand in the moral market of right and wrong. Most is an inconspicuous feature of everyday life. But it may be fateful.

Avoidance includes separation of all kinds: running away, ostracism, divorce, desertion, termination, resignation, strikes, boycotts, banishment, excommunication, suspension, segregation, migration, restrictions on migration, incarceration, and secession. Although most is nonviolent, like violence much of it is moralistic. Social control. But its identity is often mistaken. Like violence, it belongs to diverse fields whose specialists do not recognize its kinship with conflict of other kinds. Running away belongs to the field of juvenile delinquency, for instance, divorce to family relations, strikes to labor and industrial relations, migration to demography, secession to politics. Here again the sociology of conflict must protest: Foreign fields dominate and mistreat its subject matter.

Now consider the field of race and ethnic relations. It constantly addresses the nature of interaction between groups, such as blacks and whites in American history or Jews and gentiles in European history. Conflict is central. Avoidance, for example, is extremely common and includes all the forms noted above: exit, exclusion, expulsion, and exile. Also common is collective liability, where accountability for an offense or misfortune lies in a social association rather than a person (see "Compensation and the Social Structure of Misfortune" in the present volume). Whereas modern crime entails individual liability (only the guilty party is punishable), for instance, feuding in tribal societies entails collective liability (any member of the killer's clan or family is punishable). A distinctive feature of racial and ethnic conflict is that it normally involves racial and ethnic liability: All members of a group are held accountable for any misconduct attributed to any of its members. Moreover, racial and ethnic conflict commonly entails avoidance and collective liability at once: collective avoidance. Grievances are directed at all members of the race or ethnicity, and all become subject to avoidance. Collective avoidance may include voluntary migration to another locality and voluntary segregation within a locality (collective exit), employment or housing discrimination (collective exclusion), involuntary migration to another locality (collective expulsion), and involuntary residential or educational segregation (collective exile)—all frequently seen in the history of blacks in the United States. Racial and ethnic violence also involves collective liability, illustrated by riots and terrorism where any member of a race or ethnicity may be subject to injury or death (see Senechal de la Roche 1996). And collective liability is not limited to minorities such as American blacks. American whites may experience collective liability as well: Blacks may express grievances or riot against all whites, for example, or they may avoid or seek compensation from all whites.

Just as relations between blacks and whites in American history have included both collective avoidance and collective violence, so have relations between Jews and gentiles in Europe and elsewhere (see, e.g., Langmuir 1990a, 1990b). The dispersion of the Jews (known as the Diaspora) over the centuries is a history of avoidance in all its forms: Jews were collectively expelled by the Romans and others from their ancient homeland in the Near East, for instance, exited west across Africa and north into Europe, and were again collectively expelled from England and southern Italy in the 13th century, France and most of Germany in the 14th century, and Spain and Portugal in the 15th century. Next came destinations such as Eastern Europe and the Turkish Empire, followed by migrations back to western Europe, and finally North and South America. Everywhere voluntary and involuntary exclusion between Jews and gentiles pervaded everyday life—residentially, occupationally, matrimonially, and otherwise. With collective avoidance came collective violence across much of Europe, including countless anti-Jewish riots, massacres during the Crusades and the Black Death (often blamed on the Jews), and extermination by the Germans in the 20th century. The sociology of conflict could hardly be more pertinent. How else will specialists in race and ethnic relations understand the various forms of collective avoidance and collective violence so often encountered in their field? Is not segregation a form of collective avoidance? Is not racism a form of collective liability?

Or consider the field of organizations. Every organization is a moral order where conflict is a frequent feature of everyday life. The management of organizations is largely the management of conflict. Here, too, various forms of avoidance are common, including exit (resignations and lesser reductions of contact), expulsion (terminations), and exile (transfers and reassignments). So are various forms of direct and indirect aggression, including discipline, the withholding of raises and promotions, vengeance, feuding, and various forms of conciliation and therapy such as mediation, negotiation, and counseling (see Morrill 1992, 1995; Tucker 1998). One manager throws a tantrum at a colleague, for instance; another waits for weeks, months, or even years to take revenge; still another just quits. Like clans in a tribe, factions form and fight, sometimes openly, sometimes secretly. Look into executive suites and you will find conspiracies and espionage, ambushes and sabotage, exclusion and expulsion. Look at employees at the bottom and you will find grievances against employers expressed with avoidance such as absenteeism, slowdowns, and strikes, and also covert aggression such as vandalism and theft (see Baumgartner 1984; Tucker 1989). Conflict is a major product of every organization. Yet organization specialists rarely recognize that so much of their subject matter is the clash of right and wrong. The same applies to other fields. Look at international relations, the community, the family, the professions, the playground—anywhere—and you will find conflict (see, e.g., Baumgartner 1988, 1992; Mullis 1995; Tucker and Ross 1998). Justice is not confined to courtrooms.

The colonization of conflict by diverse fields of sociology is understandable: Because clashes of right and wrong occur everywhere, specialists in every region of the social universe inevitably encounter conflict in the course of their work. Even so, they often do not recognize it. Seldom can they explain it. But this is changing. The many forms of conflict are escaping the foreign fields where they have long been isolated and neglected. They are beginning to unite as a new and independent field of sociology.

PURE SOCIOLOGY

This book is not merely a field guide for the identification and classification of conflict in social life. Nor is it merely a collection of theoretical formulations about conflict. It is not about conflict alone. It contains a new sociology that discards several features familiar in the sociology of the past. The reader should therefore note what is missing: the presence of several absences.

I have discarded all that makes sociology an unending debate about unresolvable questions and unobservable subjects. I have discarded all that makes sociology little more than ideology. I have discarded all that obstructs the development of sociology as a science. What remains is a new paradigm: pure sociology (see "A Strategy of Pure Sociology" in the present volume; see also Black 1995).

Absent, for example, is psychology. Sociology can have a distinctive role in the division of scientific labor: It can truly be the science of social life. It need not speculate about the contents of the human mind. You will therefore find nothing in this book about how people think or feel or see, nothing about subjectivity, nothing about attitudes, nothing about socialization, nothing about motivation, nothing about the meaning of anything to anyone (see Black 1995:848–850).

Absent, too, is teleology—the understanding of anything as a means to an end. Teleology is metaphysical: beyond the facts. Unobservable. It disappeared from sciences such as physics and astronomy centuries ago. But teleology still pervades sociology (see Black 1995:861–864). You will therefore find nothing in this book about the preferences or purposes of any person or any group of persons. You will find nothing about needs, functions, values, interests, or goals. You will find no assumptions, imputations, or inferences about the means or ends of anyone.

Even absent is the person. The centrality of the individual in sociology is a form of anthropocentrism, a presumption that people are the center of the social universe, a claim long dead in the sciences of the physical universe and biological universe. The centrality of the person is a human conceit. Social life is greater than any person and cannot be understood as the behavior of people themselves. I have therefore eliminated people entirely by reconceptualizing human behavior as the behavior of something else: social life. The formulations in this book pertain only to various forms of social life, entities in their own right, understandable with their own principles of behavior. We can predict and explain the behavior of law, for example, the behavior of music, the behavior of science, the behavior of God (see Black 1976, 1995:858–861).

But pure sociology is not merely pure. It is not merely the absence of various features found in the sociology of the past. It is not merely minimalism. Less is more: Pure sociology is more scientific than most sociology (see Black 1995:830–847). Its subject matter—social reality—is more readily observable than psychological or teleological reality. It is more predictive and testable. It is more general—applicable to a greater diversity of empirical variation across societies and situations. It is simpler. It is more powerful: It orders more facts. And it is new.

Social life inhabits a universe of its own: social space (see Black 1995:852–858). This space is created by human interaction itself. It is multidimensional, including vertical space (social stratification), horizontal space (social morphology), symbolic space (culture), corporate space (organization), and normative space (social control). It has various elevations (such as levels of wealth, conventionality, or authority), various directions (such as upward or downward from one elevation to another), and various distances (such as degrees of relational, cultural, or functional closeness). Every form of social life therefore has a multidimensional location and direction—higher or lower, upward or downward, closer or farther—in relation to everything else. Everything has a geometry. And the shape of social space in every setting—its social structure—predicts and explains the behavior of every form of social life. Some forms appear primarily at higher or lower elevations in social space, for instance, some reach upward to higher elevations or downward to lower elevations, some span considerable distances in social space, while some flourish only in small worlds where social distances are close.

The pure sociology of conflict illustrates the paradigm: Every conflict has a multidimensional location and direction in social space. A social structure. A geometry. And the social structure of each conflict predicts and explains what happens (see Black 1989): Will it attract law, violence, avoidance, or something else? How much will it attract? Will it attract vengeance, expulsion, conciliation, a riot, a prayer, sorcery, an apology, or only gossip? Will it attract partisans? Will liability be individual or collective? We can identify litigious structures and violent structures, for example, gossipy structures, therapeutic structures, vengeful structures, expulsive structures, and genocidal structures. These structures—particular locations and directions in social space—and not the people in them, predict and explain what happens. There are no litigious or violent or gossipy persons: No one is litigious or violent or gossipy in every setting all of the time. The person predicts and explains nothing. Neither does the society, community, or group: No society, community, or group is litigious or violent or gossipy in all of its settings all of the time. What matters is the particular structure of a particular conflict.

Social structures, large and small, predict and explain everything that happens in the social universe. We can identify supernatural structures and atheistic structures, authoritarian structures and democratic structures, selfish structures and altruistic structures, metaphysical structures and scientific structures, competitive structures, sexual structures, musical structures, and creative structures (see Black 1995:847–870). We can also identify social structures that predict and explain the behavior of sociology itself. New structures generate new sociology. This book is thus a kind of sociological behavior with a social structure of its own. In this sense, the author is more than a person. The author is a multidimensional location in social space—a social structure. The person has disappeared. All that remains is pure sociology.

ENDNOTE

*I thank M. P. Baumgartner and Roberta Senechal de la Roche for commenting on the Prologue and the latter more generally for assistance on the Revised Edition.

REFERENCES

Baumgartner, M. P.
>   1984   "Social control from below." Pages 303–345 in *Toward a General Theory of Social Control*, Volume 1: *Fundamentals*, edited by Donald Black. Orlando: Academic Press.
>   1988   *The Moral Order of a Suburb*. New York: Oxford University Press.
>   1992   "War and peace in early childhood." Pages 1–38 in *Virginia Review of Sociology*, Volume 1: *Law and Conflict Management*, edited by James Tucker. Greenwich: JAI Press.

Black, Donald
>   1976   *The Behavior of Law*. New York: Academic Press.
>   1989   *Sociological Justice*. New York: Oxford University Press.
>   1995   "The epistemology of pure sociology." *Law & Social Inquiry* 20:829–870.

Collins, Randall
>   1975   *Conflict Sociology: Toward an Explanatory Science*. New York: Academic Press.

Cooney, Mark
>   1994   "Evidence as partisanship." *Law and Society Review* 28:833–858.

Dahrendorf, Ralf
>   1959   *Class and Class Conflict in Industrial Society*. Stanford: Stanford University Press (revised edition; first edition, 1957).

Hirschman, Albert O.
>   1970   *Exit, Voice, and Loyalty: Responses to Decline in Firms, Organizations, and States*. Cambridge: Harvard University Press.

Horwitz, Allan V.
>   1982   *The Social Control of Mental Illness*. New York: Academic Press.
>   1990   *The Logic of Social Control*. New York: Plenum Press.

Langmuir, Gavin I.
>   1990a   *History, Religion, and Antisemitism*. Berkeley: University of California Press.
>   1990b   *Toward a Definition of Antisemitism*. Berkeley: University of California Press.

Morrill, Calvin
>   1992   "Vengeance among executives." Pages 51-72 in *Virginia Review of Sociology*,

Volume 1: *Law and Conflict Management*, edited by James Tucker. Greenwich: JAI Press.

1995 . *The Executive Way: Conflict Management in Corporations*. Chicago: University of Chicago Press.

Mullis, Jeffery

1995 "Medical malpractice, social structure, and social control." *Sociological Forum* 10:135–163.

Sciulli, David

1996 "Courage and care in Blackian social theory: a word in praise of Senechal de la Roche." *Sociological Forum* 11:129–133 (comment on Senechal de la Roche 1996).

Senechal de la Roche, Roberta

1996 "Collective violence as social control." *Sociological Forum* 11:97–128.

1997 "The sociogenesis of lynching." Pages 48–76 in *Under Sentence of Death: Lynching in the South*, edited by W. Fitzhugh Brundage. Chapel Hill: University of North Carolina Press.

Tucker, James

1989 "Employee theft as social control." *Deviant Behavior* 10:319–334.

1998 *The Therapeutic Corporation*. New York: Oxford University Press.

Tucker, James, and Susan Ross

1998 "Corporal punishment and Black's theory of social control." Forthcoming in *Corporal Punishment in Theoretical Perspective*, edited by Michael J. Donnelly and Murray A. Strauss. New Haven: Yale University Press.

Preface

The handling of right and wrong, known in sociology as *social control* or *conflict management*, occurs throughout the social universe, wherever people intermingle. It includes phenomena as diverse as litigation, violence, mediation, gossip, ostracism, psychotherapy, sorcery, sabotage, and suicide. It occurs unilaterally (by one party against another), bilaterally (between two parties), and trilaterally (by a third party). It involves groups as well as individuals — lynching and rioting as well as fist-fighting and wife-beating — and covers everything from a glance of disapproval to the bombing of a city. This volume contains formulations that predict and explain the nature of social control anywhere and everywhere, throughout the world and across history.

The application of morality varies with the social structure of each conflict: Who has a grievance against whom? Who else participates? What is their location in social space — their degree of intimacy, wealth, organization, interdependence, and homogeneity? Is the social direction of the grievance downward (against an inferior), upward (against a superior), or lateral (against an equal)? Such variables predict and explain the handling of every case: who wins and loses (if anyone) and what happens thereafter (if anything). In this sense, we can specify the structural relativity of right and wrong.

The theoretical strategy pursued here has several characteristics that may be unfamiliar to some readers. First, it is radically sociological. It pertains to social reality alone. It neither assumes nor implies anything about the psychology of anyone, the subjective meanings of anything, or even the behavior of individuals as such. It specifies only how one variable feature of social life generates another, how, in particular, the social location and direction of a conflict predict and explain its fate. Social space is a universe unto itself, populated by entities conceptually distinct from people in the ordinary sense and subject to understanding in its own terms. (For further details, see the Appendix, "A Strategy of Pure Sociology.")

The strategy also favors formulations applicable to the widest range of facts possible—to human conflict everywhere it arises, across societies and communities, from one relationship to another. Such formulations specify how the social structure of conflict determines the way it is handled, regardless of the unique circumstances of its occurrence, such as its cultural or historical setting or the blend of personalities involved. Formulations of this kind illustrate the character and scope of general theory in sociology.

Finally, the strategy is uncompromisingly scientific. It conforms to a conventional philosophy of science sometimes viewed as inappropriate to the study of human beings. It seeks to develop a body of theory not only radically sociological and maximally general but also entirely free of value judgment and falsifiable in the face of the facts. Every formulation is quantitative in language, predictive in content, and testable by simple procedures of observation and measurement (i.e., by counting something). Every formulation is a model of social reality.

The first chapter, "Social Control as a Dependent Variable," introduces the sociological study of moral phenomena, including the origins, mission, and theoretical logic of this field. It begins with the observation that law (governmental social control) is a comparatively small part of this subject matter, less significant in everyday conflict than might be supposed. Even so, the theoretical strategy originally applied to law in my earlier book—*The Behavior of Law* (Academic Press, 1976)—readily extends to social control of every sort. Chapter 1 also introduces several variable aspects of social control: its form (unilateral, bilateral, trilateral), its style (penal, compensatory, therapeutic, conciliatory), and its quantity (amount applied).

The second chapter, "Crime as Social Control," suggests that much conduct regarded as criminal in modern societies is moralistic: It involves the handling of a grievance by unilateral aggression—self-help—a primary mode of social control in many societies of the past (such as tribal and peasant societies). Most homicides and assaults, for example, are cases of self-help. Criminal behavior of this kind belongs to the same family—social control—as law itself. This view implies an understanding of crime that departs considerably from traditional criminology.

The third chapter, "Compensation and the Social Structure of Misfortune," identifies structural conditions associated with the compensatory style of social control, whereby a grievance is handled by a payment to the aggrieved, and also the conditions associated with differing degrees of liability, whether relative, strict, or absolute. The so-called litigation explosion in modern society partly reflects a proliferation of these conditions. Organizations are more vulnerable than individuals to claims for compensation, for example, and to broader standards of liability. Hence, the growing population of organizations and the growing dependency of individuals on them partly explains why organizations such as business corporations and government agencies are increasingly subject to lawsuits by aggrieved individuals.

Chapter 4, "Social Control of the Self," explores the use of social control by individuals against themselves and proposes that it obeys the same principles as social control in general. Individuals may submit themselves to their victims or to third parties such as parents, priests, or psychotherapists. They may also punish themselves (including self-execution). In legal cases, they may plead guilty — a self-application of law — according to the same principles that predict and explain the application of law by complainants, police, judges, or anyone else.

Chapter 5, "The Elementary Forms of Conflict Management," identifies five modes of handling grievances — self-help, avoidance, negotiation, settlement, and toleration — and illustrates the diverse phenomena they embrace. Each arises in a social field with its own peculiarities. For example, self-help (by vengeance) is most extreme in stable agglomerations of equal but socially distant groups, whereas avoidance is most extreme in unstable aggregations of independent individuals with fragmented relationships. Social fields such as these may prove to be elementary forms of social life itself.

Chapter 6, "Toward a Theory of the Third Party" (co-authored with M. P. Baumgartner), classifies third parties (those who participate in the conflicts of others) according to the nature of their intervention. It presents a typology of twelve roles, including partisans (such as advisers and advocates), settlement agents (such as mediators and judges), negotiators (who combine partisan and settlement behavior), and healers (who handle conflict without defining it as such). In addition, the chapter offers formulations that predict and explain the behavior of third parties according to their social location.

The volume concludes with Chapters 7 and 8, a complementary pair of essays that examine the structural relativity of partisanship and moralism (extending the theory of the third party introduced in Chapter 6). Chapter 7, "Taking Sides," proposes a principle of social gravitation and outlines its impact on partisan behavior in various settings. This chapter also out-lines the evolution of partisanship from its earliest days as an expression of primordial intimacy to its modern incarnation as a commodity in the marketplace and a service of the state. Chapter 8, "Making Enemies," proposes a principle of social repulsion to predict and explain moralistic behavior, the opposite of partisanship. It focuses primarily on third-party moralism, expressed by formalism (an emphasis on rules), decisiveness (winner takes all), coerciveness (the use of force), and punitiveness (pain or deprivation as a remedy). Unilateral moralism by one party against another is discussed as well. The chapter closes by noting that modern society is losing the structural conditions most conducive to the production of enemies.

Because it is completely factual in orientation, this book neither ad-vances a moral argument nor logically implies anything of a moral nature. Even so, the structural relativity of right and wrong — the major theme — may have a human significance worthy of further contemplation.

The empirical evidence indicates that a universal morality, indifferent to the social structure of individual cases, nowhere exists in human society, never has, and never will. Any claim of universality in the application of morality is sociologically naive if not meaningless. Nonetheless, an unso-ciological program of this kind — morality in a social vacuum — is advanced by nearly everyone, including philosophers, theologians, and jurisprudes.

But should we now conclude that moral universalism is obsolete? Are we entering a new stage of moral evolution when right and wrong are explicitly defined partly by particular locations and directions in social space — among intimates, strangers, organizations, nations, against supe-riors and inferiors? Or is a relativistic morality a contradiction in terms and the death of morality itself? The answer is not self-evident. And precisely how the structural relativity of morality and moral universalism should be reconciled, if at all, is unanswerable by science alone.

Acknowledgments

Most of these essays appeared in earlier publications cited in the text. All benefited from funding awarded by the National Science Foundation's Program in Law and Social Science and by the National Institute of Law Enforcement and Criminal Justice. All were written in the past decade at Harvard Law School's Center for Criminal Justice and the University of Virginia's Department of Sociology. I thank everyone involved — institutions and individuals — for their support.

I also thank the colleagues and students who have worked closely with me over the years, always providing encouragement, stimulation, and diverse forms of assistance. Without them, my ideas and writings would undoubtedly be inferior to those that have resulted. Among the most important have been M. P. Baumgartner, Mark Cooney, John Griffiths, John Herrmann, Allan V. Horwitz, Candace Kruttschnitt, Maureen Mileski, Calvin Morrill, Jeffery Mullis, Frank Romo, Roberta Senechal de la Roche, and James Tucker. M. P. Baumgartner contributed especially greatly to the evolution of my work and co-authored Chapter 6 ("Toward a Theory of the Third Party"). Roberta Senechal de la Roche contributed especially greatly to Chapters 7 and 8 ("Taking Sides" and "Making Enemies") and to the planning and preparation of this volume. Others are acknowledged at the beginning of each chapter.

In addition, I take this opportunity to thank Albert J. Reiss, Jr., whose lectures at the University of Michigan long ago inspired my pursuit of pure sociology and whose invitation to study the police provided my first scientific experience with the subject of this book. Afterward, at Yale Law

School, Stanton Wheeler offered support and colleagueship during a crucial period of my development. Finally, I am grateful to Joan Snapp for typing countless drafts, J. Scott Bentley, Nikki Fine, Cynthia Fulton, Jacqueline Garrett, Barbara Heiman, and Michael Remener for editorial and other help, and Academic Press for their longstanding willingness to publish my work.

1

SOCIAL CONTROL AS A
DEPENDENT VARIABLE*

This chapter introduces the general theory of social control.[1] Little theory of this kind presently exists, and the time has come to announce its appearance, plan its future, and encourage its growth. The following pages advance a concept of social control, survey its variable nature, offer formulations that predict and explain aspects of social control from one setting to another, and suggest how we might construct models applicable across particular cases of human conflict as well as larger social formations such as communities and societies. But first we note how recent developments in social science have stimulated our project.

BEYOND LAW

Despite a flurry of attention during the early years of social science (e.g., Durkheim 1893; Ross 1901; Weber 1925; Malinowski 1926), the phenomenon of social control was largely neglected until the second half of the twentieth century; even then, scholarly work concentrated on a single category of this broader class: law. An emphasis on law — governmental social control (Black 1972:1096) — has been particularly characteristic of sociologists, political scientists, and lawyers, most of whom have further narrowed their concerns to legal life in modern societies such as the United

States. This work has resulted in a sizable body of information about diverse aspects of social control through law, especially criminal justice but also such processes as the operation of regulatory agencies, the distribution of legal services, civil litigation, and adjudication (see, e.g., the materials collected in Aubert 1969; Black and Mileski 1973; Sanders and Daudistel 1976; Friedman and Macaulay 1977; see also Vago 1981). Anthropologists have similarly concentrated on what they regard as law — typically the most formal and dramatic aspects of social control in tribal and other simple societies — although this often includes nongovernmental as well as governmental processes (for overviews and collections see, e.g., Hoebel 1954; Nader 1965; Bohannan 1967; Nader and Todd 1978; Roberts 1979). In fact, much of legal anthropology pertains to stateless societies where law, by definition, cannot exist (e.g., Barton 1919; Llewellyn and Hoebel 1941; Gulliver 1963; Koch 1974).[2] In recent years, historians have also turned increasingly to the study of legal life, particularly criminal justice in early Europe (e.g., Macfarlane 1970; Samaha 1974; Hay, Linebaugh, Rule, Thompson, and Winslow 1975; but see also Baumgartner 1978; Abel 1979; Reid 1980; Kagan 1981; Snyder 1981).

Leaving aside the question of why law has dominated the study of social control (terminologically[3] and otherwise), we can at least appreciate that knowledge about how people define and respond to deviant behavior has grown considerably. Moreover, the many facts that have accumulated provide a substantial foundation for theoretical development: How does law vary across social space? When does it come into play, how, against whom, and with what consequences? What predicts and explains who is arrested by the police? Who brings lawsuits? Who wins? A number of formulations addressing questions of this sort have already appeared, following as well as stimulating research about how law behaves as a natural phenomenon (see Black 1976). At the same time, it has increasingly come to be recognized that law is but one among many kinds of social control.

The more we study law, indeed, the more we realize how little people actually use it to handle their conflicts (see, e.g., Kawashima 1963; Macaulay 1963; Biderman 1967; Curran 1977:Chapter 4; Baumgartner 1985). And as we discover the radically uneven pattern by which it appears across the social landscape — every society has settings where law is virtually never used — we wonder precisely what is the range of mechanisms to which people resort when they have grievances against one another. What, beyond law, constitutes the larger universe of social control? How is it situated in social space? To be more specific: It is now abundantly clear, for example, that people of lower status, such as the poor and the disreputable, rarely use law against their social superiors (see Black 1976:Chapters 2–6). Some of those at the very bottom of society, such as slaves and children, are generally not permitted to use law at all, whereas some of the highest, such as feudal lords and monarchs, are practically immune to it. How, then, do people of lower status express grievances against those above them? It happens that "social control from below" is not nearly so uncommon as might be supposed and is in its own way as orderly as law itself (Baumgartner 1984a). People at the bottom also use relatively little law among themselves, but this does not mean that they do not express grievances against one another. Far from it. A significant part of their social control, however, especially that which is violent, is regarded as crime by the authorities (see Black 1983).

Besides social status, another condition associated with the distribution of law is intimacy: People who are very close, such as blood relatives and married couples, use comparatively little law against one another[4]; the same applies to those at the opposite extreme, separated by the greatest distances in social space, such as those from different tribes or nations (Black 1976:40–46). But, again, a scarcity of law does not necessarily indicate that social control in general is unavailable. Intimates such as members of the same family typically have numerous means by which to express grievances against one another, including direct criticism, ridicule, ostracism, deprivation, resort to third parties (e.g., another relative, a friend, or a psychotherapist), desertion, self-destruction,[5] and violence. In the case of total strangers such as people from alien tribes or nations, the variety of social control is not so lush, but its scale and severity may be enormous. An invasion of one society by another, for instance, often expresses a grievance, and warfare invariably does. In any event, the limited conditions under which legal life appears and flourishes raise new questions about what people do when they are uninclined or unable to have recourse to law. The scientific study of legal life thus leads naturally to other species of social control, to normative life in general, to all that expresses how people ought to behave.[6] Moreover, scholarship on the social nature of law has produced a rich endowment of intellectual resources readily applicable to other processes involving right and wrong — in and between families, organizations, or nations, and among friends, colleagues, neighbors, or strangers. A program of theory and research embracing all of this at once, including law, is now feasible.

THE CONCEPT OF SOCIAL CONTROL

First advanced at the turn of the twentieth century by Edward Alsworth Ross (1901), the concept of social control has long been associated with the normative aspect of social life. In one usage, which dominated the earlier literature, social control refers broadly to virtually all of the human practices and arrangements that contribute to social order and, in particular, that influence people to conform (see, e.g., Ross 1901; Park and Burgess 1921:Chapter 10; Mannheim 1940:274–311; Hollingshead 1941; La Piere 1954; Cohen 1966:39; for an overview of this conception, see Gibbs 1981:Chapter 3). These practices may be intentional, as when someone is punished to deter others from similar misconduct, or unintentional, as when parents unconsciously implant habits of behavior in their children. In a second and more recent usage, which is followed throughout this chapter, social control refers more narrowly to how people define and respond to deviant behavior (Black 1976:105; see also Clark and Gibbs 1965).[7] It thus includes punishment of every kind — such as the destruction or seizure of property, banishment, humiliation, beating, and execution — as well as a demand for compensation by an aggrieved person or group, an accusation or application of sorcery, gossip, scolding, or merely a facial expression of disapproval such as a scowl or stare. It also includes various modes of intervention by third parties, such as mediation, arbitration, and adjudication. In this sense, social control is present whenever and wherever people express grievances against their fellows.[8]

When social control is understood as a kind of influence, the central problem in its study is the degree to which it has an impact on human conduct. How much does each means of social control contribute to social order? How effective is each? What are the consequences of each? To what extent, for example, does punishment deter deviant behavior? Scientifically speaking, in this earlier and broader view social control is approached as an independent variable. It predicts and explains something else: how people behave. When conceived more narrowly as a reaction to deviant behavior, however, social control invites analysis as a dependent variable.[9] From this point of view, every manifestation of social control itself requires study. Why, for example, does punishment occur at all? Why is one person punished more severely than another? Under what conditions might a wrongdoer be asked to pay compensation to the aggrieved party, to enter psychotherapy, or to just go away? Why does a third party intervene in one conflict but not another? When are rules invoked? When does law occur? Vengeance? Gossip? Now the question of the extent to which these phenomena influence human behavior is left aside, and the impact of each on conformity and social order is ignored. But this is not because it is claimed that social control has no influence or impact. Nor is it because the consequences of social control are uninteresting or unworthy of study. Rather, it is simply because a different question is being asked: What predicts and explains social control itself? This question acknowledges that social control is a thing in its own right, variable in its own way, and worthy of study for its own sake. Furthermore, precisely how it varies in social space is the central problem of a general theory of social control.[10]

VARIETIES OF NORMATIVE BEHAVIOR

Across societies and history, and from one conflict to another, the phenomenon of social control appears in many different structures, levels of complexity, and magnitudes. Leaving aside for now how such diversity might be understood, this section briefly outlines several kinds of variation that a general theory of social control might address.

Form

A form of social control is a mechanism by which a person or group expresses a grievance. It is a mode of conducting normative business, such as a court of law, a face-to-face discussion, a public protest, or an act of violence. It might involve a small number of people, each with a specialized role, as in a judicial process; large numbers with similar roles, as in a war or a lynching; or simply a lone individual showing displeasure toward another. It might occur without the knowledge of the offending party, as in gossip, or it might have other elements of secrecy, as in anonymous complaints. It might entail many stages or episodes spaced over time, so that the pursuit of a grievance requires weeks, months, years, or even lifetimes of commitment; or it might begin and end literally in a matter of seconds with an angry glare, rebuke, or other situational display. The forms of social control thus vary enormously, and an exhaustive classification of all that have been observed would be a challenge in itself.

For present purposes, suffice it to say that the forms of social control divide into two major categories: those involving only the principals (with or without the help of supporters) and those involving also a third side who relates to the conflict as an agent of settlement.[11] In the former category, social control may be unilateral, flowing in a single direction from the aggrieved to the offending party (as when a parent scolds a child or a citizen assassinates a government official), or it may be bilateral, flowing in both directions at once (as in a duel, fight, or feud) where each side pursues a grievance against the other (called "negative reciprocation" by Warner 1958:162; compare Sahlins 1965:148–149). In the latter category, social control is trilateral, entailing the intervention of a settlement agent who relates authoritatively to both sides, even if ultimately a preference is expressed for one or the other. Examples are peacemakers, mediators, and judges. Considering all these possibilities, we may speak of a theory of self-help that addresses the conditions under which people aggressively pursue their own grievances, such as by unilaterally admonishing or injuring their antagonists or by entering bilaterally into a verbal or physical fight (see Black 1983), and a theory of avoidance that addresses the conditions under which people simply withdraw — whether unilaterally or bilaterally — when conflict erupts (see Homans 1950:308; Fürer-Haimendorf 1967:22; Felstiner 1974; Baumgartner 1984b, 1988:Chapter 3). We may also speak of a theory of support that specificies when and how third parties relate to conflict as partisans and a theory of settlement that specifies when and how they become involved as nonpartisans (see generally Black and Baumgartner 1983). Each form of social control is worthy of study in its own right and worthy of its own theory.

Style

Another variable aspect of social control is its style, or the language and logic by which it defines and responds to deviant behavior. Four styles have been identified: penal, compensatory, therapeutic, and conciliatory (Black 1976:4–6; see also Horwitz 1982:122–127). In modern societies, for example, the penal style is seen in criminal law, the compensatory style in tort and contract law, the therapeutic style in juvenile justice and psychiatric care, and the conciliatory style in the negotiation, mediation, and arbitration of marital, labor–management, and international disputes. Each style has its own standards, questions, and solutions. Thus, each attributes a different identity to the person or group who enters its jurisdiction. Whereas in the penal style the deviant is regarded as an offender who has violated a prohibition and who should therefore suffer pain, deprivation, or humiliation, in the compensatory style the party in jeopardy becomes a debtor and is liable for damages resulting from a failure to fulfill an obligation. In the therapeutic style, the deviant is understood as a victim who needs help and, in the conciliatory style, as a disputant in a conflict that needs to be settled.

Each style also involves a different focus. When the penal style is applied, the point of reference is the conduct itself, typically a particular act. Punishment may be justified as a means of discouraging similar conduct by the offender or by others (designated, respectively, as "specific deterrence" and "general deterrence" by Andenaes 1966), or it may be levied for its own sake as vengeance. In the compensatory style, the focus is not so much the conduct as its consequences, and because identical acts may have different consequences, they may require different amounts of compensation. The same act might result in a death in one case but a lesser injury in another, for example, and one death might deprive a family of its primary source of support, whereas another might have little economic impact. When damages are assessed, differences such as these are likely to be taken into account.[12] The therapeutic style has still another focus: the person.[13] A course of treatment depends on the particular nature of the deviant's condition, not the conduct associated with it or the consequences that result from it. In fact, the deviant is not viewed as responsible for what happened: The conduct was not chosen; it could not be avoided. When the person has been helped back to normality, the conduct and its consequences will disappear. Finally, the conciliatory style of social control shifts the focus to the relationship between the parties involved. An effort is made not to become exclusively preoccupied with any one person's or group's conduct, its consequences, or any one of the individuals or groups embroiled in the dispute. A relationship has been disturbed and needs attention: A resolution of the conflict must be found; social harmony must be restored.

Virtually any kind of deviant behavior may be handled with any of the four styles of social control. Moreover, in cross-cultural and historical perspective, there has been enormous variation in when and how each is applied. Consider, for example, the handling of homicide. In modern societies, we tend to assume that an intentional homicide committed with malice is a crime that should be punished, but over the centuries in many simpler societies compensation of the victim's family has been a common response to the same behavior (see, e.g., Pollock and Maitland 1898:Volume 1, 47–48; Evans-Pritchard 1940:150–176; Jones 1974:66–69). In other cases, homicide may be regarded therapeutically as the symptomatic behavior of someone possessed by a supernatural spirit or disabled by a mental illness (see, e.g., Middleton 1965:51; Peters 1967:272); in still others, it may be taken primarily as an aspect of a conflict in need of resolution, possibly by a ritual of forgiveness or other gesture of reconciliation (see, e.g., Hasluck 1954:Chapter 25; Barth 1959:96–98; van den Steenhoven 1962:82).[14]

Each style of social control occurs in a wide range of settings, from the most formal and legalistic to the most informal and casual. Violent self-help (which may extend to homicide) is penal in style, for example, as is the modern system of criminal justice. So is banishment. So are most forms of social control in hierarchical relationships, whether directed against people of lower status by their social superiors (beatings by husbands and parents, evictions by landlords, dismissals by employers) or against people of higher status by those below (rebellion and retaliation by slaves, servants, and other underlings; Baumgartner 1984a). Compensation also occurs in a variety of settings. It is commonly found as a remedy in modern courts of law, for example, but it is sometimes even more developed in simple societies that have no legal institutions of any kind, particularly herding societies, where cattle, camels, or other livestock serve as a standard of value for reckoning damages (see, e.g., Evans-Pritchard 1940:150–176; Howell 1954; Lewis 1959; Goldschmidt 1967:100–106).[15] The therapeutic style is practiced by modern professionals such as psychiatrists, psychologists, and social workers, but it also occurs as a response to spirit possession, "soul loss," and witchcraft in many tribal societies; ideological deviation in the People's Republic of China; or habitual drunkenness and drug addiction in associations such as Alcoholics Anonymous and Synanon (Horwitz 1982:148–160,180–181; 1984). Even friends and relatives might behave therapeutically by withholding blame and showing sympathy for an associate whose misconduct they dislike but attribute to circumstances the individual did not choose and could not avoid. Conciliation is found in diverse settings as well — between intimates or strangers, individuals or organizations — in all societies and walks of life, wherever quarrels arise, feelings are bruised, or pride and self-respect are jeopardized. The conciliatory style is strikingly illustrated by specialists in human relations observed by anthropologists in tribal societies, such as the "camp clown" of the Mbuti Pygmies of Zaire (Turnbull 1965:182–183), the "leopard-skin chief" of the Nuer of the Sudan (Evans-Pritchard, 1940:172–176; Greuel 1971), the "saint" of the Swat Pathan of Pakistan (Barth 1959:Chapter 8), and the "crosser" of the Yurok Indians of California (Kroeber 1926:514–515), but social control of this kind is no more difficult to find at an international conference, in the workplace, on a playground, or at a breakfast table.

Yet the several styles of social control described here do not exhaust the possible responses to deviant behavior. Whereas the penal style of social control focuses on an act, the compensatory style on its consequences, the therapeutic style on a person, and the conciliatory style on a relationship, still another strategy focuses on the opportunity to engage in deviant behavior, either by altering the situation of potential deviants or by altering the habits of potential victims. This is prevention. Potential deviants might be subjected to greater surveillance (known in modern police work as preventive patrol), for example, or they might be deprived of their freedom of movement to some degree (known in modern penology as preventive detention and incapacitation), and potential victims might be encouraged to reduce their vulnerability (known by modern specialists in crime prevention as target hardening).[16] Still another strategy focuses on the causes of deviant behavior: reform. It entails a manipulation of environmental conditions — such as poverty and unemployment — that are believed to generate deviant behavior.[17] Whether prevention and reform should be understood as styles of social control in a narrow sense is debatable, but both should clearly be included in the broader study of how people adapt to deviant behavior. Each may augment or even replace the handling of individual cases by punishment, compensation, therapy, or conciliation.[18]

Quantity

Because the several forms and styles of social control vary in the degree to which they define and respond to deviant conduct, each may be measured as a quantitative variable, or counted. This is especially apparent in the realm of law, where responses to deviant behavior often have an explicitly numerical character, whether punishments involving specific periods of time in prison or payments of compensation involving specific amounts of money. Even where law is not dispensed in uniform intervals such as days or dollars, however, we can identify various phenomena that may be construed as increments in the quantity of law, such as a call to the police, an arrest, the filing of a lawsuit, a prosecution, a conviction, a decision in favor of a plaintiff, a prison sentence, or an award of damages. Each of these actions increases the degree to which someone's conduct is regarded as deviant within a governmental framework, and so each may be understood as an increase in law itself (see Black 1979a.)

Social control of every sort varies in its degree or magnitude, and we may speak of the quantity of self-help, therapy, expiation, gossip, or whatever. In the case of self-help, this magnitude increases with the force and violence applied by the aggrieved: A homicide is more self-help than a lesser injury or property destruction, for instance, whereas each of these is more self-help than a mere threat or admonishment. And just as a code of law may specify a quantity of governmental social control appropriate in each case — such as the years in prison that must be served — so may other codes specify how much social control should be applied in other settings. There is, so to speak, a jurisprudence of self-help and of every other kind of social control. In traditional societies, a "code of honor" may prescribe when and how much violent self-help should occur from one incident to another (see Peristiany 1966, especially the chapters by Pitt-Rivers and by Bourdieu). In medieval Europe, handbooks called penitentials listed in great detail the many sins that might be committed and the penance appropriate for each, such as a particular period of silence, prayer, singing of psalms, fasting, seclusion, sleeping on nutshells, flagellation, or exile (see McNeill and Gamer 1938; see also Tentler 1977). Modern prisoners and children, among others, are commonly subject to disciplinary codes (see Foucault 1975). Where a third party intervenes in a conflict in a largely nonpartisan fashion, we may measure the degree of authoritativeness involved in each case (see Gluckman 1965b:222), ranging from the friendly peacemaker who merely distracts or separates the principals to the mediator who acts as a broker between them, the arbitrator who gives an opinion but cannot enforce it, the judge who gives an opinion and is able to enforce it, and, finally, the repressive peacemaker who handles each conflict as a punishable offense in itself (see Black and Baumgartner 1983, for a detailed overview of these roles).

The quantity of social control has no necessary association with its form or style. Violent self-help, for example, may be just as severe as the most extreme punishments applied by a court of law, in modern as well as in traditional societies. And penal practices are not always more severe than other styles of social control. The enforcement of traffic law is penal in style, for instance, but typically less severe than compensation awards and treatments for mental illness.

In any event, whatever its form or style, the quantity of social control should never be taken for granted. It requires explanation. In fact, in most cases people with a grievance against someone else probably do nothing at all. They just "lump it" (see Felstiner 1974:81; Galanter 1974:124–125). Accordingly, the very existence of social control itself requires explanation. Although we have long sought to understand why people commit crime and other kinds of deviant behavior, the investigation of why conduct is regarded as criminal or otherwise deviant has largely been ignored.[19] Now we have a new question: Why do people commit social control?

To approach social control as a dependent variable is to acknowledge that it differs from one situation to another and to assume that it is possible to predict and explain these differences. As noted earlier, the sociological study of law has yielded a number of formulations about how legal life varies across social settings, and these provide a point of departure for the study of social control in general. In particular, law varies in specifiable patterns with its location and direction along every known dimension of social space. It varies with the vertical dimension, or inequality of wealth, increasing and becoming more penal when it is directed downwardly from higher against lower ranks. It varies with the horizontal dimension, or the distribution of people in relation to one another, including their degree of intimacy, specialization, and integration. In a given community, for instance, intimacy tends to reduce the use of law. Also relevant is the corporate dimension: Groups use more law against individuals than vice versa, and they use proportionately more against one another as well. But groups are not punished as much as individuals; more often they are asked to compensate their victims. Law further varies with culture, the symbolic dimension of social space: Homogeneity, like intimacy, apparently retards the use of law, and unconventionality involves legal disabilities similar to those associated with poverty or a lack of organization. Social control itself describes yet another dimension — the normative — and it too is related to the incidence of law. Law varies inversely with other social control, for instance, strengthening when normative life of other kinds is weaker, and vice versa.[20] (For an elaboration of these and other formulations about legal variation, see Black 1976.)

It seems plausible that not only law but every other kind of social control varies with its location and direction in social space. Surely, for example, inequality is relevant to what happens not only in courtrooms but also in private homes, organizations, the community, and international affairs. Surely it is relevant to the occurrence of scolding, gossip, beating, deprivation, desertion, expulsion, destruction, and — considering the behavior of third parties — the occurrence of adjudication, arbitration, mediation, negotiation, and advocacy. Surely the structure of intimacy is also relevant, as well as the division of labor, social participation, corporate action, cultural heterogeneity, and so on. What predicts and explains the behavior of law may also predict and explain social control in general.[21]

THE QUANTITY OF NORMATIVE VARIATION

Although social control varies from one setting to another in its form, style, and magnitude, and although our central mission is to understand this variation, it should not be assumed that social control always varies to the same degree. Under the right conditions, how people define and respond to deviant behavior may even approach perfect uniformity from one case to the next. For example, a traffic officer checking parking meters normally writes a citation (a "ticket") for every violation discovered, and for every violation the fine is exactly the same. Under other conditions, however, traffic enforcement is highly selective (see Black 1980:32–36). Similarly, the compensation that must be paid for a wrongful injury — say, an accidental death — differs greatly across the many cases handled in a modern society such as the United States, though the circumstances involved, such as drunken driving or medical malpractice of a particular kind, might be the same. But in a tribal society such as the Nuer of the Sudan or the nomads of northern Somalia, compensation for accidental homicide differs relatively little from one case to the next (see Howell 1954:54; Lewis 1959, 1961:Chapter 6).[22] Accordingly, the quantity of normative variation is a variable in its own right and requires explanation.

We can predict and explain the degree to which social control varies from one setting to another with a single formulation applicable across cases, groups, communities, and societies: *Normative variation is a direct function of social diversity.* Differences in the form, style, and quantity of social control increase and decrease with the differences across social settings themselves. For example, social control varies case by case with the social characteristics of everyone involved — the principals, their supporters, and other third parties. The participants might be high, low, or mixed in social status; they might be more or less intimate, interdependent, and homogeneous in culture; they might be groups, individuals, or both. Characteristics of this kind may or may not differ a great deal from one case to the next. If such differences exist, they will be reflected in the social control that occurs — for example, in whether a case is taken to an official agency, whether a winner is declared, and, if so, what consequences befall the loser. In modern societies, for instance, where the social diversity of cases is much greater than in tribal societies, there is more variation in social control from one case to the next. This explains why, as noted earlier, an incident in modern America such as an accidental homicide has numerous possible consequences, ranging from no reaction at all to imprisonment or huge amounts of money in compensatory damages, whereas in a tribal society such variation is far narrower. About the only differences across the members of a tribe are those of age, sex, and intimacy, and so only these will be reflected in the handling of a given grievance.[23]

Even within a modern society, cases are not always as diverse as those arising from accidents, wherein practically anyone — organization or individual, rich or poor, married or single, employed, educated, conventional, respectable, or whatever — might be involved with practically anyone else. For example, a larger number of criminal cases than accident cases are interchangeable in their social characteristics, and so there is less variation in how criminal cases are handled. Prostitutes are typically processed by the authorities in much the same fashion from one to the next, as are "skid row" drunks, burglars, and robbers. In these cases the alleged offenders are nearly always poor and otherwise lacking in social status. They differ among themselves primarily in the nature and length of their criminal records, which in turn appear to be the major source of variation in how they are handled (see, e.g., Spradley 1970:176–177; Wiseman 1970:89–90; Mileski 1971:504–505; Farrell and Swigert 1978).[24]

Social diversity varies not only across legal settings but across normative settings of all kinds, and everywhere the same principle applies: The more diversity, the more differences in social control. The more families vary in their social composition, for example, the more their normative life varies. The manner in which husbands express grievances against their wives, and vice versa, therefore varies greatly across modern America, where some marital relationships are patriarchal in structure, others matriarchal, and still others egalitarian. Wife-beating — as a form of disci-pline — occurs frequently in some families but not others, and the same is true of desertion, avoidance, conciliation, and psychotherapy. In tribal and peasant societies, by contrast, the structure of each marital relationship is much the same as the next, and so conflict management is much the same as well. Wife-beating has roughly the same likelihood from one family to the next, and the same redundancy applies to other modes by which griev-ances are expressed.

As mentioned earlier, variation in social control depends not only on social diversity among people who have conflicts with one another but also on social diversity among those who intervene as third parties. Although settlement agents such as police officers and judges have historically been quite homogeneous in their social characteristics — for example, judges have nearly always been male, middle-aged or elderly; economically pros-perous; and racially, ethnically, and religiously conventional — this homo-geneity began to decrease during the twentieth century. If the trend toward greater diversification continues, we should expect an increasing degree of variation in judicial dispositions. This should be all the more pronounced if the diversification of third parties is accompanied by a diversification of the cases in other respects. And this appears to be happening. Hence, during the past century or so (at least in the United States), it seems to have become increasingly difficult to predict the disposition of cases with the written law alone. Technically similar cases have increasingly been handled differently. In this sense, the rules have been losing their importance. The widely held view that law is essentially an affair of rules (e.g., Hart 1961; Fuller 1964) may thus be an historically grounded conception that is becom-ing obsolete.

Finally, it should be added that the amount of variation in social control does not automatically reflect the amount of social diversity across the cases handled. This relationship depends on the extent to which the social characteristics of the cases are known when they are processed. Knowl-edge of this kind, or social information, cannot be taken for granted; it is itself variable (see Black and Baumgartner 1980:204, note 18). For example, police officers handling parking violations in a large city generally have little or no social information about the diverse owners and drivers of improperly parked automobiles, and (as noted earlier) there is little or no variation in how parking violations are processed. But when the police handle so-called moving violations, such as speeding or disobeying traffic signals, they encounter the drivers and learn some of their social charac-teristics. These characteristics differ considerably across the population of violators, and so there is more variation in how moving violations are handled (see Black 1980:32–35). Judges sentencing convicted criminals have still more social information about offenders and their victims, and so there is still more variation in the handling of otherwise identical cases (except, as mentioned above, where the parties are largely the same in their social characteristics).

The quantity of social information entering a process of social control is not random, however; it is predictable with various features of each case. The more intimate the parties, for example, the more their social characteristics will be known among themselves. Hence, social information is abundant in the tribunals of tribal and peasant villages where everyone is well-acquainted with everyone else, but it is often sparse in the courtrooms of modern cities. Social information may vary with the social status of the parties as well, if only because higher-status people may be more likely to advertise their own social superiority. And social information varies with social control itself: The greater the amount of social control applicable to each case, the more information about the social characteristics of the principals is generated. At one extreme is the parking violation, where the owner or driver usually remains socially anonymous and risks only a small monetary fine; at the other extreme is the capital case, where the accused criminal's entire life history is commonly compiled and presented to the court. Whenever social control is potentially greater, then, social diversity across the cases is likely to be better known, and this in turn increases the degree of variation in how the cases are handled. Accordingly, all else constant—including the social diversity across the cases—the following principle may be proposed: *Normative variation is a direct function of the quantity of social control.* This principle explains why the handling of capital crimes involves more variation than the handling of lesser offenses such as traffic violations (compare, e.g., Bowers and Pierce 1980 with Lundman 1979).[25] In sum, it appears that uniformity in the application of law and other social control is reserved for two situations: (1) those in which the cases are—or seem to be—socially identical and (2) those in which the cases are trivial.

MODELS OF SOCIAL CONTROL

When each party has complete knowledge of the social characteristics of the others involved, the social structure of a conflict predicts and explains how it will be handled. Accordingly, the more economically we can describe the conflict structure, the more effectively we can predict and explain the social control it attracts. Because our theoretical formulations imply how various social conditions are associated with various kinds of social control, we can construct models that depict all these conditions at once. By comparing these models with actual instances of social control, the validity of the models can be assessed.

Consider first the place of intimacy in the theory of social control, in particular, the theory of the third party. There is reason to believe that the likelihood that a settlement agent will intervene in a conflict varies with the degree of intimacy, or relational distance,[26] between the parties in conflict. In particular, this likelihood seemingly increases with the relational distance between the parties until they are complete strangers (such as members of different societies), at which point the likelihood of intervention declines: *Settlement behavior is a curvilinear function of relational distance.*[27]

We can also specify the kind of settlement behavior that is likely to occur under varying conditions of intimacy. Recall that five modes of settlement behavior can be distinguished on a continuum of increasingly authoritative intervention: friendly pacification, mediation, arbitration, adjudication, and repressive pacification. How do these vary with the structure of intimacy? Leaving aside the relational distance between the principals themselves, we might first observe that settlement behavior seems to occur only when the amount of intimacy between the third party and each of the principals is largely equal (see Simmel 1908b:149–153). Otherwise, the third party is likely to act as a partisan on behalf of the principal who is closer: *Intimacy breeds partisanship.*[28] People tend to support their friends and family members against strangers, for example, and in such cases generally would not be able, or allowed, to claim objectivity about the merits of each side in the manner of an arbitrator or judge. Even to intervene less authoritatively as a friendly peacemaker or mediator would be difficult. Thus, for example, among the Ifugao of the Philippines, the traditional settlement agent known as the *monkalun* (who seemingly may choose to act as a mediator, arbitrator, or judge) cannot be a close relative of either principal: "Were he closely related to the plaintiff, he would have no influence with the defendant, and mutatis mutandis the opposite would be true" (Barton 1919:87). Similarly, among the nomads of northern Somalia, elders who arbitrate disputes must be acceptable to both sides, and neither side will allow a relative of the other to perform this function: "Kinship ties to either party are regarded as prejudicial to a fair judgment" (Lewis 1961:229). In a Druze village of Lebanon, the selection of mediators obeys the same principle: "Anyone nearer to one disputant than the other is not likely to be acknowledged a disinterested party by both" (Ayoub 1965:13). In modern societies as well, unequal intimacy with the principals normally disqualifies a judge from hearing a case. In short, *the settlement agent and the principals form an isosceles triangle of relational distance, with the settlement agent at the apex* (Black and Baumgartner 1983:113).[29]

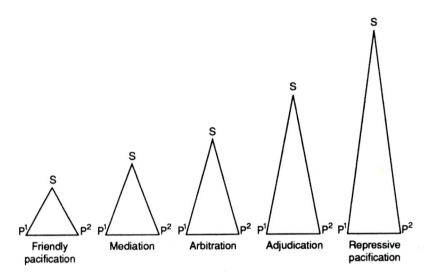

Figure 1.1 The relational structure of settlement behavior. (S = settlement agent; P¹ and P² = principals; length of sides = relational distance.)

Now consider the relational structure of each mode of settlement behavior. How does a mediation structure differ from an arbitration structure or an adjudication structure? When is pacification friendly rather than repressive? In other words, what predicts and explains the degree of authoritativeness with which a settlement agent intervenes in a conflict?

The pattern seems to be as follows: *The authoritativeness of settlement behavior is a direct function of the relational distance between the settlement agent and the principals* (Black and Baumgartner 1983:113). On the continuum of authoritative intervention described earlier, friendly pacification — the least authoritative — should thus be most frequent when the settlement agent is highly intimate with the parties in conflict, mediation when a bit less intimacy is found, arbitration when there is still less intimacy, adjudication when there is hardly any intimacy, and repressive pacification when the settlement agent is the most distant of all. Accordingly, the five modes of settlement behavior arise in isosceles triangles of intimacy with different distances between the settlement agents and the principals (see Figure 1.1).

Another feature of a conflict structure that a model of settlement behavior (and, for that matter, any model of social control) should include is the structure of social support, if any, that each side enjoys. The model should describe the relationship between each supporter and all of the other participants. Because intimacy is conducive to partisanship, we may

expect that advisers, advocates, allies, and other supporters will be relationally closer to one side than to the other (for a typology of support roles,
see Black and Baumgartner 1983:88–98). And, in fact, this pattern is often
reported in the literature on conflict management. Among the Kabyles of
Algeria, for example, support behavior perfectly obeys a principle of differ-
ential intimacy:

> *A sense of solidarity obliged one to protect a kinsman against a non-
> kinsman, a member of one's own party against a man from another moiety,
> an inhabitant of the village — even though of a rival party — against a
> stranger to the village, a member of the tribe against a member of another
> tribe. (Bourdieu 1966:201)*

The same tendency is found everywhere. Moreover, whether closer to one
of the principals or not, some partisans may have ties to the other side or
possibly to a settlement agent involved in the conflict. Configurations such
as these would also bear on the kind of settlement behavior likely to occur
and must be included in a maximally predictive model. But the relational
structure of a conflict is only one of many factors relevant to its processing.
A more powerful model would include a number of variables at once, such
as the status structure of the conflict, the involvement of groups, the cultural distances between the various parties, and the availability of alternative modes of social control.

For example: *Settlement behavior is more likely to occur when a third party
is higher than the principals in social status.*[30] And the nature of the intervention varies accordingly: *The authoritativeness of settlement behavior is a direct
function of the relative status of the third party* (Black and Baumgartner
1983:113; see also Baumgartner 1985). We would therefore expect friendly
peacemakers to be closest in social status to the principals, mediators to be
higher than those whose conflict they mediate, arbitrators higher yet,
judges still higher, and, finally, repressive peacemakers to be the highest
of all in social status, relative to the principals. Social status is relevant to
support behavior as well, and the status of the supporters on each side is
relevant to how, if at all, a settlement agent might intervene. Here again the
point is simply to illustrate the kind of theoretical formulations we seek to
develop. Ultimately it should be possible to specify every aspect of a conflict structure that is associated with every kind of settlement behavior and,
more generally, every kind of social control that might occur. These models
might then be compared with any conflict in the natural world to predict
and — if successful — explain how it is handled. The closer a model fits
reality in any case, the more precisely we can apprehend the kind of social
control that will actually occur. If, for instance, a conflict structure includes
no one equally distant from the principals and no one superior to both in

social status, a model combining elements noted earlier would predict no settlement behavior at all. On the other hand, if someone in the conflict structure is equidistant from the principals and also higher than both in social status — increasing the likelihood of settlement behavior[31] — measurements of the relational and status distances involved would further predict the level of authoritativeness likely to occur, whether arbitration, adjudication, or whatever. An ideal model of social control of any kind would show simultaneously how it is situated along every dimension of social space: vertical, horizontal, corporate, symbolic, and normative.

Models of social control may be applied not only microscopically to predict and explain the handling of a particular conflict but also macroscopically to a community, society, or other setting in which numerous conflicts arise from one day to the next. Each larger setting typically contains one or more recurrent conflict structures that, theoretically speaking, imply a limited range of social control. For example, hunters and gatherers such as the Mbuti Pygmies of Zaire (Turnbull 1961, 1965), the Hadza of Tanzania (Woodburn 1979), and the !Kung San Bushmen of Botswana (Lee 1979) live in small bands in which everyone is intimately related and status differences among adults are negligible. It is therefore structurally impossible for these people to have a conflict among themselves that would fit our models of relatively authoritative intervention, such as adjudication or repressive pacification: There is literally no one in their everyday world who is socially distant enough to be a judge or a repressive peacemaker. In fact, these societies generally do not even have mediators or arbitrators.[32] Their only settlement agents seem to be the least authoritative of all — friendly peacemakers. For example, the only settlement agent found among the Mbuti Pygmies is the so-called camp clown, who handles conflicts primarily by making a fool of himself, thereby distracting the principals from their dispute and possibly making them join together in laughter as well (Turnbull 1965:182–183). For our purposes, then, the hunters and gatherers might be regarded as friendly-pacification societies. Another step beyond these in social complexity, including status differentiation, are the herding societies, such as the Nuer of the Sudan and the nomads of Tibet, who are neither as intimate among themselves nor as egalitarian as those who forage for their livelihood (see Evans-Pritchard 1940; Ekvall 1964, 1968). These societies understandably have mediators but rarely anyone more authoritative, for their conflicts do not — cannot — have the social characteristics associated with modes of intervention further along the continuum of authoritativeness. Herding peoples might thus be classified as mediation societies. Following the same reasoning, we can also identify arbitration societies: Typically these include more sedentary people who engage in at least some horticulture and have still more social distance and inequality in their communities, such as the ancient Irish (Ginnell 1924), the Swat Pathan of Pakistan (Barth 1959), and various societies in Polynesia (Hogbin 1934; Sahlins 1958). And there are, so to speak, adjudication societies, such as the nations of the modern world, where the social structure induces a still more authoritative mode of settlement behavior.[33] Perhaps we can even speak of repressive-pacification societies, illustrated in recent history by the colonial regimes of Africa, Oceania, and other areas where rulers and ruled have been separated by vast distances in social space and where tribal modes of conflict management such as feuding and fighting have been handled by the authorities as "disturbances of the peace," or crime, and not as the pursuit of justice at all (see, e.g., Evans-Pritchard 1940:152; Harner 1972:210; Koch 1974:223; Reay 1974:205, 209). In short, it is possible to construct models of social control with applications across the entire range of social life, from face-to-face encounters to communities and societies.

THE GOOD, THE TRUE, AND THE BEAUTIFUL

This chapter has introduced social control as a natural phenomenon that varies with its location and direction in social space. The central theme has been that it is possible to develop a body of sociological theory that will predict and explain how normative life differs from one setting to another or, in other words, to understand social control as a dependent variable. A general theory of law — a single species of social control — has already been initiated, and we can now expand our program to include the behavior of virtually anything else that is normative — all of the social practices that define and respond to conduct as right or wrong, good or evil, proper or improper. Yet within a still more general perspective, social control itself proves to be only a limited instance of a larger phenomenon: evaluation.

People everywhere apply standards to everything. Whether the standards pertain to what is good or bad, true or false, beautiful or ugly, useful, delightful, or disgusting, all of this and more is evaluation. Seen in this context, social control is but one mode of evaluation, known by its normative character, its standards of right and wrong. A second mode of evaluation has an intellectual character: It is concerned with the truth and importance of ideas about the nature of reality, including their practical application and the determination of what is effective, prudent, and wise. From an intellectual standpoint, people may be regarded as intelligent, insightful, inventive, smart, stupid, fatuous, or foolish. Finally, a third mode of evaluation has an aesthetic character: It pertains to what is or is not worthy of appreciation, whether graceful, attractive, awesome, exciting, delicious, ordinary, distasteful, vulgar, or gross. These three modes of evaluation — normative, intellectual, and aesthetic — are the major frameworks in which people make value judgments.[34] Furthermore, we can identify similarities in how they come into play in social life.

It seems, for example, that people of higher status enjoy an advantage whenever they are evaluated, whether normatively, intellectually, or aesthetically. Thus, just as a downward offense by a person of higher status against someone of lower status is less likely to be punished than an offense in the opposite direction (see generally Black 1976:Chapters 2–6), so an idea that is presented downwardly by a person of higher status to someone of lower status is more likely to succeed — to be recognized as interesting or important — than is an idea presented upwardly (Black 1979b:158). People of higher status are also likely to be regarded as aesthetically superior, with better taste in music, clothing, food, and everything else (see Black 1979b:160–161). Even their recreational activities are considered more sophisticated. And, to mention another pattern, just as people are less likely to invoke law against their intimates (Black 1976:40–42), so their intellectual and aesthetic reactions to relatives, friends, and acquaintances are more positive. In general, therefore, the degree of consensus about questions of quality in science, art, or any other field is predictable from the social structure of evaluation in each: What are the social characteristics of the evaluators? How similar are they? What is their relationship to those they evaluate (see Black 1979b:161)? It should be possible to formulate propositions that predict and explain evaluations of every kind.

We may also ask why each mode of evaluative behavior occurs at all. Why is something evaluated in the language of right and wrong in one case, in terms of its cleverness or stupidity in another, its attractiveness or vulgarity in still another? The same conduct or object may evoke entirely different standards among different people. A book, speech, or film, for example, may be judged in terms of its truth, its artistic merit, or its morality. Similarly, some might consider a theft as immoral and outrageous, others might regard it as clever or stupid, and still others might relate to it aesthetically as attractive ("cool") or enjoyable ("fun").

It seems that the particular mode of evaluation employed depends on the social conditions that prevail in any given case. Each tends to appear in a limited range of locations and directions in social space. Some people are highly moralistic, constantly asking whether whatever they encounter is proper or not: Does it conform to the rules? Is it legal? Should it be punished? To others, all that matters is efficiency. They intellectualize everything: How smart is this or that? Is it rational? What does it accomplish? Does it work? And still others care only about aesthetics: Is it in good taste? Is it graceful? Pleasurable? Does it feel good? Particular settings also generate one mode of evaluation more than another. Entire societies may be dominated by a single evaluative mode, so that we might speak of moralistic societies such as Puritan New England or Soviet Russia, intellectual or technocratic societies such as those of modern Scandinavia, and aesthetic societies such as traditional Japan or Bali.

Just as the conduct of people does not by itself predict and explain the social control to which it will be subject, neither can conduct or anything else tell us how people will evaluate it, whether normatively, intellectually, or aesthetically. And just as social control cannot be taken for granted, so ultimately we must ask why value judgments — of any kind — occur at all. Although the scientific study of social control is only now beginning, then, already it is possible to imagine a general theory of evaluation.

ENDNOTES

*Reprinted with permission (and minor revision) from pages 1–36 in *Toward a General Theory of Social Control*, Volume 1: *Fundamentals*, edited by Donald Black. Orlando: Academic Press, 1984.

I thank M. P. Baumgartner, Marc Clinton, Mark Cooney, John Griffiths, Calvin Morrill, and Trevor Nagel for commenting on an earlier draft of this chapter.

1. The concept of social control is elaborated later in this chapter. Suffice it to say for now that here social control refers to any process by which people define and respond to deviant behavior. Accordingly, a general theory of social control is a body of formulations that predict and explain variation in how people define and respond to deviant behavior.

2. A qualification: Although stateless societies cannot have law on a permanent basis, they may have it temporarily, such as during warfare, communal hunts, and other collective undertakings (see, e.g., Karsten 1923:8; MacLeod 1937; Lowie 1948; see also Black 1976: 87–91).

3. A number of scholars classify as "law" many instances of social control that have no connection to government in a formal sense, so that law is said to exist even in stateless societies (e.g., Barton 1919; Howell 1954; Pospisil 1958). Nongovernmental social control has often been called "customary law" or "unwritten law," though a number of other labels are sometimes preferred, including "folk law," "people's law," "unofficial law," and "indigenous law" (see, e.g., Fuller 1971:171–186; Berman 1978; Galanter 1981). Another strategy is to treat the "legalness" of social control as a matter of degree (see Griffiths 1984).

4. A seeming exception to this principle in some societies is the frequent resort to law by married people seeking a divorce. Yet divorce generally is a legal matter only where the state participates in and guarantees the marriage contract. Where this is not the case, people simply end their marriages when one or both partners are so inclined — a practice seen in many tribal societies (e.g., Turnbull 1965:140, 274–275; Reid 1970:117–118; Lee 1979:452–453) as well as in modern societies among couples who live together without certification by the state.

5. On suicide as social control, see Jeffreys (1952), Koch (1974:75–76), Counts (1980), and Baumgartner (1984a:328–331).

6. Just as the sociology of law is also known as legal sociology, so a larger sociology of social control might appropriately be known as normative sociology.

7. For these purposes, deviant behavior refers to any conduct regarded as undesirable from a normative standpoint, that is, any conduct that *ought not* to occur. Although to some readers the concept of deviant behavior may suggest conduct that is subject to penal or possibly therapeutic responses (such as psychiatric care), any connotations or limitations of this sort are unintended here (see Black 1979a:97, note 2). Similarly, although the concept of social control may also seem to have penal or even coercive connotations, these are unintended in this discussion as well. Unfortunately, at present no word or phrase adequately captures the wide range of phenomena to which the concept of social control is meant to refer. Alternatives such as "dispute settlement" and "conflict management" — terms favored by many anthropologists and lawyers — do not seem appropriate in the context of penal and therapeutic modes of normative life and thus appear to be no more inclusive than the concept of social control. Another possibility, "social ordering" (Fuller 1978:357), implies an outcome that might better remain problematic — whether social control necessarily results in "order." Still another, "reglementation" (Moore 1978:1–31), not only suggests an orderly result but also places what may be an overly restrictive emphasis on explicit expectations about how people should behave, or "rules." It should not be assumed that people always define and respond to deviant behavior according to rules. This seems to occur under limited social conditions and should be treated as a problem for investigation (see, e.g., Toulmin 1982).

8. Even so, social control should not be conceived entirely at the case level, where one individual or group complains about another. It also appears — and invites study — in larger units that transcend particular cases. Social control includes prescriptions, proscriptions, and other kinds of exhortations and promulgations that define how people should or should not behave, for example, and it includes all manner of mechanisms and arrangements for processing people with complaints and people defined as deviants, such as courts, police forces, mental hospitals, witch finders, and lawyers. The varieties of punishment might be studied as well, and so might strategies of therapy or mediation, modes of fighting or duelling, and so on.

9. This is not to say that any concept such as social control logically implies the approach to be pursued in its study. In principle, one could conceive of social control as a process of influence and investigate why it occurs, or conceive of it as a reaction and investigate its impact on other phenomena. Even so, those who have conceptualized social control as influence have generally been more concerned with its consequences than with the social conditions under which it occurs, whereas the view that social control is a reaction to conduct regarded as deviant seems to lead in the opposite direction to the question of why reactions of a particular kind come into being.

It should also be noted that a single approach might understand social control as both an independent and a dependent variable. For example, social control might be regarded as a reaction to deviant behavior that counteracts its disequilibrating effects on the social system in which it occurs (see Homans 1950:301–312; Parsons 1951:297–321).

10. This usage assumes that the identity of a scientific theory resides in what it seeks to predict and explain so that, for instance, a theory of earthquakes or cancer tells us when and why these phenomena occur. It treats them as dependent variables. Accordingly, a theory that inquires into the impact of social control on other aspects of social life such as deviant behavior or social order is not a theory of social control but rather a theory of those other phenomena (see Gibbs 1981:Chapter 6). A theory of the conditions under which punishment deters crime, for example, is a theory of crime, not a theory of social control.

To speak of *a* general theory of social control is not to suggest that the formulations comprising this theory should be considered final or complete. Instead, what is meant is a body of theory about social control, an organic network of formulations, more or less inter-related, that are forever subject to revision and refinement. It might therefore be more appro-priate to speak of *the* general theory of social control in this context.

Finally, we are concerned here entirely with the development of sociological theory about social control and not in any way whatsoever with the psychology—or subjective aspect—of this phenomenon.

11. A "side" of a conflict may be an individual, a group, or an aggregate. Hence, nothing is assumed here about the number of people who participate in cases of social control, though surely most involve only two and occur in face-to-face encounters. Regardless of the number involved, however, it seems that most (if not all) such cases exhibit a two- or three-sided structure.

12. Another variable aspect of social control is the system of liability that specifies who is subject to social control, given the occurrence of an event regarded as deviant or injurious. Where compensation is expected, for instance, the system of liability specifies who will be asked to pay, whether the party deemed responsible or someone else, such as the responsible party's family or organization. (For a discussion of liability in cross-cultural perspective, see Koch 1984; see also Moore 1972.)

13. A group as well as a person might be handled therapeutically. Although an organi-zation, for instance, would not ordinarily be regarded as insane or possessed by supernatural spirits, it might nevertheless have its misconduct attributed to a malfunction of some kind, possibly to a matter needing the attention of a management consultant or other specialist in organizational behavior (see Gluckman 1972:7–40). Occasionally an even larger collectivity might be described in therapeutic language, as when people speak of a "sick society."

14. For a cross-cultural study of stylistic and other variation in the social control of homicide, see Cooney (1988).

15. It might seem that compensation would tend to supplant vengeance—"an eye for an eye"—wherever money, livestock, or other means of payment are available, but in some societies only vengeance is believed to be appropriate and adequate when certain wrongs occur, while the acceptance of compensation is viewed as cowardly and dishonorable (e.g., Barth 1959:85; Bourdieu 1966:216).

16. The vocabulary used here should not suggest that prevention is found only in modern societies or where an effort is made to reduce conduct that might be regarded as criminal. Although the technology of prevention is most highly developed in societies such as modern America—where, for instance, it involves diverse methods of surveillance by governmental and private police, electronic devices, and locks of all kinds to make victimi-zation more difficult—earlier and simpler societies have often used preventive techniques as well. In ancient Rome, for example, slaves were sometimes branded on the forehead or required to wear iron collars to make their apprehension easier if they ran away, and they were sometimes placed in chains to eliminate the possibility of escape altogether (see Wiedemann 1981:173–174, 193–194). For centuries, vicious dogs have been used to protect herds and dwellings (see, e.g., Hasluck 1954:73, 204), and fences have been erected for the same purpose (e.g., Chagnon, 1977:29). Prevention also seems to be a common strategy for reducing the deviant behavior of children: Prohibited objects may simply be hidden or placed out of reach, for example. Children may also prevent a certain amount of adult misconduct by wandering freely and exercising surveillance in private places or other situations where adults might not have access. (For a discussion of preventive behavior by and toward children in a tribal society, see Maybury-Lewis 1967:67–72.)

17. Social scientists have developed a number of theories that they and others put forth to guide reform of this kind. Some believe these theories demonstrate that society itself is responsible for crime and other deviant behavior. In contrast, the penal and compensatory

styles of social control imply that the deviant actor is responsible, the therapeutic style that an abnormal condition such as a mental illness is responsible, and the conciliatory style that everyone involved in a particular conflict is responsible to some degree.

The two modes of prevention noted earlier may shift the responsibility for deviant behavior in still other directions: When preventive behavior is oriented toward potential deviants, as in surveillance programs, any deviant behavior that occurs may be blamed on those who are charged with preventing it, such as when the police are blamed for a crime or an adult is held responsible for the activities of a troublesome or destructive child. If a prevention program is victim-oriented, however, the victim of a deviant act may be held responsible for failing to take the proper precautionary measures, such as when the theft of an automobile is blamed on the owner because he or she left the keys in the ignition or when a woman is blamed for her own rape because she made herself available by walking alone on the street at night.

18. Another possible focus of social control is the supernatural. The anthropological literature describes many practices designed to neutralize or otherwise counteract responses to deviant behavior by gods or other spirits. Typically the standard of conduct is a taboo, the violation of which — a sin — automatically creates a condition of spiritual pollution and danger. This condition may result in a misfortune such as a sickness, injury, or unhappy afterlife unless appropriate measures are taken to expiate the sin and placate the supernatural spirits concerned. Expiation is normally achieved by a sacrifice, confession, or other ritual (see generally Radcliffe-Brown 1952; Douglas 1966). Among the Nuer of the Sudan, for example, it is believed that incest may result in yaws or syphilis for both partners (and possibly also for close relatives) and that adultery may strike at the lumbar region of the cuckold (Evans-Pritchard 1956:183–185). In fact, any sickness at all is taken by the Nuer as evidence that a sin has been committed (Evans-Pritchard 1956:191–193), a presumption made by Arctic Eskimos and other tribal people as well (see Hoebel 1954:70–73). Among the Cheyenne of the North American Plains, murder is regarded as "putrid" and is believed to bring misfortune on the entire tribe — such as failure in war or hunting — unless the killer is banished and a ritual known as the Sacred Arrow Ceremony is performed (Llewellyn and Hoebel 1941:132–135). The Tallensi of Ghana believe that any homicide, regardless of the circumstances, is a sin against the mystical power of the earth and will result in the destruction of the killer's family unless "heavy sacrifices" are made (Fortes 1945:176–177).

Such beliefs and practices might be construed as a style of social control in their own right: the expiatory style. On the other hand, perhaps expiation should more properly be viewed as a religious equivalent of the other styles. It might involve a belief in supernatural punishment of the sinner, for example, a demand for compensation to the gods (as in a sacrifice), a curing ritual to cleanse the sinner's soul, or a ceremony of spiritual reconciliation.

19. In the early 1960s, a number of sociologists called attention to the processes whereby crime and other deviant behavior are "labeled" as such (see, e.g., Erikson 1962; Kitsuse 1962; Becker 1963). This movement, known as "labeling theory," constituted a shift away from the traditional emphasis on the characteristics of deviants and their behavior. Yet initially it did not lead so much toward a theory of social control as toward a new theory of why people engage in deviant behavior: the theory of "secondary deviation," which holds that the labeling of people as deviant increases the likelihood that they will engage in more deviant behavior in the future (Lemert 1967; see also Scheff 1966; Matza 1969). For example, a criminal record may make it more difficult for people to find legitimate employment, thereby increasing their motivation to turn to illegal sources of income. Despite the direction in which labeling theory first led, it encouraged research on criminal justice, the treatment of mental illness, and other processes of social control and so helped to lay the foundation for the theory of social control now being developed.

The theory of social control provides a radical alternative to theories of deviant behavior of every kind. Because deviant behavior is conduct that is subject to social control, every instance of deviant behavior is also an instance of social control. Thus, to say that poor people are more likely to commit crime is also to say, simultaneously, that poor people are more likely to be defined as criminals. Variation in the nature and rate of deviant behavior—across a population, across time, or whatever—necessarily entails variation in the nature and rate of social control. It is therefore possible to explain deviant behavior with the theory of social control (Black 1976:9–10).

20. This does not imply that the total quantity of social control in a given setting is constant. When law replaces other forms of social control (or vice versa), the extent to which a particular kind of conduct is punished or otherwise regarded as deviant may change considerably.

21. This is not to say that other kinds of social control necessarily behave according to the same principles as law — though this may be true in some cases — but only that the same features of the social environment may be relevant to both. Precisely how these features are relevant, if at all, remains a problem for investigation. In the case of witchcraft accusations, for example, it appears that the patterns resemble legal behavior to a remarkable degree: The social location of witches is significantly similar to that of defendants in legal cases, particularly criminal cases (see Black 1976:56–59). Witchcraft accusations even fall within the jurisdiction of law in some societies. The labeling of people as mentally ill has much in common with law as well (see Horwitz 1982). Some forms of social control, however, appear to have patterns that are quite unlike law: Whereas more law appears to flow downwardly than upwardly in status structures, for instance (Black 1976: Chapters 2–6), such forms as flight, self-destruction, and covert retaliation by the aggrieved seem to occur primarily in the opposite direction (see Baumgartner 1984a). Social status apparently is relevant both to law and to these other normative phenomena, then, but in different ways.

22. Compensation in tribal settings is not, however, totally indifferent to the social characteristics of the parties involved. The killing of a man may require more compensation than the killing of a woman or a child, for example, and the degree of intimacy or genealogical distance between the parties may be relevant as well. Nevertheless, the life or limb of all people of the same sex, age, and social distance is typically worth approximately the same from one case to the next. This is not true in modern societies such as the United States.

23. No matter how little social diversity a society or community might have within its population, the handling of grievances may vary greatly with the number of supporters that each side of a conflict is able to mobilize (see, e.g., Barth 1959: Chapter 9, especially 119–120; Gulliver 1963:297–302; 1969, 1971: Chapter 5).

24. Criminal cases of other kinds differ considerably in their social characteristics, and their handling varies accordingly. An example is homicide in modern societies such as the United States (see, e.g., Lundsgaarde 1977: 90–92, 224–229, 232; Bowers and Pierce 1980).

25. It might seem that this pattern would arise naturally from the wider range of responses to deviant behavior that higher levels of social control allow. When capital punishment is the maximum penalty, for example, a vast range of lesser penalties is theoretically possible, whereas this range is not available when the maximum is lower, as in small monetary fines. But this difference has no logically necessary relation to how these penalties are applied. Thus, if capital cases were socially identical in every respect, there would be no reason to expect that the application of the death penalty would display any more variability than the levying of $2 parking fines.

26. Relational distance refers to the degree to which people participate in one another's lives. It is measured by such variables as "the scope, frequency, and length of interaction

between people, the age of their relationship, and the nature of links between them in a social network" (Black 1976:41).

27. This is a more general formulation of a proposition about the behavior of law (see Black 1976:40–46 for the original formulation and a summary of the empirical evidence supporting it).

28. Research on helping behavior shows that the likelihood that a person in distress will receive help increases with the intimacy between the potential helper and the potential beneficiary (see Black and Baumgartner 1980:200–201).

29. Unequal intimacy with the principals does not, however, always result in the withdrawal or removal of a settlement agent. For practical reasons a replacement might be difficult to obtain, for example, or the disadvantaged principal might have social disabilities that would undermine an appeal for a replacement. Yet when the triangle formed by a third party and the principals is radically obtuse, with highly unequal relational distances between the third party and the two principals, the mode of intervention is not predicted to be settlement behavior at all. Instead, the third party is predicted to favor the closer side at the expense of the more distant side, thus acting more as a supporter than a settlement agent. This pattern is illustrated by the manner in which police officers tend to deal with complaints by citizens against fellow officers: Typically they side with their colleague from the beginning and function as supporters in opposition to the citizen (see, e.g., Chevigny 1969; Black 1980:174).

30. Social status refers here to the location of a person or group in social space (see Black 1979b:153). It might consist in a level of wealth, a degree of integration in a community (by employment, marriage, or other kinds of social participation), a degree of cultural conventionality, respectability, or other characteristics.

31. Settlement agents do not necessarily have both of these characteristics, but settlement behavior is especially likely when both occur together. (For an example of settlement agents who are equidistant from the principals but apparently equal to them in social status, see the description of mediators among the Ndendeuli of Tanzania in Gulliver 1969, 1971:Chapter 5).

32. Although settlement agents of this kind are not regularly available within their own ranks, people from outside the tribe may be recruited to intervene in a more authoritative fashion. For example, !Kung San Bushmen have been known to approach members of a neighboring Bantu tribe, the Tswana, for mediation services (Lee 1979:393). Mbuti Pygmies have tried to bring cases to the tribunal of the Ndaka (also Bantu), but have been turned away (Turnbull 1961:234–235). Under colonial rule, European officials were asked to provide the same services, and missionaries and even anthropologists have undoubtedly been approached as well.

33. Societies such as modern America, where people initiate a relatively large number of legal complaints but usually settle them without a formal trial, could arguably be described as negotiation societies.

34. These modes of evaluation seemingly correspond to the three "action orientations" delineated by Talcott Parsons—the evaluative, the cognitive, and the cathectic—which he suggests have direct parallels in three "culture patterns," namely, systems of value orientation, systems of belief, and systems of expressive symbols (Parsons 1951:12–14 and 327). Years ago, Leon Mayhew remarked to a class in which the present author was enrolled that Parsons meant to be classifying three fundamental concerns of human beings: the good, the true, and the beautiful.

2

CRIME AS SOCIAL CONTROL*

There is a sense in which conduct regarded as criminal is often quite the opposite. Far from being an intentional violation of a prohibition, much crime is moralistic and involves the pursuit of justice. It is a mode of conflict management, possibly a form of punishment, even capital punishment. Viewed in relation to law, it is self-help. To the degree that it defines or responds to the conduct of someone else — the victim — as deviant, crime is social control.[1] And to this degree it is possible to predict and explain crime with aspects of the sociological theory of social control, in particular, the theory of self-help.[2] After an overview of self-help in traditional and modern settings, the following pages briefly examine in turn the so-called struggle between law and self-help, the deterrence of crime, the processing of self-help by legal officials, and, finally, the problem of predicting and explaining self-help itself.

TRADITIONAL SELF-HELP

Much of the conduct described by anthropologists as conflict management, social control, or even law in tribal and other traditional societies is regarded as crime in modern societies. This is especially clear in the case of violent modes of redress such as assassination, feuding, fighting, maiming, and beating, but it also applies to the confiscation and destruction of property and to other forms of deprivation and humiliation. Such actions

27

typically express a grievance by one person or group against another (see Moore 1972:67–72). Thus, one anthropologist notes that among the Bena Bena of highland New Guinea, as among most tribes of that region, "rather than being proscribed, violent self-help is prescribed as a method of social control" (Langness 1972:182).[3] The same might be said of numerous societies throughout the world. On the other hand, violence is quite rare in many traditional societies, and at least some of it is condemned in all. What follows is not intended as a representative overview, then, since only the more violent societies and modes of self-help are illustrated. First consider homicide.

In one community of Maya Indians in southern Mexico, for example, any individual killed from ambush is automatically labeled "the one who had the guilt." Everyone assumes that the deceased individual provoked his own death through an act of wrongdoing: "Homicide is considered a *reaction* to crime, not a crime in itself" (Nash 1967:456). Similarly, it has been observed that in a number of equatorial African societies homicide is rarely predatory — committed for gain — but is nearly always related to a grievance or quarrel of some kind (Bohannan 1960:256; see, e.g., Fallers and Fallers 1960:78; La Fontaine 1960:103). Arctic Eskimos also kill people in response to various offenses, including adultery, insult, and simply being a nuisance (Hoebel 1954:83–88; van den Steenhoven 1956:32, 63; 1962:Chapter 4). The Ifugao of the Philippines hold that any "self-respecting man" must kill an adulterer discovered *in flagrante delicto* (Barton 1919:66–70). Under the same conditions, the Sarakatsan shepherds of Greece prefer that the wife be killed first and then her lover (Campbell 1964:152, 199). Societies such as these have, in effect, capital punishment administered on a private basis.

Unlike penalties imposed by the state, however, private executions of this kind often result in revenge or even a feud — a reciprocal exchange of violence that might last months or years (for cross-cultural studies of feuding, see Thoden van Velzen and van Wetering 1960; Otterbein and Otterbein 1965; see also Rieder 1984). Moreover, the person killed in retaliation may not be himself or herself a killer, for in these societies violent conflicts between nonkin are virtually always handled in a framework of collective responsibility — or, more precisely, collective liability — whereby all members of a social category (such as a family or lineage) are held accountable for the conduct of their fellows (see, e.g., Moore 1972; Koch 1984). Among the Cherokee Indians of southeastern North America, for example, "the relatives of the dead man had the duty and the right to kill the manslayer or one of his relatives" (Reid 1970:74; see also 75). Blood vengeance is also common among the Eskimo, though in some cases retaliation does not occur until years after the original killing (see Hoebel 1954:87–88).

Within a given society, vengeance against a killer may be allowed under some conditions but prohibited under others. For example, the Gisu of Uganda permit a man to kill anyone he finds stealing his property or having sexual relations with his wife or whom he suspects of witchcraft, and in these cases the relatives of the person killed are prohibited from reciprocating in kind (La Fontaine 1960:99). The Sarakatsan shepherds distinguish between a killing that should be avenged and counteravenged by the families involved (in theory, until all the men on one side are dead) and a killing that should be allowed to stand as a private execution: The former normally arises in response to an insult or during a quarrel, whereas the latter is essentially the punishment of someone who has offended the sexual honor of a woman, such as by seducing or raping her (Campbell 1964:201–202). In some societies the killer's family or other group may be expected to compensate the victim's survivors for their loss, even when it is recognized that the killing was intended as social control (see, e.g., Howell 1954:39–58; Diamond 1957; Lewis 1959; Koch 1974:82, 86–89; Jones 1974:68–69, 99–100).

Violence of other kinds also expresses a grievance in most instances. Among the Yanomamö of Venezuela and Brazil, for instance, women are routinely subjected to corporal punishment by their husbands:

> *Most reprimands meted out by irate husbands take the form of blows with the hand or with a piece of firewood, but a good many husbands are even more brutal. Some of them chop their wives with the sharp edge of a machete or ax, or shoot them with a barbed arrow in some nonvital area, such as the buttocks or leg. Many men are given over to punishing their wives by holding the hot end of a glowing stick against them, resulting in serious burns. (Chagnon 1977:82–83)*

In parts of East Africa, "husbands often assault their wives, sometimes with a slap, sometimes with a fist, a foot, or a stick" (Edgerton 1972:164). Among the Qolla of Peru, a husband may beat his wife "when her behavior warrants it," such as when she is "lazy" or "runs around with other men" (Bolton and Bolton 1973:64). Women among the Aborigines of Australia are subject to beatings, spearings, and other forms of violence which are, it might be added, "less likely to be avenged or compensated than injuries to men" (Hiatt 1965:126).[4] Another punishment for women in some societies is rape by a group of men, or "gang rape" (see, e.g., Llewellyn and Hoebel 1941:202–210; Murphy 1960:109). The punishment of children may also reach a degree of violence that would be viewed as criminal in a modern setting. For instance, the Jalé of highland New Guinea will "severely beat or even burn" a young boy who does not perform his chores satisfactorily (Koch 1974:51). The Kirghiz of western Siberia traditionally allow parents to kill their children if they see fit, so it seems likely that they practice a good deal of other corporal punishment as well (Riasanovsky 1938:10). Beating, maiming, and related forms of social control of women and children occur in only a limited range of societies, however, and are viewed primarily as offenses in many others (see, e.g., Fried 1953: 292; van den Steenhoven 1962:44–45; Maybury-Lewis 1967: 67–71).

Property destruction may also be a mode of social control. An extreme form is house-burning, a practice quite frequent in parts of East Africa (Edgerton 1972:164) and India (Fürer-Haimendorf 1943: 318). Animals, gardens, or other property might be destroyed as well. Among the Cheyenne of the American Plains, a man's horse might be killed (Llewellyn and Hoebel 1941:117), and in northern Albania, a man's dog might be killed, though under some conditions the latter is regarded as equivalent to the murder of a person (Hasluck 1954:76–78). In one case in Lebanon (later punished as a crime), an aggrieved man cut the branches off his adversary's walnut tree (Rothenberger 1978:169). Among the Qolla, crops are sometimes damaged as a punishment, such as "when a man methodically uproots his enemy's potato plants before they have produced any tubers" (Bolton 1973:234). Netsilik Eskimo parents may subtly encourage their children to destroy an offender's cache of food so that what appears to be mischief or vandalism may actually be a carefully orchestrated act of revenge (van den Steenhoven 1962:74). Young people are similarly mobilized to deal with offending adults in rural Wales (Rees 1950:80–84, 126–130; Peters 1972:109–124).

Property may also be confiscated as a form of social control, so that what might at first appear to a modern observer as unprovoked theft or burglary proves to be a response to the misconduct of the victim. Among the Mbuti Pygmies of Zaire, for instance, a seeming theft may be recognized by all as an "unofficial sanction" against a person who has incurred "public disapproval for some reason or another" (Turnbull 1965:199). Among the Qolla, the moralistic character of a theft is especially clear "when the object stolen has no value to the thief" (Bolton 1973:233), and it is a standard practice for the relatives of a murder victim to seize the presumed killer's livestock (Bolton 1970:233). Lastly, where women are regarded as the property of their fathers or husbands, rape may provide a means of retaliation against a man. This seems to have been the case in some of the gang rapes recorded as crimes in fourteenth-century England, for example, where even a widow might be attacked by a group of men as an act of revenge against her deceased husband (Hanawalt 1979:109, 153).[5] In some cases, then, rape may be another kind of confiscation.

MODERN SELF-HELP

A great deal of the conduct labeled and processed as crime in modern societies resembles the modes of conflict management — described above — that are found in traditional societies that have little or no law (in the sense of governmental social control; Black 1972:1096). Much of this conduct is a punishment or other expression of disapproval, whether applied reflectively or impulsively, with coolness or in the heat of passion. Some is an effort to achieve compensation, or restitution, for a harm that has been done. The response may occur long after the offense, perhaps weeks, months, or even years later; after a series of offenses, each viewed singly as only a minor aggravation but together viewed as intolerable; or as an immediate response to the offense, perhaps during a fight or other conflict, or after an assault, theft, insult, or injury.

As in tribal and other traditional societies, for example, most intentional homicide in modern life is a response to conduct that the killer regards as deviant. In Houston during 1969, for instance, over one-half of the homicides occurred in the course of a "quarrel," and another one-fourth occurred in alleged "self-defense" or were "provoked," whereas only a little over one-tenth occurred in the course of predatory behavior such as burglary or robbery (calculated from Lundsgaarde 1977:237). Only one-fifth of the offenders were strangers to their victims (Lundsgaarde 1977:230). Similar patterns were found in Philadelphia during a five-year period (Wolfgang 1958:191). Homicide is often a response to adultery or other matters relating to sex, love, or loyalty; disputes about domestic matters (financial affairs, drinking, housekeeping) or affronts to honor; conflicts relating to debts, property, and child custody; or other questions of right and wrong. Cases mentioned in the Houston study include one in which a young man killed his brother during a heated discussion about the latter's sexual advances toward his younger sisters, another in which a man killed his wife after she "dared" him to do so during an argument about which of several bills they should pay, one where a woman killed her husband during a quarrel in which the man struck her daughter (his stepdaughter), one in which a woman killed her 21-year-old son because he had been "fooling around with homosexuals and drugs," and two others in which people died from wounds inflicted during altercations over the parking of an automobile (Lundsgaarde 1977).[6] Like the killings in traditional societies described by anthropologists, most intentional homicide in modern society may thus be construed as social control, specifically as self-help, even if it is handled by legal officials as crime.[7] From this standpoint, it is apparent that capital punishment is quite common in modern America — in Texas, homicide is one of the ten leading causes of death — though it is nearly always a private rather than a public affair.[8]

Most conduct that a lawyer would label as assault may also be understood as self-help. In the vast majority of cases the people involved know one another, usually quite intimately, and the physical attack arises in the context of a grievance or quarrel. For example, most arrests for assault in the United States involve offenders and victims with a prior relationship (see, e.g., Vera Institute 1977:23–42), even though the police are far less likely to invoke the law when this is the case (Black 1971:1098; see also Black 1980:155–164). Commonly the assault is a punishment, such as when a husband beats or otherwise injures his wife because she has not lived up to his expectations. In one case that came to the attention of the Boston police, a woman complained that her husband had beaten her because supper was not ready when he came home from work (Black 1980:161), a state of affairs, incidentally, which might have been the woman's own way of expressing disapproval of her husband (see Baumgartner 1984a). In a case handled by the police in Washington, D.C., a woman hit her father-in-law with a baby bottle because he had become intoxicated and "called her vile names" (Black 1980:161). Other standards are enforced violently as well. In one instance that occurred in a major northeastern city and that apparently was not reported to the police, a young woman's brothers attacked and beat her boyfriend "for making her a drug addict"; in another, a young man was stabbed for cooperating with the police in a burglary investigation (Merry 1981:158, 180–181). In a case in Washington, D.C., that resulted in an arrest, a boy shot his gang leader for taking more than his proper share of the proceeds from a burglary (Allen 1977:40–43). Years later, the same individual shot someone who had been terrorizing young women — including the avenger's girlfriend — in his neighborhood. Although he pleaded guilty to "assault with a deadly weapon" and was committed to a reformatory, not surprisingly he described himself as "completely right" and his victim as "completely wrong" (Allen 1977:62–66, 69–70).

Indigenous people arrested for violence in colonial societies are likely to have a similar point of view: They may be proud of what they have done and admit it quite openly, even while being prosecuted as criminals by the foreign authorities.[9] Those apprehended in Europe for the crime of duelling — also a method of conflict resolution — typically lacked remorse for the same reasons (see Pitt-Rivers 1966:29–31). Thus, when asked by a priest to pray for forgiveness before being hanged for killing a man with a sword, one such offender in France exclaimed, "Do you call one of the cleverest thrusts in Gascony a crime?" (Baldick 1965:62). As in duelling, moreover, violence in modern societies is often prescribed by a code of honor. He who shrinks from it is disgraced as a coward (see generally Peristiany 1966; Werthman 1969; Horowitz and Schwartz 1974).

Many crimes involving the confiscation or destruction of property also prove to have a normative character when the facts come fully to light. There are, for example, moralistic burglaries, thefts, and robberies. Over one-third of the burglaries in New York City resulting in arrest involve people with a prior relationship and not infrequently express a grievance the burglar has against the victim (Vera Institute 1977:82). In one such case handled by the Boston police, a woman learned from a neighbor that while she was away "her estranged husband had entered her apartment, wrecked it, loaded all of her clothes into his car, and driven away, presumably headed for his new home several hundred miles away" (Black 1980:115). Although the specific nature of this man's grievance was not mentioned, it seems apparent that his actions were punitive and possibly compensatory to some degree, and surely his estranged wife understood this as well. In a New York City case resulting in two arrests for burglary, two black women barged into the home of an elderly white woman at midnight to confront her because earlier in the day she had remonstrated with their children for throwing rocks at her window (Vera Institute 1977:88). A crime may also be committed against a particular individual to express the disapproval of a number of people in a neighborhood or community. A former burglar thus notes in his autobiography that early in his career he selected his victims partly to avenge his neighbors:

> We always tried to get the dude that the neighbors didn't like too much or the guy that was hard on the people who lived in the neighborhood. Like, some storekeepers wouldn't let people have credit till the end of the week. We used to call them just plain cheezy. Say you go in there for a loaf of bread and a loaf of bread cost seventeen cents and you didn't have but fifteen cents — he wouldn't let you out there! People like that — just plain scrooges. . . . I like to think that all the places we robbed, that we broke into, was kind of like the bad guys. (Allen 1977:39–40)

The victims of moralistic crime may nevertheless be entirely unaware of why they have been selected, especially when the offender is unknown. Such crimes may therefore be understood as instances of secret social control (compare Becker 1963:20).[10]

Another possible mode of self-help is robbery, or theft involving violence. In New York City, where over one-third of the people arrested for robbery are acquainted with their victims, the crime often arises from a quarrel over money (Vera Institute 1977:65–71). In one case, a woman reported that her sister and her sister's boyfriend took her purse and $40 after assaulting her and threatening to kill her baby, but she later explained that this had arisen from a misunderstanding: The boyfriend wanted reimbursement for a baby carriage he had bought for her that she thought had been a gift (Vera Institute 1977:69–70). It seems, in fact, that robbery is frequently a form of debt collection and an alternative to law. The same applies to embezzlement, though it may also express other complaints against the employer who is victimized (see Cressey 1953:57–59, 63–66).

Conduct known as vandalism, or malicious destruction of property, proves to be a form of social control in many cases as well. Far from being merely "malicious," "non-utilitarian," or "negativistic," with "no purpose, no rhyme, no reason" (Cohen 1955:25–30, including quoted material in note 4), much vandalism in modern society resembles the moralistic destruction of crops, animals, and other valuables in traditional societies. But whereas, say, a Plains Indian might kill a horse, a modern agent of justice might damage the offender's automobile. In one American neighborhood where parking spaces on the street are scarce, for example, the residents have their own distribution system with customary rules and enforcement procedures: In the winter, one rule is that whoever shovels the snow from a parking space is its "owner," and persistent violators may find their automobile pushed into a snow bank, spray-painted, or otherwise abused (Thomas-Buckle and Buckle 1982:84, 86–87). Vandalism may also be reciprocated in a feudlike pattern of mutual destruction. In one such case in a northeastern city, a young man found that someone had broken the radio antenna on his automobile, learned from some children who had done it, and thereupon proceeded to slash the tires of the offender's automobile (Merry 1981:179).

Business places and dwellings are often damaged to punish their owners or inhabitants. Arson, or burning, has a long history of this kind.[11] Less severe sanctions, however, are far more frequent. In one case handled by the police in Washington, D.C., the proprietor of a bar advised his customers to ignore a deaf-mute man trying to solicit money from them, so the man, enraged, broke one of the windows (Black 1980:179). In a case occurring in a suburb of New York City, a young man drove his car across someone's lawn during a quarrel, and in another incident in the same town several young men spray-painted an older man's house in the middle of the night because he had called the police to disperse them when they were sitting in their cars drinking beer and listening to music (Baumgartner 1984b:92–93). If all the facts were known, then, it seems likely that much seemingly senseless and random vandalism would prove to be retaliation by young people against adults (see Greenberg 1977:202–204). Some may even be done by children on behalf of their parents in a pattern analogous to that found among the Eskimos mentioned earlier (for a possible example, see Black 1980:167–168). If parents themselves are the offenders, however, other strategies might be followed. Among the Tarahumara Indians of northern Mexico, children with a grievance against their parents often "run away" from home, staying with an uncle or grandparent for a few days before returning (Fried 1953:291). Qolla children have a similar custom, locally known as "losing themselves" (Bolton and Bolton 1973:15–16). Modern children do this as well, though like vandalism it is regarded as a form of juvenile delinquency.

Finally, it might be noted that the practice of collective liability — whereby all the people in a social category are held accountable for the conduct of their fellows — occurs in modern as well as traditional societies. This is most apparent during a war, revolution, or riot, when anyone might suffer for the deeds of someone else, but during peaceful times, too, seemingly random violence often follows the same logic. Today a police officer might become the victim of a surprise attack by a stranger, for example, because of the conduct of one or more fellow officers in the past. Seemingly random crime of other kinds may also involve collective liability. Thus, for instance, a black rapist described his selection of white victims as vengeance against white people in general:

> It delighted me that I was defying and trampling upon the white man's law, upon his system of values, and that I was defiling his women — and this point, I believe, was the most satisfying to me because I was very resentful over the historical fact of how the white man has used the black woman. I felt I was getting revenge. (Cleaver 1968:14)

Similarly, a former burglar and robber remarked that he once selected his victims primarily from a relatively affluent neighborhood, but not simply because this provided a chance of greater material gain: "I really disliked them people, 'cause it seemed like they thought they was better 'cause they had more" (Allen 1977:32–33). People might be held collectively liable because of their neighborhood, social class, race, or ethnicity. Crime by young people against adult strangers may have this logic in some cases as well: All adults might be held liable for the conduct of those known personally, such as police, teachers, and parents.[12] Among young people themselves, particularly in large American cities, rival "gangs" may engage in episodic violence resembling the feud in traditional settings, where each member of a feuding group is liable — to injury or even death — for the conduct of the other members (see, e.g., Yablonsky 1962). A significant amount of crime in modern society may even resemble what anthropologists describe as "raiding," a form of predatory behavior often directed at people collectively defined as deserving of revenge (see, e.g., Sweet 1965; Tanner 1966:41; Ekvall 1968:52–53; Schneider 1971:4). And some might properly be construed as "banditry," a form of primitive rebellion by those at the bottom of society against their social superiors (see Hobsbawm 1959: Chapter 2; 1969). In short, although much crime in modern society directly and unambiguously expresses a grievance by one person against another, this may be only the most visible portion of a much broader phenomenon.

THEORETICAL CONSIDERATIONS

When a moralistic crime is handled by the police or prosecuted in court, the official definition of the event is drastically different from that of the people involved, particularly the alleged offender. In the case of a husband who shoots his wife's lover, for example, the definition of the offender and the victim is reversed: The wife's lover is defined as the victim, even though he was shot because of an offense he committed against the woman's husband. Moreover, the lover's offense is precisely the kind for which violent social control — by the husband — is viewed as acceptable and appropriate, if not obligatory, in numerous tribal and other traditional societies. Even in modern society, it might be said that the husband is charged with violating the criminal law because he enforced his rights in what many regard as the customary law of marriage. The victim thus becomes the offender, and vice versa. The state prosecutes the case in its own name, while the original offender against morality (if alive) testifies as a witness against the man he has victimized — surely a perverse proceeding from the standpoint of the defendant (compare Christie 1977). It is also enlightening in this regard to consider criminal cases arising from quarrels and fights, where each party has a grievance against the other. Here the state often imposes the categories of offender and victim on people who were themselves contesting the proper application of these labels during the altercation in question. Whether there was originally a cross-complaint or not, however, in all these cases the state defines someone with a grievance as a criminal. The offense lies in how the grievance was pursued. The crime is self-help.

It should be apparent from much of the foregoing that in modern society the state has only theoretically achieved a monopoly over the legitimate use of violence (compare, e.g., Weber 1919:78; 1922:156; Elias 1939:201–202). In reality, violence flourishes (particularly in modern America), and most of it involves ordinary citizens who seemingly view their conduct as a perfectly legitimate exercise of social control. It might therefore be observed that the struggle between law and self-help in the Western world did not end in the Middle Ages, as legal historians claim (e.g., Pike 1876:Chapter 13; Pollock and Maitland 1898:Volume 2, 574; Pound 1921:139–140; see also Hobhouse 1906:Chapter 3). It continues.[13] Many people still "take the law into their own hands." They seem to view their grievances as their own business, not that of the police or other officials, and resent the intrusion of law (see Matza 1964:Chapter 5). They seem determined to have justice done, even if it means that they will be defined as criminals.[14] Those who commit murder, for example, often appear to be resigned to their fate at the hands of the authorities; many wait patiently for the police to arrive; some even call to report their own crimes (see generally Lundsgaarde 1977). In cases of this kind, indeed, the individuals involved might arguably be regarded as martyrs. Not unlike workers who violate a prohibition to strike — knowing they will go to jail — or others who defy the law on grounds of principle, they do what they think is right and willingly suffer the consequences.[15]

Deterrence and Self-Help

To the degree that people feel morally obligated to commit crimes, it would seem that the capacity of the criminal law to discourage them — its so-called deterrent effect — must be weakened. For example, homicides committed as a form of capital punishment would seem to be more difficult to deter than those committed entirely in pursuit of personal gain (on the deterrability of the latter, see Chambliss 1967). This is not to deny that moralistic homicide can be discouraged to some extent. In fact, one former resident of Harlem (in New York City) noted that the inhabitants of that unusually violent area seem to debate in their own minds whether moralistic homicide is ultimately worth its legal consequences: "I think everybody was curious about whether or not it was worth it to kill somebody and save your name or your masculinity, defend whatever it was that had been offended — whether it was you or your woman or somebody in your family" (Brown 1965:220). He adds that during his years in Harlem this question loomed especially large whenever anyone was executed in prison (Brown 1965:220). That the desirability of killing another person is entertained at all is remarkable, however, particularly when the death penalty is believed to be a possible result (a belief that is largely unfounded; see next section). Furthermore, because other crimes of self-help carry fewer legal risks than homicide, they should be even harder to discourage. In any event, a theory of deterrence should recognize that the power of punishment to discourage crime partly depends on whether a given crime is itself a form of social control (for other relevant variables see, e.g., Andenaes 1966; Chambliss 1967; Zimring 1971).

A related question is the extent to which crime itself is deterred by self-help rather than by — or in addition to — law. Although many citizens are entirely dependent on legal officials such as the police to handle criminal offenders, others are prepared to protect themselves and their associates by any means at their disposal, including violence. It is well-known among potential predators in one American neighborhood, for example, that a number of the residents would be dangerous to victimize, in some cases because they enjoy the protection of family members who act as their champions (see Merry 1981:178–179). Such people are left alone. Entire segments of a community may also be avoided from fear of retaliation. For this reason, some thieves and robbers may avoid the poor: "One of the most dangerous things in the world is to steal from poor people. . . . When you steal from the poor, you gamble with your life" (Brown 1965:214; see also Allen 1977:50–52). Moreover, since the deterrent effect of social control generally increases with its severity (for qualifications, see Zimring 1971:83–90), it is noteworthy that self-help is often more severe than law. A burglar or robber might be executed by the intended victim, for example, though burglary and robbery are not capital crimes in modern codes of law. Accordingly, to the degree that self-help is effectively repressed by the state, crime of other kinds might correspondingly increase. Among the Gusii of Kenya, for example, rape dramatically increased after the British prohibited traditional violence against rapists and instituted a less severe system of criminal justice (Le Vine 1959:976–977).[16] Perhaps some of the predatory crime in modern society is similarly a result of a decline in self-help.

The Processing of Self-Help

Even while the ancient struggle between law and self-help continues, the response of legal officials to those handling their own grievances by violence and other aggression is not nearly as severe as might be supposed. In fact, crimes of self-help are handled with comparative leniency. An extreme of this pattern occurred in medieval England, for example, where the concept of "self-defense" was often generously applied to the otherwise capital crime of homicide: In cases in which a killing involved social control, juries routinely avoided a conviction by fabricating a version of the incident in which the victim had first attacked the defendant, forcing him to resist with violence in order to save his own life (Green 1972, 1976:428–436). Likewise, in later centuries, European authorities and juries were generally reluctant to enforce laws against duelling (see Baldick 1965:Chapters 4–7; Andrew 1980). Early in the twentieth century, the same applied to the handling of lynchings in the American South — executions carried out by a group of private citizens, usually against a black man believed to have victimized a white: Typically no one was arrested, much less prosecuted or punished, though the killers were frequently well-known and readily available (see, e.g., Raper 1933). Today, much violent self-help continues to be tolerated by American officials and juries. Incidents that a lawyer would normally classify as felonious assault, for example — involving severe bodily injury or the threat thereof — are unlikely to result in arrest if the offender and victim are intimately related (see, e.g., Black 1980:180–185; see also Black 1971:1097–1098). Where an arrest is made, prosecution and conviction are less likely when the offense entails an element of self-help. In Houston, for instance, people arrested for homicide are often released without prosecution, and in many cases this seems to be related to the moralistic nature of the killing.[17] In 1969, 40% of those arrested for killing a relative (such as a spouse or sibling) were released without prosecution, as were 37% of those arrested for killing a friend or other associate and 24% of those arrested for killing a stranger (Lundsgaarde 1977:232). And when self-help is involved, such as when a burglary or robbery is committed to collect an unpaid debt, offenses that initially result in prosecution are likely to be abandoned or dismissed at a later point in the process (see, e.g., Vera Institute 1977:69–70, 87–88). At every stage, then, crimes of self-help commonly receive a degree of immunity from law.

The capacity of law to deter crimes of self-help is seemingly weak in the first place, and surely any degree of leniency in the handling of these crimes — if known among the population — makes it weaker still. But still it might be wondered why so much self-help occurs in a society such as modern America. Why do so many people criminally pursue their own grievances in a society where law is so highly developed? Why, in particular, are they so violent?

The Theory of Self-Help

Several centuries ago, Thomas Hobbes argued that without a sovereign state — without law — a "war of every one against every one" would prevail, and life would be "solitary, poor, nasty, brutish, and short" (1651:100). Many stateless societies have since been observed by anthropologists, however, and Hobbes's theory has proven to be somewhat overstated: Life without law is not nearly as precarious as he believed (see, e.g., Middleton and Tait 1958; Gluckman 1965b; MacCormack 1976; Roberts 1979). Even so, the idea that violence is associated with statelessness still enjoys considerable support. With various refinements and qualifications, an absence of state authority is used to explain high levels of violence in settings as diverse as the highlands of New Guinea (Brown 1964; Koch 1974:Chapter 7),

Lake Titicaca in the Andes (Bolton 1970:12–16), and western Sicily (Blok 1974: 210–212).[18] It is also used to explain war and other violent self-help in international relations (e. g., Hoffman 1968; Arendt 1969:5; Koch 1974:173–175). A version of the same approach may be relevant to an understanding of self-help in modern society.

Hobbesian theory would lead us to expect more violence and other crimes of self-help in those contemporary settings where law — governmental social control — is least developed, and this prediction appears to fit the facts: Crimes of self-help are more likely where law is less available. This is most apparent where legal protection is withheld as a matter of public policy, such as when a contract violates the law. A gambling debt is not legally enforceable, for example, and the same applies to transactions in illicit narcotics, prostitution, stolen goods, and the like. Perhaps for this reason many underworld businesses find it necessary to maintain, in effect, their own police, such as the "strong-arms" of illegal loan operations and the "pimps" who oversee the work of prostitutes (see, e.g., Allen 1977:100). Furthermore, it appears that social control in these settings is relatively violent (but see Reuter 1984).

Law is unavailable, or relatively so, in many other modern settings as well, though not necessarily as a matter of public policy. A teenager with a grievance against an adult, for example, will generally be ignored or even reprimanded by the police (Black 1980:152–155). Lower-status people of all kinds — blacks and other minorities, the poor, the homeless — enjoy less legal protection, especially when they have complaints against their social superiors, but also when conflict erupts among themselves (see Black 1976:Chapters 2–6). To the police and other authorities, the problems of these people seem less serious, their injuries less severe, their honor less important.[19] A fight or quarrel among them may even be viewed as itself a "disturbance of the peace," an offense in its own right, regardless of the issues dividing the parties (see Black and Baumgartner 1983:106–107). People in intimate relationships, too, such as members of the same family or household, find that legal officials are relatively unconcerned about their conflicts, particularly if they occur in private and do not disturb anyone else (see Black 1976:40–44; 1980:Chapter 5).[20] In all these settings neglected by law, crimes of self-help are comparatively common. There are, so to speak, stateless locations in a society such as modern America, and in them the Hobbesian theory appears to have some validity.[21]

Yet the likelihood of self-help is not merely a function of the availability of law, and, moreover, crimes of self-help are not always handled leniently by legal officials. Different locations and directions in social space have different patterns. In particular, the relation between law and self-help depends on who has a grievance against whom.

Four patterns can be identified: First, law may be relatively unavailable both to those with grievances and to those who are the objects of self-help, as when people of low status and people who are intimate have conflicts with one another (on the distribution of law, see generally Black 1976). This pattern was emphasized earlier in the chapter. Second, law may be relatively unavailable to those with grievances in comparison to those who have offended them. Should the former employ self-help, they may be vulnerable to harsh treatment by legal officials. This is the situation of people with a grievance against a social superior, such as a teenager with a grievance against an adult, and may help to explain why they tend to develop their own techniques of social control, including covert retaliation, self-destruction, and flight (see Baumgartner 1984a). Those with grievances against a social inferior illustrate a third pattern: Law is readily available to them, but not to those against whom they might employ self-help. In this situation, the aggrieved party seemingly has a choice of law or self-help. A father might easily obtain legal help against his teenaged son, for example, but if instead he simply beats the boy—a form of self-help—he is unlikely to be handled with severity by the police or other officials (see Black 1980:152–155). The fourth possibility, where law is readily available both to those with grievances and to those who have offended them, is seen when people of high status and people who are strangers have conflicts with one another. Here self-help seems to be relatively infrequent. In sum, law and self-help are unevenly distributed across social space, and each is relevant to the behavior of the other.[22]

CONCLUSION

The approach taken in this chapter departs radically from traditional criminology (as seen, e.g., in Cohen 1955; Miller 1958; Cloward and Ohlin 1960; Sutherland and Cressey 1960). Indeed, the approach taken here is, strictly speaking, not criminological at all, since it ignores the characteristics of crime as such (including, for example, how criminals differ from other people and how their behavior differs from that which is not prohibited). Instead, it draws attention to a dimension of many crimes usually viewed as a totally different—even opposite—kind of human behavior, namely, social control. Crime often expresses a grievance.[23] This implies that many crimes belong to the same family as gossip, ridicule, vengeance, punishment, and law itself. It also implies that to a significant degree we can predict and explain crime with a sociological theory of social control, specifically a theory of self-help. Beyond this, it might be worthwhile to contemplate what else crime has in common with noncriminal conduct. As remarked earlier (in Note 7), for instance, some crime is economic behavior, and some is recreation. In other words, for certain theoretical purposes we might usefully ignore the fact that crime is criminal at all.[24] The criminality of crime is defined by law, and therefore falls within the jurisdiction of a completely different theory (see especially Black 1976).

ENDNOTES

*Reprinted with permission (and minor revision) from pages 1–27 in *Toward a General Theory of Social Control*, Volume 2: *Selected Problems*, edited by Donald Black. Orlando: Academic Press, 1984. A shorter version appeared in the *American Sociological Review* 48 (February, 1983): 34–45, and permission was also obtained from the American Sociological Association.

The following people made helpful comments on an earlier draft: M. P. Baumgartner, John L. Comaroff, Mark Cooney, Jack P. Gibbs, Richard O. Lempert, Craig B. Little, Sally Engle Merry, Alden D. Miller, Calvin K. Morrill, Trevor W. Nagel, Lloyd E. Ohlin, Alan Stone, and Sheldon Stryker.

1. The concept of social control employed here refers to any process by which people define or respond to deviant behavior (Black 1976:105). It is a broad category that includes such diverse phenomena as a frown or scowl, a scolding or reprimand, expulsion from an organization, an arrest or lawsuit, a prison sentence, commitment to a mental hospital, a riot, or a military reprisal. This concept entails no assumptions or implications concerning the impact of social control on conformity, social order, or anything else, nor does it address the subjective meanings of social control for those who exercise or experience it (see generally Black 1984b). In some cases, for example, an arrest might harden a criminal's commitment to crime, disrupt the order of a community, or violate the moral preferences of the officer who makes it, but in the present usage every arrest is nevertheless construed as an instance of social control.

2. Self-help refers to the expression of a grievance by unilateral aggression. It is thus distinguishable from social control by third parties such as police officers or judges and from avoidance behavior such as desertion or divorce. (This conception of self-help derives from collaborative work with M. P. Baumgartner.)

3. Illustrations of traditional self-help are given here in the present tense (known in anthropology as the "ethnographic present"), although many of these practices have changed considerably — if not disappeared altogether — since they were originally observed.

4. In cross-cultural perspective, Aborigine women are notable for their vulnerability to violence. If two men quarrel over a woman, for example, a third man may attack and kill the woman, or threaten to do so, justifying this by saying, "She is really the cause of all the trouble" (Hiatt 1965:119, note 3; 139–140). A man will attack his own sister with a spear if he hears someone swear at her, possibly because he holds her responsible for the disturbance and for his own distress in the situation. He might also subsequently attack his other sisters, since he strives to treat each of his sisters "in exactly the same manner" (Warner 1958:110–113; Hiatt 1965:112–119).

5. For an overview of self-help in fourteenth-century England, see Pike (1873:246–255), who notes — remarkably in the spirit of the present discussion — that "the criminal tendencies of modern times seem in many cases to have been handed down from a period when that which is now considered crime was thought very nearly akin to virtue" (247).

6. Similar conditions apparently accompany most homicide everywhere. In modern India, for example, typically the killer "correctly or incorrectly perceives of the victim as a violator of important social norms" such as those pertaining to sexual infidelity, property, or the treatment of women and children (Driver 1961:157).

7. Crimes of self-help are distinguishable from other categories of conduct regarded as criminal, such as certain kinds of economic behavior (e.g., predatory robbery or the selling of illicit goods and services) and recreation (e.g., gambling or underage drinking of alcoholic beverages). Some crime is also multidimensional. For instance, an incident might be both moralistic and predatory at once, as when someone is killed in a quarrel but then robbed as well.

It is presently impossible to specify with precision what proportion of all crimes involves self-help, and in any case this varies across societies and other settings. We can surmise from available evidence, however, that in modern societies such as the United States, at least three-fourths of the non-negligent criminal homicides are cases of social control (see Wolfgang 1958: Chapter 10; Lundsgaarde 1977:237).

8. Compare Wolfgang and Ferracuti's (1966) argument that homicide (and related conduct) reflects a "subculture of violence." For a criticism of their view in light of cross-cultural evidence, see Haft-Picker (1980).

9. This reportedly applied, for example, to the Nuer of the Sudan when they lived under British rule:

A Nuer dispute is usually a balance of wrongs, for a man does not, except in sexual matters, wantonly commit an act of aggression. He does not steal a man's cow, club him or withhold his bride-cattle in divorce, unless he has some score to settle. Consequently it is very rare for a man to deny the damage he has caused. He seeks to justify it, so that a settlement is an adjustment between rival claims. I have been told by [a British] officer with wide experience of Africans that Nuer defendants are remarkable in that they very seldom lie in cases brought before Government tribunals. They have no need to, since they are only anxious to justify the damage they have caused by showing that it is retaliation for damage the plaintiff has inflicted earlier. (Evans-Pritchard 1940:171–172)

Another observer of the Nuer notes that "it is rare that a killer attempts to conceal his guilt, even if in the heat of battle there are no witnesses" (Howell 1954:66). This honesty seemed remarkable to the British, for they were accustomed to their own system of justice in which only one side could be recognized as right or wrong, and in which the moral claims of an accused criminal were not generally regarded as relevant.

In Australia, the Aborigines have long been subject to what they call "whitefella law" for certain practices pertaining to the enforcement of "blackfella law," particularly religious taboos. In one such case, six Aborigines were prosecuted after admittedly following their tradition of killing a fellow tribesman who had violated a major taboo (by stealing a number of sacred relics and selling them to a white tourist). A white lawyer successfully argued for reduced sentences on the ground that "according to tribal law they were doing only what they had to do" and that "if Your Honour took too severe a view of their breach of our law, Your Honour would in effect be punishing them for adherence to their own code" (Eggleston 1976:289–293; see also Maddock 1977; Australian Law Reform Commission 1980:37–40).

10. To some readers, "secret social control" might seem a contradiction in terms. Perhaps such a contradiction would exist if the concept of social control meant an effort to influence the future conduct of a population or, at least, the future conduct of a particular deviant. But recall that social control here refers simply to any process by which people define or respond to deviant behavior (see Note 1). This does not imply that social control influences conduct (though it obviously does in many cases) or that it is intended to do so (though often it is).

People of lower status may be especially prone to use secret forms of social control against their superiors (see Baumgartner 1984a). A secret mode used more widely in social space — apparently in all societies — is gossip (see Merry 1984).

11. On "revenge arson" in fourteenth-century England, for example, see Hanawalt (1979:90–91); on anonymous letters threatening arson in eighteenth-century and nineteenth-century England, see Thompson (1975).

12. Subpopulations such as women, old people, and the poor may be particularly vulnerable to vengeance of this kind. In cross-cultural perspective, this is not inconsistent with the practice of collective liability. In some tribal societies, for example, retaliation may be taken against those who are physically less dangerous, such as women and children, and against those who are less likely to be avenged, such as social isolates and visitors (e.g., Koch 1974). Anyone who happens to be available may also be considered a satisfactory victim (e.g., Harner 1972:172). On the other hand, a "code of honor" may govern revenge and limit it, for instance, to adult males able to defend themselves (e.g., Hasluck 1954:Chapter 24; see also Stauder 1972:166).

13. The struggle, however, was once more rancorous and spectacular, and sometimes included open confrontations between those engaging in self-help — along with their supporters — and the authorities who defined their conduct as criminal. In medieval England, for example, a prisoner's friends might forcibly seize him from the sherriff, or an armed band might violently challenge the authorities in the courtroom itself (see, e.g., Pike 1873: 257–258).

Like so much else, the struggle between law and self-help has become more individualized and is mostly invisible to the general public. Only an occasional riot harkens back to the earlier pattern.

14. Criminologists have suggested that offenders may condemn their victims to "neutralize" their own feelings of guilt (Sykes and Matza 1957:668; see also Fattah 1976). But the argument here is that many of these condemnations may be authentic. Some criminals may be telling the truth.

15. Others become fugitives and are driven further into a life of crime. In southern Italy, for example, young men often become bandits after first committing an act of violence in defense of their honor: Despite popular approval of their behavior, they are sought by the police (who define their violence as crime) and thereafter lead a life of banditry merely to survive without a legitimate livelihood (Brögger 1968:233–234). Such banditry is a classic example of "secondary deviation" — deviant behavior that results from social control (Lemert 1967). At least a few robbers and thieves in modern societies such as the United States probably have a similar history.

16. It appears that predatory behavior within tribal and peasant villages is often effectively deterred by the threat of self-help. Such was the impression, for example, of an anthropologist who studied the Nuer of the Sudan: "It is the knowledge that a Nuer is brave and will stand up against aggression and enforce his rights by club and spear that ensures respect for person and property" (Evans-Pritchard 1940:171; see also Howell 1954:231–232).

Why people in any society refrain from victimizing their fellows raises difficult questions of motivation, however, and lies beyond the scope of the present discussion.

17. Until 1973, Texas expressly permitted a husband to kill a man he discovered in an act of adultery with his wife. As of 1972, New Mexico and Utah also had statutes defining such a killing as "justifiable homicide," while Georgia did so by judicial decision. The rest of the American states traditionally regard adultery as a "provocation" that reduces the seriousness of a homicide from murder to voluntary manslaughter (La Fave and Scott 1972:576). Even so, juries in these latter states have long been reputed to ignore the written law and to

treat such cases as justifiable homicide as well. This is known as an "unwritten law" (see, e.g., Roberts 1922).

In modern American law, homicide committed as self-help is everywhere permitted as "justifiable" if it qualifies as "self-defense," "defense of another," or "prevention of felony" (see, e.g., Torcia 1979: Sections 125, 127–128).

18. A cross-cultural survey of 50 societies indicates that those with the least "political integration"—which means, *inter alia*, those without a state—are the most likely to have "coercive self-help" as their dominant mode of conflict management (Koch and Sodergren 1976:454–455).

19. Such individuals are relatively unlikely to bring their grievances to legal officials in the first place. For instance, most teenagers would not consider calling the police about an adult, and the same generally applies to those with a grievance against an intimate such as a spouse or friend (but see Black 1980:Chapter 5, especially 124–128). It might even be said that many people choose statelessness as a way of life. This may undermine still further the capacity of law to deter crimes of self-help.

20. Self-help may occasionally function—whether by design or not—as a mechanism by which law is mobilized among those who might otherwise be ignored. It appears that the Metá of the Cameroon consciously employ violence as a technique of this kind: Because village elders are empowered to arbitrate disputes only if the parties become violent, individuals may initiate a fight to obtain a hearing of their case (Dillon 1980:664; see also Gluckman 1967:79). Children may use the same technique to mobilize adults. Some violence in modern society may likewise serve as a cry for help from people less able to attract legal attention without it. Reports of violence may even be fabricated to ensure that the police will handle cases that the callers fear—possibly with justification—would otherwise be dismissed as trivial (for a likely example, see Black 1980:151). But then, as noted earlier, the police are likely to respond with indifference anyway.

21. The opposite of statelessness can occur as well, with opposite results: The availability of law can expand to such a degree that it nearly displaces self-help. People may become so dependent on law that they are unwilling or unable to handle their own grievances. It appears, in fact, that this extreme is almost reached by so-called totalitarian societies, such as the Soviet Union under Stalin or Germany under Hitler, where the state insinuates itself throughout a population by actively encouraging citizens to make use of its coercive apparatus whenever they have a grievance of any kind. Since apparently nearly anyone can have nearly anyone else sent to prison, each person is dangerous to others, yet vulnerable to them at the same time (see Gross 1984). The result resembles what Hobbes called a "war of every one against every one," but within the framework of a state. And self-help tends to wither away.

22. Other conditions are also relevant to the incidence of self-help. But no effort will be made here to develop a comprehensive theory. The point is merely to promote a sociological theory of self-help and to offer a single formulation that it might include. Furthermore, despite the emphasis in the present discussion on contemporary society, such a theory would apply to all instances of this phenomenon, traditional as well as modern.

Self-help in traditional societies may provide insights into modern self-help, and vice versa. For example, whereas anthropological descriptions of violent self-help in tribal societies might suggest that people resort to this mode of social control in direct relation to the social distance between the aggrieved and the alleged offender (see, e.g., Evans-Pritchard 1940:150–172; Middleton 1965:46–52; Koch 1974:Chapters 4–6), the evidence from modern societies indicates that this tendency is not universal. As noted earlier, for instance, violent self-help frequently occurs in families and other settings where the parties involved are extremely close. But not all modern intimates are violent when they have a grievance: Middle-class people, for example, are more inclined simply to avoid one another and, for that matter, are highly unlikely to use violence against strangers (Baumgartner 1984b). In any event, a theory of self-help should be constructed on an empirical foundation broader than that characteristically employed by either anthropologists or sociologists.

23. This analysis could also be extended to other kinds of illegal behavior. A case legally regarded as a breach of contract or as slander or libel, for example, might similarly qualify as self-help.

24. The definition of conduct as criminal may also be relevant to its form and frequency. Even so, a particular category of crime may share more with noncriminal conduct than with other crime. The use of illicit drugs seemingly resembles the legal consumption of alcoholic beverages more than robbery or rape, for example, and extortion seemingly resembles the practices of many landlords, physicians, and corporations more than vandalism, trespassing, or treason.

3

COMPENSATION AND THE SOCIAL STRUCTURE OF MISFORTUNE*

Compensation is a style of social control in which a grievance is handled by a payment to the aggrieved.[1] The following discussion introduces and elaborates the sociological theory of this phenomenon. It concludes with an application of the theory to the evolution of compensation, including its explosive growth in modern societies such as the United States.

COMPENSATION AS A DEPENDENT VARIABLE

Compensation falls within the jurisdiction of a field of sociological inquiry ultimately concerned with the prediction and explanation of social control of every kind. It is one of several major styles in which particular grievances are handled. Each style has its own language and logic, including its own standards, questions, and solutions (see Black 1976:4–6; 1984b:8–12; see also Horwitz 1982:122–127).

Styles of Social Control

The penal style of social control speaks in a language of prohibitions, violations, guilt, and retribution. Illustrated in modern law by criminal justice, it focuses on conduct and punishes those who violate its prohibitions.

The conciliatory style focuses on relationships and seeks to restore harmony between those in conflict. It is seen in the mediation of marital, industrial, and international conflict. The therapeutic style focuses on persons who suffer from abnormalities and seeks to help them. Modern psychiatry is an example. In contrast to these, the compensatory style of social control focuses primarily on the consequences of conduct rather than on the conduct itself, the relationship it might disrupt, or the person who is its agent. It speaks of obligations, damages, debts, and restitution. It examines the misfortune of a particular victim and addresses the question of who, if anyone, should provide a remedy. An example is the modern law of accidental injuries.

Although each style of social control may seem a natural or even automatic reaction to the problem it addresses in contemporary life, crosscultural and historical evidence indicates that this is far from true. What is compensated in one setting is punished in another; in a third, the restoration of social harmony takes priority, while in still another the problem is defined as spiritual possession or mental illness. Consider violence.

In a modern society such as the United States, violence is often regarded as criminal and worthy of punishment, but it might also result in mediation to repair the relationship involved, psychotherapy to treat a "violent personality," or a civil lawsuit to obtain compensatory damages. Variation in the response to violence across societies and history is even more dramatic. Although a killing brings punishment or retaliation by the victim's family in many societies, in others compensation is a common response (for examples of the latter, see Howell 1954; Lewis 1959; Gulliver 1963; Jones 1974; Koch 1974). And everywhere there are exceptions. Among the Bedouin of Cyrenaica in Libya, for instance, killings are frequently compensated with a payment of camels, but when a killing occurs between people widely separated in social space, feuding or warfare is more likely (Peters 1967:267–269). On the other hand, a killing between people in the same camp is endured as a misfortune that cannot be remedied, though the killer (scorned as one who "defecates in the tent") typically goes into temporary exile (263–264). If the victim is a close relative of the killer, the latter is regarded as "out of his mind," for the offense is otherwise inconceivable (272). If a man kills his father, this too is inconceivable and proves that the killer is not really the victim's son: The killer must therefore be illegitimate, and his mother is condemned as an adulteress (275). If a woman is killed under any circumstances, however, the death is always regarded as accidental, since a man would never do such a thing intentionally (270).

Similar variations occur elsewhere. The Lugbara of Uganda, for instance, consider it unthinkable that a man would deliberately kill his brother, and when this happens they avoid the killer as "unnatural" and dangerous. But they demand neither revenge nor blood money. Other killings within the clan might require a payment of cattle to the survivor's immediate family. Those beyond the clan call for violent retaliation, sometimes (when the killer is especially distant) accompanied by mutilation and cannibalizing of the person killed in revenge (Middleton 1965:51–52). Among the Jalé of New Guinea, killings across great distances in social space may also involve cannibalism ("People whose face is known should not be eaten"; Koch 1974:80), whereas others provoke only simple vengeance against the killer or one of his relatives, seizure of a pig from the killer's family, or payment of a "guilt pig" by the killer's family to the victim's family (Chapter 3). Patterns such as these abound in the anthropological literature.

Since none of the styles of social control seems to be inherently associated with particular grievances, the application of any style in any situation requires explanation. Moreover, each style is itself highly variable. In compensation, the amount demanded and given may vary greatly from one instance of misfortune to another, as may the system of liability specifying who must make such a payment to whom and the process by which the payment is reckoned and collected.

Dimensions of Compensation

One life or limb is worth more than another. Some herding societies, for example, reckon a man's life to be worth twice as much as a woman's (see, e.g., Hasluck 1954:239; Lewis 1959:277; 1961:163; Peters 1967:270). Slave societies value a freeman's life considerably more than a slave's (see, e.g., Wiedemann 1981:174; Patterson 1982:194–195). In tribal Europe, the value of a man's life increased with his rank (see, e.g., Maitland 1881:213–214; Pollock and Maitland 1898: Volume 1, 47–48). In modern America, civil courts calculate the value of a life according to the person's earning power.

The degree of liability, or the extent to which a person or group is accountable for the grievance of another, varies as well (compare Cooney 1988:74–79).[2] In a compensatory context, liability entails a debt, and its extent depends on the conditions creating such a debt. At one extreme, liability is limited to a specific category of misfortune inflicted on one party by another in a specific manner with a specific subjective orientation (such as a physical injury inflicted by a careless driver). At the other extreme, liability is literally unconditional, since it arises from any misfortune whatsoever befalling anyone at all. In the Anglo-American legal tradition, compensatory liability may arise from intentional injuries of various kinds (such as civil assault), unintentional injuries resulting from negligence (such as an injury suffered in an accident involving a lack of reasonable care), injuries simply caused by a particular party (such as an injury involving a defective product), and injuries merely associated with a particular party (such as an injury occurring in a workplace that is not caused by the employer). Liability may thus depend on both conduct and subjectivity, conduct alone, or neither conduct nor subjectivity. Liability requiring both injurious conduct and a particular state of mind has been called *relative liability* (Koch 1984:98), that requiring injurious conduct alone is known as *strict liability* (e.g., Lieberman 1981:40–42), and that requiring mere association is known as *absolute liability* (e.g., Lieberman 1981:42, 47). The key difference between strict and absolute liability is that in the former an injury is allegedly caused by the liable party, whereas in the latter no such allegation is made. In neither, however, is the subjectivity of the liable party regarded as relevant.

In simple societies, compensation may be demanded and paid when the liable party seems to a modern observer to be only remotely related to the misfortune in question. The Jalé of New Guinea, for example, hold a man's clan liable for the death of his wife during childbirth. Compensation is owed the woman's family because she would not have died unless her husband had impregnated her: "She died by his penis" (Koch 1974:88). If a Jalé man is invited to go hunting and suffers a fatal fall or other misfortune, the clan of the man who proposed the trip must pay a "guilt pig" to the dead man's relatives (Koch 1974:88). Similarly, among the Tlingit Indians of the Northwest Coast of North America, "if a man was injured or accidentally killed while out hunting with the members of another clan, this clan would have to compensate the dead or injured man's clan by a payment of goods" (Oberg 1934:150). The Ifugao of the Philippines hold the givers of certain feasts liable for compensation if any guests are injured or killed during the occasion, accidentally or otherwise. Had there been no feast, they reason, the misfortune would not have occurred (Barton 1919:72–73). Among the Yurok Indians of California, a man who falls ill might accuse someone (such as a known enemy) of bewitching him, and demand and receive compensation from the alleged witch's family (Kroeber 1925:37). And a man who asks another to ferry him across a river becomes liable for damages if the boat owner's house burns down during his absence, for had he not been asked and remained at home, he might have saved his house (Kroeber 1925:35). Much the same standard of compensatory liability occurs in post-tribal societies such as medieval England and the Arab nations adhering to traditional Islamic law (see, e.g., Pollock and Maitland 1898: Volume 2, 170–171; Black 1987b). In contrast, the Carib Indians of Guyana totally excuse all accidental injuries, including those involving negligence, on the grounds that they are supernaturally caused by the violation of a taboo (Gillin 1934:337). These illustrations are not, however, meant to suggest that tribal and earlier people have no understanding of issues such as causation, intention, or fault.[3] Rather, the point is that the application of these notions cannot be taken for granted but requires explanation.[4]

The administration of compensation also varies. It is not, as a modern reader might suppose, the exclusive responsibility of courts and judges. In fact, in cross-cultural and historical perspective, a trilateral process in which two adversaries argue their case before a formal tribunal is unusual. Many societies are stateless and have no courts or judges at all, yet they have highly developed compensatory procedures. (This applies to all of the tribal societies cited earlier.) In such societies compensation is commonly negotiated bilaterally by the principals or their representatives. It also may occur unilaterally, by a voluntary payment to the victim or a seizure of property by the victim. For that matter, modern lawyers and citizens negotiate vastly more payments of compensation than are ordered by courts (see, e.g., Macaulay 1963; Ross 1970; Trubek, Grossman, Felstiner, Kritzer, and Sarat 1983:S-19, S-23). Unilateral compensation occurs in today's society as well. If examined closely, for instance, a significant amount of property crime such as embezzlement, employee pilfering, and even burglary is compensatory self-help by people taking what they regard as rightfully theirs (see Black 1983:37; Tucker 1989).

THE THEORY OF COMPENSATION

The sociological theory of compensation addresses the social conditions under which the compensatory style of social control occurs. It also addresses the variable aspects of compensation itself.

Style and Societal Structure

The classical point of departure in the theory of compensation is Emile Durkheim's *Division of Labor* (1893), where he proposes that the compensatory style is directly related to the degree of interdependence in society[5]: Since over time societies tend to develop an ever greater division of labor, which implies interdependence, compensation becomes increasingly prominent and progressively displaces the penal style of social control. Durkheim's formulation does not entirely withstand a test of the facts (see, e.g., Diamond 1957; Schwartz and Miller 1964; Spitzer 1975),[6] but it nevertheless illustrates a distinctively sociological approach to this subject.

Later investigators have proposed other conditions associated with compensation. Richard Posner suggests, for example, that it appears only in societies that enjoy a degree of surplus wealth (1980:43; see also Rohrl 1984:198–199). Accordingly, he attributes the evolutionary drift from a vengeance-dominated system of social control to one increasingly compensatory

> not to . . . diminishing bloodthirstiness . . . but simply to growing wealth. A system of compensation will not work unless injurers and their kin have a sufficient stock of goods in excess of their subsistence needs to be able to pay compensation for the injuries they inflict on others. (Posner 1980:43)

But Posner does not recognize that people without surplus resources might perform labor or other services to compensate their victims. The Yurok Indians, for instance, had a system of slavery based completely on debts of this kind (Kroeber 1925:32–33). Nor does Posner's proposition explain why vengeance and warfare play a significant role in many tribal societies and in international relations despite abundant resources available for compensatory purposes. The acceptance of compensation may even be viewed as "cowardly and dishonorable" (Black 1984b:10). For example, the Ifugao of the Philippines routinely accept compensation for many injuries but prefer vengeance for others: "No Ifugao would dream of taking a payment for the deliberate or intentional murder of a kinsman. He would be universally condemned if he did so" (Barton 1919:9). The Kabyles of Algeria similarly hold in contempt anyone who accepts compensation for a killing that dishonors the victim: "He is a man who has agreed to eat the blood of his brother; for him, only his stomach counts" (Bourdieu 1966:216). Among the Swat Pathan of Pakistan, compensation for homicide "would further emphasize the superiority of the murderers," and only those without social standing will generally accept it in lieu of revenge (Barth 1959:85). Finnish Gypsies do not compensate homicide either, but prefer retaliation or, more often, mutual avoidance by the kin groups involved (Grönfors 1986: 107–121).

Various societal characteristics are associated with compensation. Mark Cooney's (1988) cross-cultural study of reactions to homicide indicates that compensation is more frequent in relatively developed societies (such as those with a written language, social classes, a state, law, and courts), but he discovered no relationship between compensation and the use of metal currency, the structure of the economy, the fixity of residence, the size of local communities, population density, the fluidity of social relations, the degree of occupational specialization, or the homicide rate itself (1988:73).

Another societal characteristic associated with compensation is organization, or the capacity for collective action (see Black 1976:Chapter 5). Apart from a state structure that organizes society, noted by Cooney, compensation is simply more likely among groups than among individuals. The mere presence of groups apparently has this consequence, apart from the issue of who allegedly injures whom (which is addressed in the next section). Thus, tribal societies with highly articulated and structurally interchangeable kinship groups, including those known in anthropology as "segmentary" (see, e.g., Service 1971:116–118), seem to have the most compensation. Moreover, it is demanded and given in the name of the groups themselves. Examples cited earlier include the Bedouin, Lugbara, Jalé, and Ifugao. More individualistic societies, such as the Eskimos of the Arctic (Balikci 1970:Chapter 9), the Yanomamö of Venezuela and Brazil (Chagnon 1977), the Hadza of Tanzania (Woodburn 1979), and the Tausug of the Philippines (Kiefer 1972), have vastly less compensation.[7]

During the past century, compensation has become an increasingly common mode of social control in modern societies. And organizations — often involved in conflicts in which compensation is demanded — have proliferated to a degree never before seen. Regardless of whether organizations or individuals participate in the cases, however, the sheer number of organizations and other groups in itself seems to nourish the compensatory style. So arises our first proposition: *Compensation is a direct function of groups.*

Now consider the cases.

Style and Case Structure

Compensation varies with the social structure of the cases: Who has a grievance against whom? What, for example, is the degree of intimacy between them? Are they members of the same family, mere acquaintances, or strangers? In his cross-cultural study, Cooney reports that payment for homicide occurs less at the extremes of intimacy, between those who are extremely close or extremely distant, and proposes this pattern as a general characteristic of compensation (1988:48, 73–74, 81; see also Gluckman 1965a:206). A payment is therefore less likely when an injury occurs between close kin or between members of different tribes or nations. Among the Nuer of Sudan, for instance,

> The killing of a stranger, especially of a foreigner, who does not come
> within the most expanded form of the social structure, is not really wrong
> (duer) at all. . . . The killing of a fellow tribesman, and to a much lesser
> extent a fellow Nuer of another tribe who is within the orbit of the killer's

social sphere, is a wrong because it is an offense against the stability of society in its most extended form. But it is a private delict and not a crime, and demands only retaliation or restitution. The closer the relationship between the component tribal segments involved, the greater the sanction for restitution. . . . Finally, in the narrowest definition of blood-relationship, where kinship is a reality and not merely a fictional social form — that is, within the lineage or the extended family group — restitution becomes less and less necessary because the persons who assist in the payment of compensation are also the recipients. [Thus] a man does not pay compensation at all if he kills his own wife — a rare occurrence — for he would have to pay it to himself. (Howell 1954:207–208, 57–58; see also Scott 1976)

Among the Lugbara of Uganda, "beyond the major lineage and section no blood money is payable," but "if a fight within the same major lineage leads to death, the killer gives compensation of two bulls and two cows to the victim's sons." When this happens between those still closer, within the minimal lineage, "it is a sin for which there is no humanly awarded punishment" (Middleton 1965:51). The Ifugao similarly pay compensation in cases between but never within families: "A family cannot proceed against itself" (Barton 1919: 8; italics omitted). In modern life, compensation is often paid when injuries occur within the same society but is less likely between members of different societies. At the other extreme, courts generally do not allow compensation when the parties are very closely related, such as family members in the same household, and under these conditions it is rarely demanded anyway. Even people who are friends or residents of close-knit communities are reluctant to ask each other for these payments (see, e.g., Engel 1984; Ellickson 1986). Compensation is most likely to be paid across intermediate distances in social space. More precisely: *Compensation is a curvilinear function of relational distance* (Cooney 1988:74).

The social status of the principals is relevant to the use of compensation as well.[8] In particular, a case against a social superior of the aggrieved — an upward case — appears more likely to be handled in the compensatory style than a case against a social inferior — a downward case. Modern law illustrates this pattern: Downward grievances are commonly prosecuted as criminal cases, whereas upward grievances are rarely prosecuted but instead typically entail a demand for compensatory damages, whether because of negligence, malpractice, breach of contract, failure to abide by administrative regulations, or the like. Status superiors may also unilaterally mollify their victims by giving them money or other valuables — even masters are known to have compensated their slaves after injuring them (see, e.g., Wiedemann 1981:180–181). In other cases the aggrieved inferior may appropriate some of the superior's property, usually covertly, a practice common among peasants, servants, and slaves throughout history (Baumgartner 1984a:309–310). The more compensatory character of upward cases does not merely reflect the greater resources of social superiors but may as well involve a reluctance by social superiors to accept payment from inferiors in lieu of other forms of justice (illustrated earlier by the Swat Pathan view of compensation as humiliating to the recipient). In any event, the available evidence indicates the following: *Upward cases are more compensatory than downward cases* (see Black 1976:29).[9]

Another variable is organization: *Cases against groups are more compensatory than cases against individuals* (see Black 1976:98). In tribal societies, it is virtually always a group — usually a kinship group — that is asked for compensation. In modern societies, groups, particularly business organizations, are often sued for compensatory damages. In fact, this seems to be all that people normally want from the organizations they claim have victimized them. In the United States, for example, self-described victims of consumer fraud rarely demand punishment of the business organization involved; typically, all they want is a financial settlement (Steele 1975:1138). But criminal cases are rarely brought against groups. An even more extreme illustration is legal action against governments. Apart from court orders such as injunctions, the usual claimant demands only compensation. Governments are rarely asked to pay punitive damages or to suffer other penalties. The punishment of governments occurs almost exclusively in international relations, when one nation uses violence against another.

Liability and Case Structure

It would be impossible to explore here all the variable aspects of compensation itself. Instead, let us consider only the system of liability,[10] since this will be pertinent to our closing speculations.

Recall that liability is a matter of degree. In compensatory cases, it defines the conditions under which one party's misfortune requires payment by another. The broader these conditions, the greater the liability, and in this sense liability is a quantitative variable. As noted earlier, various degrees of liability collapse into several categories: Relative liability arises from both injurious conduct and subjectivity of a particular kind, strict liability from injurious conduct alone, and absolute liability without regard to either injurious conduct or subjectivity. Since liability varies independently of styles of social control, however, we address a general theory of the subject rather than a theory of compensatory liability alone. Patterns of vengeance and punishment as well as compensation are therefore mentioned to illustrate propositions about the social structure of liability.

Again social distance is relevant. As Max Gluckman observes: "The less close the relationship. . . , the more absolute the liability, and the less the regard paid to intention" (1965a: 231). He refers specifically to how the degree of intimacy between the principals predicts the degree of liability and offers a number of examples from the anthropological literature. Cross-cultural evidence from Cooney's survey also conforms to this pattern (1988: 77–79). As relational distance increases, not only does the subjective orientation of the party responsible for an injury lose importance, but so does the question of responsibility itself. Liability may arise from nothing more than a lack of intimacy with a victim of misfortune, possibly combined with a social connection to the person or group actually responsible. This is illustrated by the application of collective liability, often seen in tribal and international settings, where everyone in a social category becomes liable for the conduct of a fellow member (see, e.g., Moore 1972; Koch 1984).[11] The Kwakiutl Indians of the American Northwest Coast, for example, may take vengeance for a death from illness or accident involving no human agent at all, and liability in these cases always attaches to outsiders such as members of another tribe or village. When several relatives of a Kwakiutl chief accidentally drowned during a canoe trip, for instance, his fellow tribesmen attacked and killed eight sleeping Sanetch Indians to — as he said — "let someone else wail" (Codere 1950:102, 117).

Liability increases not merely with relational distance but also with other kinds of social distance, such as status and cultural differences. Slaves and modern children may thus be held strictly, absolutely, or otherwise broadly liable for damage to property (see, e.g., Piaget 1932: 133–134; Wiedemann 1981:176),[12] even when they are relationally very close to those who demand redress. In the slaveholding states of nineteenth-century America, for instance, the death of a white person by natural causes might be attributed to poisoning by a slave. As one Kentuckian commented, "Every disease at all obscure and uncommon in its symptoms and fatal in its termination is immediately decided to be a case of negro-poison" (quoted in Wyatt-Brown 1982:424).[13] Among the Tlingit Indians, a man of very high status caught stealing is assumed to have been bewitched by someone of lower status, often a slave, who is thereupon executed (Oberg 1934:149, 155). The relevance of cultural distance is illustrated by cases in which different tribes, nations, or ethnic groups hold one another's members collectively liable for injuries committed by their fellows. So-called terrorism is one example. To include other social cleavages in our formulation, then, we might restate Gluckman's (1965a:21) proposition as follows: *Liability varies directly with social distance.*[14]

Liability also varies with organization. Strict and absolute standards of liability are more often applied to collectivities than to individuals. Evidence from Cooney's cross-cultural survey shows less concern with the subjectivity of the liable party in cases of homicide between groups than between individuals (1988:196), and he proposes that this obeys a general principle of social control (181). In modern societies, grievances between groups such as business organizations as well as those by individuals against organizations are associated with a broader conception of liability. Tort cases involving strict liability, such as recent American lawsuits dealing with defective products, are directed against organizations in virtually all instances (see Lieberman 1981:40–47). In many of these, the organization's liability may even appear to be absolute, since to some observers it may not seem causally connected to the misfortune in question (for examples, see the list of cases in the next section). Nevertheless, in each case injurious conduct is attributed to the organizational defendant. Liability is, at most, strict. Absolute liability is, however, institutionalized in American programs such as Workmen's Compensation (which makes the employer liable for all job-related injuries), the no-fault system of automobile insurance (which makes insurance companies liable for accidents without regard to their causation), and victim compensation in criminal cases (which makes states liable for losses suffered at the hands of any offenders within their boundaries). All of this suggests the following proposition: *The liability of groups is greater than the liability of individuals.*[15]

In sum, the sociological theory of compensation specifies social conditions associated with the compensatory style of social control and its variable characteristics, such as the amount of compensation demanded and paid, the system of liability applied, and the process by which it is administered.[16] Durkheim's early theory that compensation increases with the division of labor has stimulated a search for other factors. Scattered evidence indicates that compensation varies directly with the number of groups in society. It also appears to be more likely at intermediate distances in social space, in upward rather than downward cases, and in group-directed rather than individual-directed cases. The standard of liability seems to broaden with social distance and against groups as well. To assess the universality of these tendencies would require more evidence. Even so, it is clear that compensation is not inherently associated with particular kinds of misfortune but rather varies with the social structure of the cases. The history of compensation therefore reflects the changing context in which misfortune is experienced.

THE EVOLUTION OF COMPENSATION

We now turn to a recent trend in modern society: the increasing compensatory liability of organizations for the misfortunes of individuals. The trend is especially noticeable during the second half of the twentieth century in the civil courts of the United States, where organizations have been held to an ever broader standard of liability. The first stage of this development involved a new standard of strict liability for an organization causing harm to an individual, and a standard of absolute liability may even be evolving as well (see Lieberman 1981:40–47; Malott 1985). An organization's mere association with an individual's misfortune increasingly leads to demands for compensation. Although conceptions of causation and fault continue to be invoked, they grow steadily broader in their interpretation and application. A few recent lawsuits illustrate this trend:

1. A man tried to commit suicide by jumping in front of a subway train. He subsequently sued the city's transit authority, arguing that the train's operator had not stopped fast enough. He received a $650,000 settlement.
2. A man had a heart attack while trying to start a lawn mower. A jury ordered the lawn mower company to pay him $1.75 million.
3. One man shot another with a gun. A court ruled that the manufacturer of the gun was liable.
4. A man was injured when a drunk driver crashed into a telephone booth. A judge ruled that the company that designed the telephone booth was liable.
5. A man was robbed and killed on a street near his hotel. His family successfully sued the hotel and the city in which it is located.
6. A man was killed by the hijackers of the cruise ship on which he was a passenger. His wife sued not only the political organization allegedly associated with the hijacking but also the cruise ship company and the travel agency that issued her husband's ticket.[17]

The Devolution of Liability

Viewed in evolutionary perspective, the tendency to hold organizations broadly liable for the misfortunes of individuals is not altogether new. A related phenomenon occurred in earlier and simpler societies in Africa, New Guinea, and elsewhere. Recall, for example, the Jalé practice of holding a man's clan liable for compensation when his wife dies in childbirth or when someone he invited hunting is accidentally killed during the hunt. Or consider this practice observed among the Suku of the Congo: When a member of clan A steals a goat from a member of clan B, clan B will sometimes seize a compensatory goat from clan C. Liability lies with "the surrounding social universe as a whole," and any nearby group serves adequately as a source of compensation (Kopytoff 1961:65–66). These practices significantly resemble the modern cases listed above, especially those in which murder victims' families sue what seem to be simply the nearest available organizations. All involve a claim of compensatory liability against a corporate entity that would appear to be only remotely associated with someone's misfortune. All effectively recruit—or conscript—a nearby group to compensate people who would otherwise bear the burden of misfortune themselves. In this sense, the increasing compensatory liability of organizations is a devolutionary development, a return to the past (see Black 1984a:276–277). How can this be explained? Why is it happening at this moment in history?

It is well-known that one of the great transformations across the centuries in many societies, especially since the beginning of industrialization, has been the decline of the family as a major actor in everyday life. Economic, political, and religious action as well as wealth and other elements of social standing came increasingly to reside in individuals rather than families or clans. As this occurred, moreover, liability in legal and related matters shifted from families to individuals. Whereas once a man's blood relatives shared in his misdeeds and misfortunes, whether by vengeance or by compensation, increasingly he had to fend for himself. The individuation of social life was thus reflected in legal and moral individuation, and notions such as responsibility, intent, and fault became increasingly refined and important in the determination of liability. Collective liability came to be regarded as a primitive stage of legal evolution (see, e.g., Hobhouse 1906; Diamond 1935; Gluckman 1965a:Chapter 7; Moore 1972).

Now, in retrospect, the individuation of society and law in the Western world seems to have peaked in the nineteenth century, when compensatory liability was limited to the narrowest conditions ever seen. In the United States, such liability required proof of the defendant's carelessness, a lack of negligence by the victim contributing to the misfortune, an absence of known risk undertaken by the victim prior to the injury, and initiation of tort actions only by the victims themselves, which excluded cases involving death (see, e.g., James 1970; Malone 1970; Horwitz 1977: 85–99; Lieberman 1981:Chapter 2). Cases resembling those on the list above (such as the subway and lawn mower cases) were inconceivable. Since then, however, a previously uncommon form of collective life has proliferated and fundamentally altered the course of legal evolution: organizations.

Organizational Dependency

The past century has seen a dramatic growth in the number and role of organizations in modern societies such as the United States (see, e.g., Boulding 1953; Coleman 1982:Chapter 1).[18] Individuals have become increasingly dependent on organizations much as, in centuries past, they were dependent on extended families. More and more people earn their livelihoods in organizations, obtain life's necessities from them, and learn, relax, and play in them. It is increasingly difficult to do or have anything without the involvement of an organization, whether public or private. This includes the experience of misfortune. Accidents, for example, increasingly occur in, near, or because of an organization; during or after a transaction with an organization; or in circumstances insured by an organization.

The growing dependency of individuals on organizations is reflected in an ever greater propensity to recruit organizations to compensate people for their misfortunes. In lawsuits such as those listed above, this process is involuntary and entails the application of an ever broader standard of liability by which compensation may be obtained from organizations associated with injured individuals. So returns a system of collective liability resembling practices long thought primitive and even incompetent or ignorant. Meanwhile, public and private organizations have increasingly established programs to compensate their members for injury, sickness, and other losses. In New Zealand, for example, a government commission provides compensation for literally all injuries suffered by anyone in any circumstances whatsoever, regardless of fault and causation, and lawsuits pertaining to injuries have been eliminated (see, e.g., Harris 1974). An expansion of this "no-fault" approach is presently being advocated in the United States and elsewhere (see, e.g., O'Connell 1975; Saunders 1979). Compensatory liability of this breadth was once the burden of extended families, whether those of the victims or the victimizers. After a period of individualism, then, collectivism is reappearing in a new form: *The organization is replacing the family in the compensation of misfortune.*

CONCLUSION

The conscription of organizations to provide compensation to individuals is consistent with the formulations presented earlier. The population of organizations is itself positively associated with the compensatory style of social control. Moreover, the relational distance between organizations (or insured parties) and aggrieved individuals generally lies in the intermediate range in which compensation is most likely to appear. A fragmentary relationship (such as between a supplier and customer, government and citizen, or employer and employee) commonly exists between the organization and the individual before the injury occurs. And since the allegedly liable organization has more wealth and social stature than the injured individual in nearly every case, these grievances are virtually always directed upwardly rather than downwardly. The mere fact that the cases are usually brought against an organization rather than an individual is also predictable from the theory of compensation.

The broad standard of liability applied to organizations may be explained with the considerable degree of social distance that typically separates the principals (such as a consumer and the manufacturer of an allegedly defective product). That such cases are brought against a group rather than an individual also supports the formulation linking the degree of liability to organization itself. In short, the modern trend whereby organizations are held increasingly liable for the misfortunes of individuals conforms to our theoretical expectations. [19]

Conditions for the compensatory liability of organizations are, so to speak, excellent. And since there is presently no end in sight to the increasing role of organizations in modern life, we may expect that the demand for compensation of this sort will continue to grow. Once located in families and clans, the responsibility for misfortune shifts historically first to individuals and then to organizations. The evolution of compensation thus ultimately describes a circle, from one kind of collective liability to another. [20]

ENDNOTES

*Reprinted (with minor revision) by permission of the Law and Society Association from the *Law and Society Review* 21 (Number 4, 1987): 563–584.

This essay was originally prepared for a symposium entitled "Issues in Compensatory Justice," held at the University of Virginia on January 27, 1986. The symposium was organized and chaired by Ravindra S. Khare and sponsored by the Committee on the Comparative Study of the Individual and Society of the University's Center for Advanced Studies.

The following people commented on earlier drafts: M. P. Baumgartner, Mark Cooney, Robert C. Ellickson, David M. Engel, John Griffiths, Allan V. Horwitz, John Jarvis, Robert L. Kidder, Saul X. Levmore, Albert J. Reiss, Jr., Roberta Senechal de la Roche, James Tucker, and Charles O. Wood.

1. This might be called compulsory or involuntary compensation to distinguish it from payments made on a voluntary or contractual basis, such as compensation for unemployment by a government or for labor by an employer. The distinction between compulsory, voluntary, and contractual compensation is not always easily drawn or even theoretically important, however, and the latter forms do not lie entirely beyond the scope of this discussion.

2. The concept of "accountable" here is not intended to imply a claim of causation, fault, or blameworthiness on the part of the liable party.

3. Compare Frederic William Maitland's assertion of "the utter incompetence of ancient law to take note of the mental elements of crime" (1883:327).

4. Who receives the compensation for an injury is variable as well. In the case of a killing, for example, the payment might be made to a surviving spouse or nuclear family, shared with a larger group such as a clan (see, e.g., Lewis 1959:284–286; Jones 1974:69), or entirely disallowed on the grounds that the victim is not available to claim it (e.g., Lieberman 1981:38). In some African tribes, such as the Zulu, every man "belongs to the king," and compensation for any killing is always paid to him. The king may, however, give something to the deceased's family "out of generosity" (Gluckman 1965a:212). For an overview of compensation in tribal societies, see Nader and Combs-Schilling (1976).

5. Durkheim (1893) speaks of compensation as an application of "restitutive sanctions" and of interdependence as "organic solidarity."

6. For example, the societies with the least interdependence — hunters and gatherers — generally have little or no compensation *or* punishment of the sort associated with criminal justice. Of the two, moreover, compensation seems to appear at an earlier stage of societal development.

Durkheim's formulation applies more convincingly to recent legal evolution: Modern societies do seem to have more compensation than the ancient civilizations to which he often refers.

7. Various Indians of North America may be exceptions. Compensation was apparently offered and accepted with some frequency among highly individualistic Plains Indians such as the Comanche and Cheyenne (see Hoebel 1954:Chaper 7), for example, although it was sometimes contemptuously rejected as a bribe (see, e.g., Llewellyn and Hoebel 1941:135). The individualistic Yurok of California also practiced compensation (Kroeber 1925:Chapter 2).

8. "Social status" is used here as a composite concept measurable by the principal's wealth, degree of integration into society (by employment, social ties, parenthood, and the like), cultural conventionality and virtuosity, and respectability (see the various types of status treated separately in Black 1976:Chapters 2–6).

9. The use of compensation seems also to vary directly with the social status of the liable party and inversely with the social status of the aggrieved party (see Black 1976:29). This would mean that its likelihood increases with the steepness of the gradient of upward cases and decreases with that of downward cases.

The reader should be aware that upward social control appears to be relatively infrequent and lenient (see, e.g., Black 1976:21–24, 35–36; but see Baumgartner 1984a). The point here is only that upward social control is especially likely to be compensatory. A similar pattern applies to the relationship between organization and social control (see Note 19).

10. For a discussion of the relationship between liability and societal structure, see Koch (1984).

11. Vengeance seems to occur when the relational distance between people is both greater and smaller than when compensation is characteristically paid. While compensation is a curvilinear function of relational distance, then, vengeance may be a U-curvilinear function of the same variable (compare Rieder 1984:145–146).

Compensation and vengeance also seem to be kindred phenomena in some respects. Both involve a logic of reciprocity or exchange, for example, and both often appear as major remedies within the same society (see, e.g., Hasluck 1954; Howell 1954; Barth 1959; Peters 1967; see also Warner 1958:162, who speaks of vengeance as "negative reciprocation"; Gouldner 1960; Sahlins 1965:148–149, 176; Rohrl 1984:193–194). Cooney's cross-cultural study indicates that virtually all societies with compensation for homicide have vengeance as well, although many have vengeance but not compensation (1988:73).

12. Very young childen are generally not held liable at all. Instead, those in charge of them may be accountable for their damage, much as people are held liable for damage caused by their pets or livestock.

13. Often the slave accused of a poisoning was a healer who had given the deceased a medical potion of some kind, so it might be argued that the healer was held strictly or absolutely liable for the death of the patient. But simply because the evidence in a case appears extremely weak to an observer does not mean that a strict or absolute standard of liability is being applied. Since criminal intent appears to have been attributed to the accused slave in all these cases, they are properly classified as instances of relative liability with a very broad standard of evidence.

14. Cooney cites evidence of an inverse relationship between the intimacy of a group and its concern with human subjectivity (particularly Horwitz 1984:219–220) and proposes that the relational location of a victim may predict the extent to which the subjectivity of an allegedly liable party is important: The greater the degree of intimacy of the victim's group, he suggests, the less the alleged offender's subjectivity will be emphasized (1988:181–183).

If we regard the victim's social embeddedness as a kind of integration into social life, however, such a pattern might indicate that the social status of the victim (associated with integration) predicts the degree of liability that issues from a misfortune: The higher the status, the greater the liability. On the other hand, the social status of the allegedly liable party may be inversely related to the degree of this liability. These matters await further study.

15. Liability probably increases with the degree of organization as well. Large organizations such as major corporations appear to be held to a broader standard of liability than lesser organizations such as small businesses.

16. A general theory of compensation ultimately addresses the conditions associated with voluntary or contractual compensation as well. In fact, significant continuities between voluntary, contractual, and compulsory compensation may emerge. Compensation for labor, for example, is apparently more likely to be given across intermediate distances in social space (rather than, say, within families and friendships or between tribes and nations), downwardly in status structures, and by groups rather than individuals — conditions that also seem to attract compulsory compensation.

17. These cases are not meant to be representative of modern lawsuits but only to illustrate the degree to which the trend toward a broader standard of compensatory liability of organizations has advanced. Moreover, the final resolution of these cases does not matter for these purposes. The mere fact that they were filed is historically unprecedented and sociologically important.

Cases of this sort are sometimes cited to support a general claim that a "litigation explosion" is occurring in modern America. No such claim is intended here. (For discussions of the litigation explosion thesis, see, e.g., Galanter 1983; Black 1984a.) Even so, twentieth-century America clearly experienced a significant increase in both negligence claims and the size of damage awards in negligence cases (see, e.g., Friedman and Percival 1976: 281–283; Friedman 1980:664–665).

18. One sociologist estimates that the number of organizations in the United States now exceeds the number of individuals, but he includes families and households in the organizational population (Reiss 1985:303).

19. That organizations are the objects while individuals are the initiators of these cases and that the former often lose in court may appear inconsistent with existing theory proposing that the quantity of law is "greater in a direction toward less organization than toward

more organization" (Black 1976:92) and that cases brought by individuals against organizations are the least likely to succeed when compared to cases between individuals, between organizations, and by organizations against individuals (Black 1976:97). But nothing in the present analysis is inconsistent with these earlier formulations. This would require cases by individuals against organizations to rise from their contemporary level as the least likely to be brought and the least likely to succeed in modern law. As it stands, cases in which individuals seek and win compensation from organizations are significant and interesting, but they by no means dominate the legal scene. On the contrary: Organizations are both more litigious and legally successful than are individuals, and the most likely and successful cases are brought by organizations against individuals (see, e.g., Wanner 1974, 1975).

20. The evolution of compensation should not be equated with social evolution itself, however. The earliest and simplest societies — hunters and gatherers — have little or no compensation at all (see Note 6).

4

SOCIAL CONTROL OF THE SELF*

This chapter explores the self-application of social control. Groups such as public and private organizations apply standards to their own conduct and take action against themselves, but here we focus on the self-application of social control by individuals. After an overview of the subject, the discussion turns to pleading in criminal cases as an illustration and, finally, to the variability of adversariness and the general nature of self-interaction.[1]

THE DEVIANT SELF

Social control includes "any process by which people define and respond to deviant behavior" (Black 1984b:1, note 1). Examples are criticism, gossip, litigation, punishment, compensation, avoidance, psychotherapy, witch-hunting, feuding, and warfare. Most literature on social control addresses cases in which people are regarded by their fellows as wrong, negligent, crazy, or otherwise deviant. Moreover, it generally assumes that alleged deviants naturally and automatically evade or resist social control, capitulating only when their plight is hopeless. But while people may be more tolerant of themselves than of anyone else (see Cooney 1988:43), in many cases they treat their own behavior as deviant. They may apply social control to themselves unilaterally, without the involvement of anyone else, or submit to their victims or to third parties such as judges, priests, or psychotherapists. Self-initiated social control complements complainant-initiated and authority-initiated social control (compare Black 1973). People not only initiate cases against themselves but handle themselves in all respects at all stages of social control, including final dispositions. For example, they may convict themselves of a crime (by confessing or pleading guilty) or choose the appropriate remedy for their wrongdoing (by compensating a victim or resigning from an organization).

One extreme and dramatic self-application of social control is suicide. The number of suicides qualifying as self-execution is difficult to estimate, however, and varies across time and space.[2] Virtually all suicides may qualify in some societies, but few or none in others. The great majority of suicides among the Trobriand Islanders of Melanesia, for instance, seem to be self-punishment or self-exile. Typically the offender leaps from a palm tree or drinks poison after being accused of misconduct such as incest or adultery (Malinowski 1926:77–80, 94–97). Among the Chenchu of India, "self-recrimination for acts of violence committed in a fit of temper sometimes resulted in suicide" (Fürer-Haimendorf 1967:22). In traditional Japan, suicide was "a means of clearing one's name, of washing away a sin or disgrace" (Tatai 1983:18), though nowadays most self-killings apparently arise under other circumstances (see generally Tatai 1983; Iga 1986). Modern Americans kill themselves more than they kill others — about twice as often (see, e.g., Henry and Short 1954:13) — and sometimes leave a note indicating the suicide was intended to atone for misbehavior (Douglas 1967:302–304). Self-executions surely occur more than state executions.[3]

Deviants also submit to their victims or adversaries even when they might otherwise escape detection. Children may voluntarily confess and apologize to their parents, for example, and people may leave their names on unattended automobiles they damage or reveal illicit affairs to spouses or lovers. Social control of the self occurs where deviant behavior is handled by third parties as well: Criminal offenders may surrender to the police, apologize, and plead guilty to judges; sinners confess to priests; and people disturbed by their own conduct — in conflict with themselves — seek the help of psychotherapists (see, e.g., Rickett 1971; Hepworth and Turner 1982; Thoits 1985; Wagatsuma and Rosett 1986).[4] What explains this behavior?

Self-applications of social control are understandable with existing theory.

THE CASE AGAINST THE SELF

Central to the sociological theory of social control is the premise that the social structure of a case predicts and explains how it will be handled (see Black 1976, 1984b, 1989:Chapter 1). A case structure includes the social characteristics of all the parties — principals (the victim or complainant and the alleged wrongdoer), supporters (such as friendly witnesses and lawyers), and third parties (such as the judge, mediator, or jury). What is the social status of each? The degree of intimacy between them? Are they individuals or organizations?

We know, for example, that the social structure of a legal case predicts how much law (governmental social control) it will attract. Cases from higher levels of social status against people at lower levels attract more law than cases in the opposite direction: *Downward law is greater than upward law* (Black 1976:Chapters 2–6). Thus, in modern America, blacks convicted of killing a white are vastly more likely to receive the death sentence than whites convicted of killing a black. Instances of the latter are almost unknown, whereas blacks killing a white run a far greater risk of execution than whites killing a fellow white or blacks killing a fellow black (see, e.g., Bowers and Pierce 1980:594). In addition, cases between people of higher status attract more law than cases between people of lower status: *Law varies directly with social status* (Black 1976:Chapters 2–6). Predictably, therefore, whites convicted of killing a fellow white are more likely to receive the death sentence than blacks convicted of killing a fellow black (Bowers and Pierce 1980:594). And cases between strangers attract more law than cases between intimates: *Law varies directly with relational distance* (Black 1976:40–46).[5] Accordingly, convicted killers of a stranger are more likely to receive the death sentence than convicted killers of a relative, friend, or acquaintance (Gross and Mauro 1984:58–59).

Now back to the self: *The self-application of social control obeys the same principles as social control in general.* The self's response to its deviant behavior — and to allegations thereof — depends on the social characteristics of the self, the victim or complainant, the allies or other supporters, and the third parties. Self-tolerance increases when the case structure is conducive to leniency and decreases when it is conducive to severity. Because a person's relationship with himself or herself is the closest in the social universe, and because closeness breeds partisanship (see Black 1984b:21), the self is commonly its own greatest ally. But when the social conditions are right, the self offers no defense or even becomes its own enemy.

THE SELF-APPLICATION OF LAW

Although the legal process in modern societies is formally an adversary system in which people can defend themselves against prosecutions and lawsuits, the vast majority do not. They give up. Often they become witnesses against themselves. For example, over 90% of the civil and criminal cases filed in the United States conclude without a trial. Civil defendants typically settle out of court (see, e.g., Trubek et al. 1983:S-23; see also Ross 1970), and criminal defendants typically plead guilty (see, e.g., Newman 1956, 1966; Skolnick 1967; Alschuler 1968; Buckle and Buckle 1977; Mather 1979; Maynard 1984). Most criminal defendants exchange a plea of guilty for leniency (known as a "plea bargain" in modern America).[6]

A plea of guilty is a self-application of law — a self-conviction (Alschuler 1979:213). It is an increment of law, a form of self-inflicted severity that supplements and reinforces other applications of law. It specially criminalizes, stigmatizes, and disables the defendant, and it expedites and finalizes the disposition of the case.[7] In contrast, defendants pleading not guilty can sometimes win an acquittal, can forever protest their innocence and deny their criminality even when convicted, and can appeal to higher courts and possibly reverse their fate entirely. Any leniency for those pleading guilty or severity for those pleading not guilty effectively compensates for these differences.[8]

If self-applications of law obey the same principles as legal behavior in general, pleading should reflect the social structure of criminal cases. Structures attractive to law (such as cases against the victim's social inferior or against a stranger) should be more likely to generate a plea of guilty, whereas structures repulsive to law (such as cases against the victim's social superior or against an intimate) should be more likely to generate a plea of not guilty. Between the extremes most attractive and most repulsive to law should lie cases in which the defendant explicitly exchanges a plea of guilty for leniency. First consider status effects.

All else constant (including the victim's and complainant's characteristics), defendants with the least social status attract the most law (Black 1976:Chapters 2–6). Hence, defendants with the least status should be the most likely to plead guilty without bargaining for leniency and the least likely to plead not guilty. Those with the most status should do the opposite, while those between the extremes should be the most likely to plead guilty in exchange for leniency. The available evidence supports these predictions.

Of all the criminal defendants in modern America, among the lowest in social stature are the homeless men of "skid row." They exhibit virtually every characteristic attractive to law yet discovered, being at once poor, unemployed, unmarried, unorganized, unconventional, and unrespectable (see Black 1980:32). Not surprisingly, then, they experience a level of police attention (including violence and humiliation) rarely seen elsewhere in society, and their treatment in court is correspondingly harsh (see Wallace 1965; Spradley 1970; Wiseman 1970; Black 1980:29–32). But they rarely resist or complain. On the contrary, they subject themselves to law nearly as mercilessly as the police or anyone else. When arrested and charged with public drunkenness — a routine occurrence — they typically plead guilty without bargaining or asking for consideration of any kind (Spradley 1970:Chapter 6; Mileski 1971:493). Falsely charged during "clean-ups" when the police arrest every vagrant in sight for public drunkenness (Bittner 1967:704, note 24; Spradley 1970:124; Wiseman 1970:68–79), they plead guilty just the same, without bargaining for anything (Spradley 1970:180, 289). Entirely sober, they convict themselves of being drunk.

Defendants from the top of the social ladder, such as wealthy individuals and corporations, are comparatively unlikely to plead guilty, and for them to do so without bargaining for leniency is almost inconceivable. Imagine, for example, an unbargained plea of guilty by a corporation charged with murder for selling fatally defective automobiles (as in a famous American case involving a Ford Pinto). It would appear to be sociologically impossible.[9]

Between the top and the bottom of the social ladder — usually closer to the bottom — are those normally pleading guilty in exchange for leniency. Here we find the great majority of defendants, the rank-and-file criminals of modern America.

The social stature of a case also depends on whether an attorney handles it and, if so, the attorney's own characteristics. An attorney enhances the stature of a typical criminal defendant, and those so represented receive less severe treatment (see, e.g., Mileski 1971:486–492). They plead guilty at a lower rate as well (Mileski 1971:535, note 15). Only those representing themselves, such as skid-row vagrants, are likely to plead guilty without first bargaining for leniency. Attorneys thus reduce both the severity of courts toward defendants and of defendants toward themselves. Even so, attorneys often effectively convict their own clients by advising them to plead guilty. And they do this in a pattern as predictable as the behavior of police officers, judges, or anyone else in legal life: They are more likely to advise capitulation to sociologically vulnerable clients. In England, for example, attorneys are more likely to advise clients who already have a criminal record to make their record worse by pleading guilty, and the clients usually agree (McBarnet 1981:77–78).[10] Attorneys are valuable allies, but their behavior follows the natural tendencies of law.

The social status of victims is another factor in legal behavior: The greater the victim's social elevation, the more law gravitates to the case (Black 1976:Chapters 2–6). Those who victimize people of higher status should therefore be harsher toward themselves by pleading guilty. And they are: Whites in modern America usually victimize fellow whites, whereas blacks usually victimize fellow blacks (Reiss 1967), and whites plead guilty at a higher rate (Mileski 1971:494–495; Petersilia 1983:26; Cooney 1991a:98, note 5). Defendants charged with raping a white woman plead guilty at a higher rate than those charged with raping a black woman (La Free 1980:839).[11] Because organization has the same effect as social status (Black 1976:Chapter 5), it is also noteworthy that defendants charged with victimizing an organization plead guilty at a higher rate than those charged with victimizing an individual (Hagan 1982:1006).[12]

The social structure of prosecution is important as well. Whoever the victim of a crime might be, a government files and argues the case in court. Governments normally have greater social stature than any individual or private organization, and this alone explains why so many criminal defendants give up (see Black 1989:Chapter 3). When the state initiates the case, as in most public drunkenness, vice, and traffic matters, defendants are especially likely to capitulate. Those arrested during the 1960s black riots in the United States were also prone to plead guilty. In the Detroit riot cases, for example, 99% of the convictions resulted from a guilty plea (Balbus 1973:143).[13] When the prosecutor is a totalitarian state such as Stalin's Soviet Union or Hitler's Germany, defendants typically confess and plead guilty even when the charges are false (see Arendt 1958:307; Black 1976:96–97). Torture alone does not explain this phenomenon. People falsely charged with witchcraft frequently confess, too, particularly when their accusers are social superiors. In Renaissance Europe, for instance, those accused by royal officials on the Continent confessed at a higher rate than those accused by local witch-finders in England (Currie 1968: 13–14, 19). The "witch-cleansing cults" of sub-Saharan Africa have also received excellent cooperation: Alleged witches "almost invariably" confess (Willis 1970:130).[14] Again, torture is not an adequate explanation. When Imperial Rome defined Christianity as a crime, numerous Christians voluntarily surrendered, confessed, and requested execution (Ste. Croix 1963:21–24).

Still another factor in legal behavior is the closeness between the adversaries. Because relational distance attracts law while intimacy repels it, those accused of victimizing strangers should plead guilty at a higher rate than those accused of victimizing relatives, friends, or other associates. This appears true, for example, of American rape cases (see, e.g., Holmstrom and Burgess 1978:246–247). And defendants accused of crimes particularly likely to involve intimates, such as homicide and assault, are the least likely to plead guilty (Mather 1979:62; but see Cooney 1991a: 97–99).

In sum, self-applications of law obey the same principles as all applications of law. Those more vulnerable to law, sociologically, are more likely to convict themselves by pleading guilty, and the most vulnerable of all—

such as skid-row vagrants—tend to capitulate immediately, without bargaining for leniency, even when falsely charged. Moreover, these patterns occur in pleading rates despite possible biases against our theoretical predictions: Because defendants of higher status and those accused of victimizing an intimate attract less law of any kind, they are likely to face legally stronger cases when they are arrested, to be charged with lesser offenses, and to be offered more leniency for pleading guilty (see Hagan and Bernstein 1979; Stanko 1982:230–235). Those we predict to plead guilty at a lower rate may therefore have special reasons for doing so at a higher rate. Yet, as predicted, they still plead guilty less than anyone.[15]

CONCLUSION

The prominence of courtroom trials might give the impression that people accused of wrongdoing defend themselves at all costs. But they do not. They handle their own deviant behavior much as anyone else would. Intimate with themselves, they indulge themselves to some extent, but nevertheless tend to behave according to the sociological principles obeyed by social control in general. As a result, they frequently apply law and other forms of social control to themselves. In criminal cases, defendants plead guilty more often when law is predictably more harsh (such as when they offend a social superior or stranger), and they plead not guilty more often when law is predictably more lenient (such as when they offend a social inferior or intimate). Adversariness is variable, then, increasing as law and other forms of social control decrease, and vice versa. What produces social control reduces adversariness.

The intimacy between individuals and themselves affects self-oriented behavior of every sort. It leads them to value their own ideas, for example, and their own taste (Cooney 1988:43). Even so, people tend to treat themselves according to the principles by which others treat them and, for that matter, by which they treat others. Self-interaction resembles all interaction. Just as self-applications of law are greater among those more sociologically vulnerable to law, so those whose social characteristics weaken their intellectual credibility and aesthetic influence, such as social inferiors (see Black 1979b:158–159), take themselves less seriously as well. Those held in lower esteem have less self-esteem.

People may appear to learn their self-worth from their fellows—a conception known as the "looking-glass self" (Cooley 1902: 184). And they may appear to "take the role of the other" toward themselves, so that "self-criticism is essentially social criticism" (Mead 1934:254–255). But the self and others also behave the same independently.[16] Their behavior obeys the same principles, and not merely because the self mimics others. Self-interaction is a form of social interaction.

ENDNOTES

*Reprinted with permission (and minor revision) from pages 39–49 of the *Virginia Review of Sociology*, Volume 1: *Law and Conflict Management*, edited by James Tucker. Greenwich: JAI Press, 1992.

The following people commented on earlier drafts: M. P. Baumgartner, Charles Cappell, Mark Cooney, John Griffiths, John Herrmann, Allan V. Horwitz, Setsuo Miyazawa, Calvin Morrill, Steven Nock, Roberta Senechal de la Roche, James Tucker, and Charles Wood.

1. Mark Cooney calls a person's relationship with himself or herself a "monadic relationship" (1988:42) after the philosopher Leibniz's "monads," the fundamental units of physical reality (1728:251). But he does not address the self-application of social control, apart from remarking that "people rarely invoke law against themselves" (1988:43).

The concept of "self-interaction" in the text derives from modern physics: Subatomic particles are said to "self-interact" (Capra 1976:232). Cooney similarly speaks of "monadic interaction" and of "people interacting with themselves" (1988:43).

2. Paul Bohannan calls these "jural" suicides (1960:260).

Suicide as social control of the self should be distinguished from suicide as social control of another person or group, such as when it is designed to deprive an offender of the company or services of the departed individual, to bring punishment against someone who will be blamed for the suicide, or to facilitate vengeance by the suicidal person's ghost (see, e.g., Jeffreys 1952; Price 1973; Counts 1980; Baumgartner 1984a:328–330; Robins 1988).

3. In the United States, those who commit murder more often kill themselves than are executed by the state (Wolfgang 1958:Chapter 15), though not all these qualify as self-applications of social control. Some probably seek to join their victims in an afterlife, for instance, while others might want to avoid publicity or prison.

4. In its pure form, psychotherapy is initiated by the deviant individual (see Black 1976:4–5; Horwitz 1982:127).

5. More precisely, the pattern is curvilinear. People from totally separate worlds (such as different societies or tribes) are, like intimates, relatively unlikely to use law against each other. Within a single society, however, the pattern is linear: Law increases with relational distance.

6. Even defendants who do not explicitly bargain for leniency may anticipate that pleading guilty will reduce the severity of their sentence, and they may be right in many cases. As one investigator observes, "By going to trial, the defendant risks a substantially harsher sentence than if he pleads guilty" (Feeley 1979:195).

On the other hand, whether a defendant who pleads guilty actually receives leniency is difficult to measure. We do not know the sentence any given individual pleading guilty would receive if he or she were to risk a trial. Some would be acquitted and receive no sentence at all. Moreover, leniency — a sentence below the maximum legally possible — may be a common response to cases such as the defendant's, even for those pleading not guilty (see Feeley 1979:191).

7. If the adverse consequences of legal events indirectly measure the quantity of law (Black 1979a:103, note 11), pleading guilty would seemingly incur more such consequences than pleading not guilty followed by conviction. For example, a defendant pleading guilty

would probably find it more difficult to find a job, and from this we might infer that pleading guilty entails more law. (On legal disabilities in the employment market, see Schwartz and Skolnick 1962.)

8. Leniency for someone pleading guilty is thus analogous to leniency for someone serving time in jail before trial and conviction.

Legal leniency may also compensate for self-applications of nonlegal social control. For this reason, defense lawyers may encourage their clients to provide restitution to victims or to begin rehabilitation programs before sentencing (see Feeley 1979:173). Leniency in these cases is predictable from the inverse relationship between law and other social control (see Black 1976:107–111; suggested by M. P. Baumgartner).

9. A "sociological impossibility" violates the natural behavior of social life and is analogous to a physical impossibility such as an object falling up instead of down (Black 1989:55).

10. A criminal record is itself a legally disabling status — a "normative status" — commonly known as unrespectability (Black 1976:111–117).

11. In La Free's sample, however, black defendants with black victims chose to plead guilty at essentially the same rate as black defendants with white victims (1980:845, Table 4). This may reflect greater inducements to plead guilty offered to the former, a difference which would invalidate the comparison.

The effect of earlier stages of the criminal process on pleading behavior is briefly discussed below.

12. Hagan's study was conducted in Canada.

13. Chicago rioters had a greater tendency to plead guilty as well, but those in Los Angeles did not (Balbus 1973:213, 74, respectively).

14. African children accused of witchcraft by their parents usually confess as well (Brain 1970). Most nonlegal confessional behavior seems to involve a confessant who is socially inferior to the confessor. On the role of status inequality in Catholic confessions and psychotherapeutic relationships, see Hepworth and Turner (1982:56, 60–61).

15. Pleading behavior is often explained as a rational choice of defendants calculating their risk of conviction and a more severe sentence if they plead not guilty and face a trial (see, e.g., Padgett 1985). Defendants are assumed to calculate this risk partly on the basis of the state's case against them, especially the strength of the evidence. But an implication of the present analysis is that, consciously or not, defendants also plead guilty when their risk of conviction is greater for sociological reasons.

16. Cooney likewise implies that the behavior of the self may be independent of the behavior of others (1988:41–46), but not that self-interaction resembles all interaction.

5

THE ELEMENTARY FORMS OF CONFLICT MANAGEMENT*

Conflict management is the handling of grievances, including litigation, mediation, arbitration, negotiation, beating, torture, assassination, feuding, warfare, strikes, boycotts, riots, banishment, resignation, running away, ridicule, scolding, gossip, witchcraft, witch-hunting, hostage-taking, fasting, confession, psychotherapy, and suicide.[1] Although diverse, its many varieties reduce to a smaller number, each arising under distinctive conditions.

The following pages describe five forms of conflict management — self-help, avoidance, negotiation, settlement, and toleration[2] — and propose the social fields[3] where their most extreme expressions occur. These fields and forms are isomorphic.

SELF-HELP

Self-help is the handling of a grievance by unilateral aggression (Black 1983:34, note 2). It ranges from quick and simple gestures of disapproval, such as glares or frowns, to massive assaults resulting in numerous deaths. In simple societies, self-help occurs dramatically as blood revenge, feuding, and affairs of honor (see, e.g., Hasluck 1954: 219–260; Otterbein and

Otterbein 1965; Peristiany 1966; Reid 1970; Koch 1974). It also includes cursing, sorcery, and the assassination of witches (see, e.g., Evans-Pritchard 1937:Part 1, Chapter 7; Winans and Edgerton 1964; Knauft 1985). In modern societies, it includes much fighting, beating, and killing between family members, friends, acquaintances, ethnic groups, and nations. Conduct regarded as criminal is often self-help (Black 1983), as is virtually all so-called terrorism and insurrection. And, once begun, wars always involve the pursuit of justice by one or both sides.

What is the social structure of self-help? Where in social space is it most likely to occur? When, in particular, does it appear in its most extreme versions, with fatalities, severe injuries, or substantial property destruction?

The evidence indicates that self-help is not a unitary phenomenon in a single configuration of social relations. Rather, it arises in two drastically different situations. One produces vengeance, the other discipline and rebellion.

Vengeance

Pure vengeance is reciprocal. A grievance pursued aggressively begets aggression in return. The blood feud, for example, is a pattern of reciprocal homicide that may be nearly interminable (see Black-Michaud 1975:63–85; Peters 1975:xxii–xxiii). Feuds are common in the Mediterranean region, such as among Bedouin nomads (Peters 1967), the shepherds of Albania, Greece, and Montenegro (Hasluck 1954; Campbell 1964; Boehm 1984), the Jalé of New Guinea (Koch 1974:76–86), the Jívaro of Ecuador and Peru (Harner 1972:170–193), the Yanomamö of Brazil and Venezuela (Chagnon 1977:Chapter 5), the Tausug of the Philippines (Kiefer 1972: Chapter 3), and the nomads of Tibet (Ekvall 1964). In modern America, feuds develop among street gangs, Mafia families, neighbors, and ethnic groups (see, e.g., Rieder 1985:171–202; Ellickson 1986). International warfare also entails reciprocal vengeance.

Only groups can provide the continuous supply of victims needed for relatively permanent conditions of hostility. The famous Hatfield–McCoy feud of Kentucky and West Virginia, for example, lasted twelve years and included twelve deaths (see Waller 1988). But extreme vengeance also arises among individuals, sometimes regulated by a "code of honor" specifying who should seek redress against whom, under what circumstances, and how (see generally Peristiany 1966). Honor normally involves a defense of "manliness" (Pitt-Rivers 1966:44–45) and was strongly emphasized among the nobility of Europe and the rural gentry of the American South, both famous for their fatal duels (see, e.g., Baldick 1965; Wyatt-Brown 1982).

Gunfights in the frontier towns of the American West were similar (McGrath 1984:Chapters 10–11). Today, honor is important among the young men of American slums and housing projects (see, e.g., Horowitz 1983: Chapter 5).[4] Individualized vengeance is also frequent and often fatal in American prisons (see, e.g., Abbott 1981:85–90, 149–150).

What social characteristics do cases of extreme vengefulness share? A few can be suggested:

1. *equality*
2. *social distance*
3. *immobility*
4. *functional independence*
5. *organization*

To elaborate: In simple societies, vengeance typically appears between structurally interchangeable groups comparable in size and resources, such as tribes, clans, or families. Individualized vengeance, including the defense of honor, characteristically involves parties of equal standing as well:

> *The power to impugn the honor of another man depends . . . on the relative status of the contestants. An inferior is not deemed to possess sufficient honor to resent the affront of a superior. A superior can ignore the affront of an inferior. . . . A man is answerable for his honor only to his social equals. (Pitt-Rivers 1966:31; see also 35; Berger, Berger, and Kellner 1973:86)*

The Kabyles of Algeria regard challenging social inferiors as dishonorable (Bourdieu 1966:199). An insult from a black man, for example, should be ignored: "Let him bark until he grows weary of it" (Bourdieu 1966:200, 207).[5] In slave societies, slaves neither have honor nor can dishonor a non-slave (Patterson 1982:81–97). And when duelling flourished in the American South, "no gentleman ever accepted a challenge from one not considered his social equal" (Williams 1980:27). Codes of honor develop primarily in stratified societies but pertain to relations among peers, particularly elites such as aristocrats and slave owners (Berger et al. 1973: 85–86; see also Gorn 1985:41–42). In short, pure vengeance arises in egalitarian rather than stratified settings.

And vengeance varies directly with relational distance[6]: "Feud is waged and vengeance taken when the parties live sufficiently far apart, or are too weakly related by diverse ties" (Gluckman 1956:19; see also Rieder 1984:154; Cooney 1988:Chapter 2). Vengeance is therefore more frequent and severe between tribes than within them, between clans than within them, between families than within them, and so on. A survey of simple societies throughout the world indicates that homicidal vengeance fits this pattern (Cooney 1988:Chapter 2).[7] Also consistent is Colson's observation that cross-cutting ties such as marriages between members of different clans inhibit vengeance (1953; see also Gluckman 1956:Chapter 1; Thoden van Velzen and van Wetering 1960; Otterbein and Otterbein 1965; Boehm 1984: 172, 219; Cooney 1988:Chapter 2). Vengeance develops most fully with horizontal segmentation, when people are separated by chasms in relational space, and social bridges across these chasms may reduce or terminate it. The headhunting Ilongot of the Philippines encourage intermarriage between feuding groups ("let their children marry") to restore peace (Rosaldo 1980:65–66). The Yakan of the Philippines ritually establish blood ties ("blood brotherhood") to pacify feuding groups (Frake 1980:207). The same practice occurs among the tribal people of Montenegro (Boehm 1984:136–137). Similarly, interracial ties inhibit race riots, and when rioting does erupt, those with ties to the racial adversary stay home (Senechal de la Roche 1990:144–147).

Cultural distance[8] also encourages vengeance. Wide cultural differences accompany some of the most extreme cases: massacres of women and children, torture, mutilation, and genocide. Intertribal and international vengeance is more severe among those widely separated in cultural space, for instance, as is interethnic conflict within a society. So-called terrorism obeys the same principle.

But there is no vengeance where people live in different worlds. Those involved must be mutually accessible and share a social arena, however superficially. Their relations are stable and predictable. The amount of violence in tribal societies thus varies inversely with the amount of spatial movement in their way of life (Thoden van Velzen and van Wetering 1960:198). So do sorcery and the naming of witches (see, e.g., Winans and Edgerton 1964; Baxter 1972; Douglas 1973:Chapter 7; Knauft 1985). But high rates of homicidal self-help are found in prisons, where the inmates are locked together (see Cohen 1976). Nations are effectively locked into place as well. Rioters reside in the same city. Vengeance is inescapable.

Vengeance is also more likely among persons or groups who are independent of one another for their survival and well-being, economic or otherwise. Homicidal vengeance thus occurs most frequently in societies with little division of labor, indicating little economic interdependence (Cooney 1988:Chapter 2; see also Durkheim 1893:Book 1). And nations lacking a division of labor among themselves have a stronger inclination for warfare.[9] People more readily kill those they can do without.

Finally, vengeance between organized groups is more extreme than vengeance between individuals. In simple societies, conflict between primordial groups such as clans produces a great deal. Egalitarian tribes with "fraternal interest groups" (usually patrilineal clans) display a particularly high rate, typically committed in the name of the groups themselves (Thoden van Velzen and van Wetering 1960). Conflict between nations — also groups — has produced the most death and destruction in human history (see Lee 1979:398–399; Cooney 1988:Chapter 5).

In sum, vengeance is most extreme in a social field combining several characteristics — equality, relational and cultural distance, immobility, independence, and organization — a collection of largely similar elements, separate yet frozen together in physical and social space. We might call this a *stable agglomeration*.[10]

Discipline and Rebellion

Self-help also appears under conditions radically unlike those associated with vengeance. Whereas vengeance flows laterally and is heterarchical, discipline and rebellion flow vertically and are hierarchical (see Bateson 1958:98; Hofstadter 1979:133–134; compare Rieder 1984:140–144). Discipline is downward self-help; rebellion is upward self-help (for similar usages, see, e.g., Hobsbawm 1959; Stinchcombe 1964; Foucault 1975). They arise in the same settings and are complementary: Where discipline is most extreme — involving torture, mutilation, maiming, and homicide — so is rebellion. Where the former is mild, so is the latter. Both typically are penal in style and authoritarian in procedure (Baumgartner 1984a:331–336).[11] A pure case is the master-slave relationship, where grievances in either direction — from master against slave (downward) or from slave against master (upward) — may have dire consequences, including death (see, e.g., Wiedemann 1981:Chapters 9–11; Patterson 1982). Illustrations beyond slavery include relations between guards and prisoners, lords and serfs, officers and enlisted men, parents and children, and husbands and wives in patriarchal families. States employ self-help — discipline — when they seize, imprison, torture, or execute individuals without using judicial procedures (e.g., Solzhenitsyn 1973; Timerman 1981). State discipline can be more severe than slave discipline (see generally Collins 1974). Like slaves, moreover, state-dominated individuals occasionally rebel.

The social structure of discipline and rebellion — in the extreme — has at least five characteristics:

1. *inequality*
2. *vertical segmentation*
3. *social distance*
4. *functional unity*
5. *immobility*

The greater the inequality, the more severe the discipline and rebellion. The master–slave relationship, a form of parasitism[12] with social inequalities of many kinds (Patterson 1982:335–337), may entail violent discipline with various practices to intensify the suffering of those punished, even when the misbehavior seems trivial. In one Roman case, for example, a slave who accidentally broke a crystal cup during a banquet was condemned to be thrown as food to lamprey eels (Wiedemann 1981:176).[13]

Most discipline is applied to individuals who belong to a homogeneous class in a larger hierarchy of social relations. Just as a system of slavery extends beyond a slave's household, for example, so enlisted men, workers, students, and children belong to larger classes as well.[14] And a substantial distance separates them from their superiors. Vertical segmentation is analogous to the relational segmentation associated with vengeance.

The most distance of a social nature produces the most discipline.[15] Where slaves have little or no contact with their owners, for instance, such as in plantation-type farming and in mining, whipping and other corporal punishments increase (Patterson 1982:198, 206). Even so, much discipline is found in relationships combining intimacy and distance, such as long-term relationships with few shared activities and associates. Slave masters, guards, and parents have many social involvements unknown to their charges, for example; their relational structure is jagged, close in some respects but not others. Cultural distance also increases discipline. Master–slave relationships commonly are interethnic (Patterson 1982:178),[16] as is modern torture by governments (Collins 1974:439, note 37).

Those involved in discipline also tend to be functionally unified: They are likely to participate in the same enterprise, whether production, warfare, imprisonment, or education. Their roles differ, but their lives intertwine. Socially distant, they are nevertheless bound together for the long term.

Rebellion and discipline rise and fall together, though the former may be less frequent.[17] The social field conducive to both is a *parasitical hierarchy*.

AVOIDANCE

Avoidance is the handling of a grievance by the curtailment of interaction (Baumgartner 1988:Chapter 3). The aggrieved or offending party may initiate and accomplish it alone, unilaterally, or both may withdraw at the same time. Avoidance ranges from permanent flight to a temporary reduction in contact, begun and ended in a single encounter. It may be total or partial, and may entail physical separation or only decreased communication. Examples include secession from a nation, migration from a region, desertion from an army, resignation from an organization, running away, divorce, termination of a business relationship, the "cold shoulder," and suicide. Because people also curtail interaction in the absence of grievances, whether any given instance qualifies as conflict management may be difficult or impossible to determine.

Without a visible complaint, avoidance eludes identification (see Hirschman 1970:86). Its purest form is silent, and those avoiding others may even explicitly deny that they harbor a grievance. Public officials resigning from office may thus deny their reasons (such as their involvement in a scandal) and instead cite "personal" concerns (e.g., "to spend more time with my family"; Hirschman 1970:105). Similar denials are common in everyday life ("No, I'm not avoiding you. I've just been very busy.").

Hunting and gathering societies typically use a great deal of avoidance (see, e.g., Turnbull 1965:100–109; Fürer-Haimendorf 1967:17–24; Lee 1979: 372; Woodburn 1979). Eskimos, for example, move from one band to another when conflict arises and also locate their dwellings to facilitate avoidance within a single settlement:

> Whenever a situation came up in which an individual disliked somebody or a group of people in the band, he often pitched his tent or built his igloo at the opposite extremity of the camp or moved to another settlement altogether. This is common practice even today. . . . People who like each other stay together; those who do not live apart. An additional detail is significant in this respect: If for any reason two families who are not on friendly terms have to camp close by, the openings of their dwellings will face in opposite directions, indicating that there is no intercourse between the two families. (Balikci 1970:192–193; punctuation edited)

Shifting horticulturalists also favor avoidance (see, e.g., Turner 1957; Carniero 1970:734–735; Stauder 1972), as do gypsies (Grönfors 1986:119–121), consumers in the modern marketplace (Hirschman 1970), and suburbanites (Baumgartner 1984b, 1988:Chapters 3–4).

Temporary and partial avoidance is ubiquitous in social life. But again the extremes are instructive. Although avoidance rarely has homicidal consequences apart from self-destruction, it may be fatal for relationships (suggested by John Jarvis). Permanent and total avoidance is most likely under the following conditions:

1. *absence of hierarchy*
2. *social fluidity*
3. *social fragmentation*
4. *functional independence*
5. *individuation*

Avoidance is uncommon in authority relationships, though slaves sometimes flee their masters, serfs their lords, or soldiers their officers (see Baumgartner 1984a:320–324). But it frequently occurs in nonhierarchical status systems without chains of authority.

The fluidity of social life, or the rate at which relationships begin and end (relational fertility and mortality rates), predicts the amount of avoidance. The higher these rates, the more people avoid each other (Baumgartner 1984b:94–95; 1988:Chapter 3). Since avoidance itself contributes to social fluidity, the association between the two may seem trivial or self-evident. But there is no necessary reason why people in fluid relationships should handle grievances with avoidance rather than confrontational modes such as vengeance or settlement by a third party.[18]

Hunters and gatherers have more fluid relationships than sedentary peoples, and this partly explains their greater use of avoidance (Baumgartner 1988:Chapter 3; see also Cooney 1988). Fluid relationships on the wagon trails to the American West in the nineteenth century meant that avoidance predominated over the brawling and gunfighting romanticized in books and movies (see Reid 1980; compare Faragher 1979:101–102). And the highly unstable suburban world of modern America has so much avoidance it has been called an "avoidance culture" (Baumgartner 1988: Chapter 3).

People may share many activities with their associates, or they may have more limited and focused interaction.[19] The latter produces avoidance. For example, commercial relationships today are highly fragmentary, often embracing only the business at hand, and avoidance is common (see Baumgartner 1988:Chapter 3). In traditional villages and families where people have many involvements with each other, however, confrontational modes of conflict management are more likely. With the modernization of society, relationships become increasingly emaciated, and avoidance proliferates (see Baumgartner 1988:Chapter 6).

Functionally independent people also use more avoidance (Baumgartner 1988:Chapter 3). Avoidance-prone hunters and gatherers have little division of labor and can subsist almost by themselves.[20] Similarly, as modern women become more independent, they increasingly use separation and divorce to resolve their problems with men. Business executives in decentralized companies with independent subdivisions use more avoidance than those in more hierarchical companies (Morrill 1986:Chapters 2–4). And all markets entail a degree of independence between the participants: Buyers and sellers normally can and do go elsewhere when dissatisfied (Hirschman 1970). A business may be shunned by individuals for the rest of their lives and by families for generations.[21]

When independent people disperse across physical space, avoidance increases (see Baumgartner 1988:Chapter 3). Hunters and gatherers again provide the prototypical case. At the opposite extreme are prisons and other "total institutions" (Goffman 1961) where physical separation is impossible. Some social scientists even speculate that the state and law emerged when populations expanded in limited spaces and individuals could no longer avoid their enemies (Carniero 1970; Taylor 1982:129–139; Mann 1986:Chapters 3–4).

A final factor conducive to avoidance is individuation, the capacity of individuals to act autonomously without implicating groups (see Baumgartner 1988:Chapter 3). Groups avoid each other, such as organizations that terminate commercial relationships or nations that sever diplomatic relations, but individuals do so more often. Moreover, individuals frequently avoid groups. For example, avoidance is the primary means by which individuals express grievances against business organizations (Hirschman 1970).

To summarize: An avoidance structure is generally nonhierarchical, fluid, fragmented, individuated, and composed of mutually independent participants. A social field with these characteristics might be called an *unstable aggregation*.[22]

Violence varies inversely with avoidance (see Baumgartner 1984b:97; 1988). For example, killings are more likely when permanent and total avoidance is difficult or impossible: in agricultural societies; between contiguous groups such as street gangs, tribes, and nations; in maximum security prisons; and in families and households (see Cohen 1976:17). These settings differ markedly from the unstable settings where avoidance is most common: among hunters and gatherers, in suburbia, in markets — wherever relationships fluctuate and the turnover of people is high. Eliminate the conditions for avoidance, and violence increases. The nomadic Chenchu of India, for instance, traditionally handled conflict with avoidance, but after the British concentrated them in large settlements they became uncontrollably violent (Fürer-Haimendorf 1967:22).

Like homicide, suicide often originates in human conflict (see, e.g., Douglas 1967) and may be a form of avoidance (see Koch 1974:74–75). Modern suicide occurs at a higher rate among relatively isolated individuals (Durkheim 1897:Book 2, Chapters 2–3, 5), where marital separation and divorce are more frequent (Durkheim 1897:259–262), and in urban rather than rural areas (Durkheim 1897:353) — conditions conducive to avoidance in general. And suicide varies inversely with homicide (Durkheim 1897:338–352; Henry and Short 1954).[23] This is because the conditions associated with a high level of avoidance are nearly opposite those associated with violent self-help (unstable aggregations versus stable agglomerations and parasitical hierarchies).

NEGOTIATION

Negotiation is the handling of a grievance by joint decision (Gulliver 1979:5):

> The decision is made by the disputing parties themselves. . . . Each party can only obtain what the other is in the end prepared to allow. Since the two parties necessarily began with some kind of difference between them . . . , the process of decision-making therefore involves a convergence. At least one party, but usually both, must move toward the other. (Gulliver 1979:5)

This may or may not include the intervention of a third party as a negotiator (see Black and Baumgartner 1983:108–109).

Negotiation is the primary mode of handling major conflicts in many simple societies throughout the world. Often it involves haggling about compensation for a death or injury (see, e.g., Kroeber 1926:514–515; Hasluck 1954:Chapter 15; Gulliver 1963, 1969, 1971:Chapter 5; Nader 1965; Jones 1974). Lawyers in modern societies also engage in much negotiation (known in the United States as "out-of-court settlement" in civil cases and "plea bargaining" in criminal cases; see, e.g., Galanter 1983; Black 1984a, for reviews of the evidence). The rapid growth of the legal profession in twentieth-century America (see, e.g., Curran 1986:20) may thus indicate an increased demand for negotiators.[24]

When do people bargain rather than use violence, avoidance, or other forms of conflict management? When do they expend a great deal of time and energy in this fashion? Extensive negotiations occur most in social fields with the following characteristics:

1. *equality*
2. *cross-linkages*
3. *organization*
4. *homogeneity*
5. *accessibility*

Negotiation is less likely among unequal parties. Superiors usually obtain what they want from inferiors with little or no bargaining, whereas the latter may have trouble even initiating negotiations with the former. Nevertheless, equality need not exist between the adversaries themselves. Allies and other supporters on each side can transform a conflict between

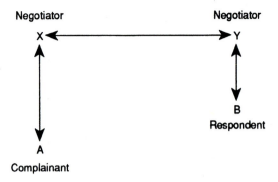

Figure 5.1   The status structure of Thai negotiation. (Vertical position = status level.)[25]

unequal parties into one between equals. In tribal societies, support typi-
cally arises from familial and residential affiliations (see, e.g., Gulliver 1963:
Chapter 7; 1969; Frake 1980). Those serving as negotiators — usually status
superiors of the adversaries — may also function as equalizers. In tradi-
tional Thailand, for example, if A has a grievance against a social superior
(B), and B refuses to discuss the matter with A, A may mobilize a superior
(X) in his own hierarchy who is acquainted with one of B's social superiors
(Y). X and Y may then negotiate a settlement and urge A and B to accept it
(Engel 1978:76–77). Negotiators can thereby flatten otherwise vertical con-
flicts (see Figure 5.1).

Lawyers frequently have the same effect. Indeed, the structural transformation of cases in highly stratified societies such as the United States
may be one of their most significant functions. As familial and other primordial alliances decline, lawyers become the great equalizers of modern
life. They offer equality as a commodity, for sale in the marketplace.[26]

The Thai practice described above illustrates another factor associated
with negotiation: cross-linkages between the parties. Negotiation between
A and B depends not only on equalization but also on A's connection to B
through X and Y. Because of his link to Y, X provides a "crossover point"
between A and B (Engel 1978:77). Indirect ties open communication, bridg-
ing social gulfs that might otherwise preclude discussion and bargaining.
As implied earlier, vengeance structures generally lack linkages of this kind
(see also Colson 1953; Nader 1965; Peters 1975:xxiv–xxvii; Cooney 1988:
Chapter 2).

Cross-linking is another function (besides equalization) provided by
lawyers. Even if not personally acquainted, the shared professional affilia-
tion and mutual accessibility of opposing lawyers provides a social bridge

between their clients. And once begun, negotiation increases intimacy between all concerned. On the other hand, adversaries who are already intimate — such as married couples, friends, or fellow employees — may find that the intervention of lawyers widens the social distance between them and compounds the fracture in their relationship. Their conflict may therefore escalate, increasing the likelihood of a permanent termination of their relationship (see, e.g., Macaulay 1963; Griffiths 1986).

Negotiation is also more extensive between corporate beings than between individuals. The conflict need not originate in groups as long as groups ultimately participate. The adversaries' allies may band together, or groups may customarily or contractually participate, such as occurs in tribal conflicts involving a system of collective liability (see, e.g., Moore 1972) or in modern conflicts involving insurance companies (see, e.g., Ross 1970). To a lesser extent, outside negotiators transform conflicts into corporate events.

Homogeneity is relevant as well. Because negotiation requires communication, cultural closeness between the parties tends to facilitate it. A shared language obviously helps, as do other shared practices — another contrast with vengeance, where the most extreme cases frequently entail cultural cleavages.

Finally, negotiation requires mutual accessibility. As noted above, this is another contribution of lawyers. Physical availability is not necessary — as in vengeance — but only the possibility of communication, such as a telephone.

Negotiation structures resemble vengeance structures in their equality, organization, and mutual accessibility, but not in their cross-linkages and cultural homogeneity. Negotiation can, however, withstand the physical separation and mobility of its participants, though its ideal setting is less fluid than an avoidance structure. Neither a stable agglomeration nor an unstable aggregation, the social field most conducive to negotiation lies between the settings of vengeance and avoidance. It is a *tangled network*. And because it combines characteristics of both vengeance and avoidance, in the pure case the adversaries neither attack each other nor run away, but do something between these extremes: They talk.

SETTLEMENT

Settlement is the handling of a grievance by a nonpartisan third party. Only a significantly nonpartisan third party can achieve the trilateral structure that distinguishes this form of conflict management. The most familiar examples are mediation, arbitration, and adjudication. The mediator acts as a broker, helping the adversaries resolve their conflict without taking sides, the arbitrator decides how to resolve a conflict but cannot compel compliance, while the judge both makes a decision and, if necessary, enforces it. These roles appear in many societies and have received extensive scholarly attention (e.g., Galtung 1965; Eckhoff 1966; Gulliver 1977; Fuller 1978; Getman 1979; Shapiro 1980; Merry 1982; Black and Baumgartner 1983).

Mediation, arbitration, and adjudication differ in their degree of authoritativeness, including their decisiveness and coerciveness. Mediation entails neither a decision nor coercion by the third party, arbitration entails a decision but no coercion, and adjudication entails both. While mediation is the least authoritative of the three, still less so is friendly pacification, a mode of settlement in which the third party seeks merely to separate or distract the adversaries (Black and Baumgartner 1983:99–100). The "camp clown" of the Mbuti Pygmies, for example, dampens conflicts by diverting attention to himself in a humorous fashion (Turnbull 1965:182–183). In modern societies, family members and other intimates may use friendly pacification. Gossip is the least authoritative of all—a kind of trial *in absentia* unknown to the principals (see, e.g., Gluckman 1963; Cohen 1972; Merry 1984).

Repressive pacification defines the other extreme of authoritative intervention. Here a third party handles the conflict as an offense in itself and seeks to crush it forcefully regardless of the adversaries' concerns or complaints (Black and Baumgartner 1983:106–107). Colonial administrators repressively pacified indigenous populations involved in feuding and warfare (see, e.g., Evans-Pritchard 1940:152; Koch 1974:223; Reay 1974:205, 209), and adults relate similarly to fighting among children (see Black and Baumgartner 1983:107).

Consider now the social conditions associated with violent or otherwise highly authoritative settlement — adjudication and repressive pacification. Several variables are relevant:

1. *inequality*
2. *relational distance*
3. *isosceles triangulation*
4. *heterogeneity*
5. *organizational asymmetry*

The authoritativeness of third parties varies directly with their social superiority (Black and Baumgartner 1983:113). Friendly peacemakers tend to be about equal to the adversaries, whereas mediators, arbitrators, and adjudicators tend to be (in the same order) increasingly elevated above the adversaries.[27] Repressive peacemakers are generally the most elevated of all, illustrated by the colonial administrators who once intervened in the tribal conflicts of Africa and Oceania. The tribesmen were effectively treated as "nonpersons" (Goffman 1961:341–342) — like wildlife — and their disputes as "disturbances of the peace" (e.g., Scheffler 1964:399; Koch 1974:223). Conditions of great inequality also produce corporal punishment such as whipping, torture, mutilation, and execution, but offenders of high status — closer to the third parties — may escape the harshest treatment. The Roman nobility, for example, were immune to crucifixion and to being thrown to wild beasts (Garnsey 1968:13).

Relational distance between the third party and the adversaries has the same effect as social superiority: The greater it is, the more violent the settlement is likely to be (see Black and Baumgartner 1983:113). Friendly peacemakers tend to be very close to those they disentangle, mediators a bit less so, followed by arbitrators, judges, and repressive peacemakers.[28] Repressive pacification in colonial settings again defines the extreme: The administrators are usually not only socially superior but also entirely unacquainted with the people they handle. So are judges who pronounce the death penalty.

The relational distance between a third party and each adversary must be approximately equal if the process is to be significantly nonpartisan (see Simmel 1908b:149–153). Imbalance breeds partisanship (see Black and Baumgartner 1980:200–201). Third parties substantially closer to either adversary are likely to be disqualified from handling the case (see, e.g., Barton 1919:87; Lewis 1961:229; Ayoub 1965:13). The third party and the adversaries therefore tend to form an isosceles triangle of relational distance, with the former at the apex (Black and Baumgartner 1983:113; see also Black 1984b:21–23). Settings lacking third parties equidistant from the adversaries — isosceles triangulation — generally have little or no settlement behavior at all. A village completely bifurcated by kinship, for example, is unlikely to have an internal system of settlement for handling conflicts that cross family lines (see, e.g., Nader 1965). When socially superior or relationally distant third parties are lacking, no settlement of an authoritative nature is likely to occur. Hunters and gatherers, typically both egalitarian and intimate among themselves, often do not even have mediation, much less arbitration, adjudication, or repressive pacification (see, e.g., Turnbull 1961, 1965; Woodburn 1979; Lee 1979).

Cultural distance — heterogeneity — has the same relevance as relational distance: The greater it is, the more authoritative the settlement procedure is likely to be. Again the extreme example is the imposition of colonial authority by a foreign power, such as when Europeans enforced their conception of law and order in Africa and elsewhere. Cultural equidistance from the adversaries — another form of isosceles triangulation — is also important, since cultural closeness, like intimacy, engenders partisanship (Black and Baumgartner 1983:114). In an intertribal conflict, for instance, a third party from either tribe — even if a stranger to all concerned — will normally not be acceptable to both sides. Culturally skewed procedures, however, appear to be considerably more common than relationally skewed procedures (see, e.g., Beidelman 1966, 1967).

Authoritative third parties usually represent a corporate entity, often a government. Capital punishment inflicted by legal officials is thus a form of corporate behavior, but it virtually always applies to individuals and is in this sense organizationally asymmetrical (see Coleman 1982:19–30). Most vengeance is organizationally symmetrical, whether between two groups or between two individuals, as is negotiation. Avoidance may be organizationally asymmetrical, but usually in the opposite direction: An individual is more likely to avoid an organization than vice versa.

The most authoritative settlement thus entails inequality between the third party and the adversaries, relational and cultural distance, isosceles triangulation, and organizational asymmetry — a social field we might term a *triangular hierarchy*.

TOLERATION

Toleration is inaction when a grievance might otherwise be handled. Although arguably not a form of conflict management at all, toleration is sometimes consciously advocated or adopted as the most effective response to deviant behavior, disagreement, or disruption (see, e.g., Parsons 1951:Chapter 7; Lemert 1967). For example, members of organizations may use "unilateral peaceableness" to handle volatile situations (Boulding 1964: 47–48). Whether to forestall further conflict or not, people continually "lump it," "turn the other cheek," or "bite the bullet" (see, e.g., Felstiner 1974:81; Galanter 1974:124–125; Yngvesson 1976; Merry 1979; Baumgartner 1984b). Toleration is the most common response of aggrieved people everywhere.

A matter of degree, toleration is measurable by comparing what might otherwise occur under the same circumstances. When a group exacts blood vengeance for one killing but does little or nothing in response to another, its behavior in the latter is extremely tolerant. The same applies when a case of inaction might otherwise result in police intervention, arrest, or prosecution. We can also compare the degree of toleration across societies and historical epochs. There is noticeable variation, for example, in reactions to drunkenness, adultery, homosexuality, and homicide. Nothing automatically attracts social control.

Moreover, we can specify the social conditions most conducive to toleration (i.e., those least likely to provoke vengeance, avoidance, or anything else). One is social inferiority. Underlings such as slaves and students are unlikely to rebel violently against their superiors, and when their superiors fight or victimize each other, they rarely do more than gossip.[29] Social inferiors may not be subjectively tolerant of their superiors, but behaviorally they are exceptionally so.

Another source of toleration is intimacy. People endure all manner of offenses by people close to them, including not only rudeness and insult of various kinds but also physical intimidation, beatings, and rape. In modern societies, criminal offenses between intimates are far less likely to be reported to the authorities (see, e.g., Block 1974; Williams 1984). In tribal societies where vengeance commonly follows homicide, within a family it is rare. The Bedouin of Cyrenaica, for instance, regard the killer of a fellow family member as "one who defecates in the tent" and, at most, temporarily exile him (Peters 1967:264; for other examples, see Goody 1957:97; Middleton 1965:51). As people grow closer, they "normalize" conduct that earlier would have spurred them to action (Lemert 1964:86). And third parties intimate with those in conflict tend to hang back or to employ the gentler modes of intervention such as friendly pacification or mediation (Black and Baumgartner 1983:113; Black 1984b:22–23).

Cultural closeness has the same effect as relational closeness. People who are vicious toward foreigners will more readily forgive their own kind. Organization induces toleration as well. Conduct regarded as outrageous in an individual—lying, cheating, violence—may be countenanced in a group such as a government or corporation (see, e.g., Black 1976:Chapter 6). Toleration increases still more when the aggrieved party belongs to the offending group itself, a situation that simultaneously combines several conditions conducive to toleration (inferiority, intimacy, homogeneity, and organization).

Much toleration also occurs in urban settings with swarms of heterogeneous strangers, social fragmentation, individuation, and continual turnover (Boswell 1980:33–38; Baumgartner 1984b, 1988). Toleration thus arises under opposite conditions, where social relations are either very tight or very loose: extremely close, homogeneous, stable, and possibly even oppressive *or* distant, heterogeneous, unstable, and free. Only in a *polarized field* of social life can all these conditions operate at once. Past societies rarely divided daily life between such drastically different worlds, but modern societies increasingly do (see Black 1976:Chapter 7).

* * *

We can identify five modes of conflict management — self-help, avoidance, negotiation, settlement, and toleration — and the social fields associated with their most extreme versions. Vengeance, a form of self-help, reaches its highest level in stable agglomerations, where people are equal, independent, organized, socially separated, and yet frozen together in physical space. Two other forms of self-help, discipline and rebellion, are characteristic of parasitical hierarchies, where people are unequal, segmented, socially distant, functionally unified, and immobile. Avoidance arises in unstable aggregations, without hierarchies of authority, where social relations are fluid and fragmented, and where people are mutually independent and individuated. Negotiation thrives in tangled networks, where people are equal, cross-linked, organized, homogeneous, and mutually accessible. Settlement develops to its highest level in triangular hierarchies, where people are unequal, socially distant, organizationally asymmetrical, and where their relational and cultural structure resembles an isosceles triangle. Lastly, toleration is most likely at opposite extremes of social life, either very tight or very loose, which only a polarized field can contain in a single setting.

CONCLUSION

The models above predict and explain the elementary forms of conflict management. The more a social field resembles one of them, the more accurately we can anticipate its pattern of conflict management.[30] Where the fit is only partial, a less developed pattern should occur. For example, a stable agglomeration of individuals should have less vengeance than a stable agglomeration of groups, a parasitical hierarchy between intimates should have less discipline than one spanning a greater distance in social space, and a triangular hierarchy with relatively little inequality should have less authoritative settlement than one with more inequality. Settings that mix characteristics of different fields should mix the forms of conflict management. Modern America's complex society contains all the social fields modeled here to some degree, and all the forms of conflict management as well. People everywhere participate in multiple fields of social relations — family, neighborhood, peer group, workplace, marketplace — each with its own pattern of conflict management. A modern adult may thus wield discipline at home, experience it at work, use avoidance in the neighborhood, seek third parties to handle strangers in the community, and demand vengeance against foreigners. Conflict management is as variable as social life itself.

But why? Why is each form of conflict management associated with a particular configuration of social relations? Why is vengeance associated with stable agglomerations, avoidance with unstable aggregations, and so on? What is their affinity? A deeper pattern underlies them all: *Conflict management is isomorphic with its social field*.

Each form of conflict management reproduces its social environment. Social settings with a high level of avoidance — unstable aggregations — exhibit much relational mortality apart from the handling of grievances. The Ndembu of Zambia, for example, have such a high rate of relational mortality that their social life is described as "fissile" (Turner 1957:xxiii). Villages, lineages, and families continually split apart, but not all this fission involves conflict. Spatial mobility is the Ndembu way of life, and their management of conflict reflects this larger tendency (see Turner 1957: Chapters 5–7). A similar pattern appears in the suburbs of modern America: The constant fluctuation of relationships in neighborhoods, associations, and workplaces often has nothing to do with grievances, yet avoidance increases this fluidity all the more (Baumgartner 1984b, 1988). In the marketplace, too, shopping for something better is both how business is conducted and how conflict is handled (see Hirschman 1970).

Discipline similarly mirrors subordination. Patriarchal families have more discipline than egalitarian families. Business organizations with strict hierarchies, such as banking firms, have more than decentralized and segmentary organizations, such as accounting firms and restaurant chains (Morrill 1986:Chapters 2, 4). Grade schools have more than universities. Where everyday life is dictated from above, so is the management of conflict.

Vengeance is an exchange. Its hallmark is balance: "an eye for an eye, a tooth for a tooth," one life for another (called "negative reciprocation" by Warner 1958:162; compare Sahlins 1965:148–149). It is most developed where wealth, armed forces, and other resources are balanced as well. In herding societies, for example, various mechanisms, including bridewealth offerings and livestock raids, commonly equalize neighboring groups (see Sweet 1965). Negotiation arises where people are interlinked and continually bargain over their conditions of life as well as their conflicts. Settlement likewise reflects its social setting. A judge is to the parties in a case what a ruler is to the ruled. In many simpler societies, judge and ruler are one and the same: the chief. Settlement mirrors not only political hierarchies but also economic, religious, and domestic hierarchies.[31]

Conflict management is not a unique genus of behavior, then, but recapitulates and intensifies its larger environment.[32] It expresses and also dramatizes its social field in a pure and concentrated fashion. Modern courts of law thus elevate the judge and require exaggerated etiquette, and similar rituals frequently accompany blood vengeance, duels, discipline, the termination of relationships,[33] and negotiations between tribes and nations. And because it resembles the whole of which it is a part,[34] conflict management may diagnostically identify various locations in social space. Ultimately it may even reveal the elementary forms of social life.

ENDNOTES

*Reprinted with permission (and minor revision) from pages 43–69 in *New Directions in the Study of Justice, Law, and Social Control*, prepared by the School of Justice Studies, Arizona State University. New York: Plenum Press, 1990.

This essay was originally presented in the Distinguished Scholar Lecture Series, School of Justice Studies, Arizona State University, Tempe, February 9, 1987. I thank the following people for commenting on an earlier draft: M. P. Baumgartner, Albert Bergesen, Albert K. Cohen, Mark Cooney, Kathleen Ferraro, John Griffiths, John Hepburn, John Herrmann, Allan V. Horwitz, Pat Lauderdale, Calvin Morrill, Michael Musheno, Annamarie Oliverio, Roberta Senechal de la Roche, and James Tucker.

1. The present chapter could as well be called "The Elementary Forms of Social Control." For a discussion of this conceptual issue, see Black (1984b:5, note 7).

2. This typology was developed with M. P. Baumgartner and presented jointly in a talk entitled "Toward a Theory of Self-Help" at the Center for Criminal Justice, Harvard Law School, Cambridge, Massachusetts, February 19, 1982.

For related typologies, see Koch (1974:27–31) and Gulliver (1979:1–3).

3. Related concepts of "field" are applied to this subject matter in Goody (1957), Collier (1973:253–255), and Moore (1973).

In physics, a field is a "region of influence" (Whitrow 1967:68).

4. Horowitz proposes that honor is more developed where men have little wealth and must achieve social status by violence and deference from others (1983:Chapter 5).

Ayers reports that honor was defended by all classes of the Old South (1984:Chapter 1) and suggests that it migrated to northern cities with blacks (1984:275).

5. A Kabyle legend tells of a particular tribe that sent blacks against an opponent in war. The opponent capitulated rather than dishonor itself by fighting such a lowly foe. The losers thereby preserved their honor while the winners lost theirs (Bourdieu 1966:200).

6. Relational distance refers to "the degree to which [people] participate in one another's lives" and can be measured by "the scope, frequency, and length of interaction between people, the age of their relationship, and the nature and number of links between them in a social network" (Black 1976:40–41).

7. Homicidal vengeance between intimates such as married couples, lovers, and friends does not fit this model (see, e.g., Wolfgang 1958:191; Lundsgaarde 1977:230). Perhaps the relationship is U-curvilinear (see Black 1987a:574, note 11).

Another exception is the killing of alleged witches, a practice that may involve neighbors, acquaintances, or even kinfolk (see, e.g., Knauft 1985:Chapter 7; 1987a:462–472).

8. Cultural distance refers to differences in the content of culture, such as differences in religion, language, and aesthetics (see Black 1976:74).

9. This pattern is consistent with Durkheim's (1893) theory that functional interdependence (the "division of labor") increases compensation ("restitutive sanctions") at the expense of punishment ("repressive sanctions").

10. In botany, a number of plants are regarded as an agglomerate if they are "crowded into a dense cluster, but not cohering" (*Random House Dictionary*, unabridged edition, 1967).

11. Baumgartner remarks that "there is considerable isomorphism between upward and downward social control — so much, in fact, that there appears to be a greater affinity between the two than between either of these and the forms of social control found among equals" (1984a:336).

12. Wilson defines parasitism as a kind of symbiosis "in which one partner benefits as the other suffers" (1971:389).

13. Slaves may be killed in non-punitive circumstances as well, such as to satisfy the grief of a bereaved master, to accompany the burial of a deceased master, or for ritual purposes (see Patterson 1982:191).

14. The same applies to women in patriarchal societies.

15. The incompatibility between discipline and intimacy may explain why military organizations discourage fraternizing between officers and enlisted men.

16. Patterson reports, however, that the treatment of slaves is not associated with ethnic differences (1982:179).

17. It is not entirely clear that rebellion is less frequent than discipline. Discipline and rebellion may tend toward a natural balance or equivalence (see Rieder 1984:142). Or rebellion may even be more frequent than discipline. Social inferiors sometimes covertly resist their superiors on a daily basis, such as by minimizing their labor, pilfering, and vandalizing property (see Baumgartner 1984a; Scott 1985:especially 265–273). And rebellion does not necessarily involve direct action against superiors but may also be self-directed, such as when a slave mutilates himself or commits suicide — technically speaking, a form of property destruction. On self-injury as "social control from below," see Baumgartner (1984a:328–331). Durkheim calls suicide of this kind "fatalistic" and explains it with "excessive regulation," a condition found among "persons with futures pitilessly blocked and passions violently choked by oppressive discipline" (1897:276, note 25).

18. Baumgartner distinguishes "confrontational" from "nonconfrontational" modes of social control and classifies avoidance as a form of the latter (1984b).

19. Gluckman calls the former "multiplex relationships" and contrasts them with "ephemeral relationships" that involve "single interests." He proposes the number of shared activities as a predictor of how disputes will be handled, arguing that those in multiplex relationships are more likely to be handled in a conciliatory than an authoritative fashion (1967:20–21).

20. In hunting and gathering societies, a division of labor usually exists between men and women but not between families, and individuals are generally not dependent for food on other individuals but rely on the multifamily band as a whole (Leacock 1982:159).

21. Such avoidance does not necessarily relate to dissatisfaction with a product or service. In one American city, for instance, blacks in the 1970s were still avoiding businesses whose earlier owners had participated in an anti-black riot over 50 years earlier (Senechal de la Roche 1990:183).

22. In biology, an aggregation is defined as "a group of organisms of the same or different species living closely together but less integrated than a society" (*Random House Dictionary*, unabridged edition, 1967).

The social context of avoidance also resembles the phenomenon known in physics as "Brownian motion": the constant and irregular movement of tiny particles observable in a liquid such as a glass of water.

23. One exception is Durkheim's "fatalistic" suicide, which apparently occurs under some of the same conditions as violent rebellion. See Note 17. Another exception would seem to be self-punishment by suicide (see Douglas 1967:302–304).

24. This need not mean that negotiation itself is increasing but could also indicate that private individuals are increasingly unwilling or otherwise unavailable to act as negotiators.

25. This diagram is adapted from Engel (1978:77), whose version does not vary the positions of A and B to signify differing levels of social status.

26. Programs providing legal services for the poor in societies such as modern America are presumably intended to remedy shortcomings of the marketplace in this respect.

27. Gossip is democratic, occurring in diverse locations in social space including those beneath the status level of the offending parties.

28. Where social superiority and intimacy occur together, third parties typically display a blend of warmth and repression, a pattern frequently seen when parents handle fighting between their children. This mixed form might be called paternalistic pacification.

Therapy is a mode of third-party intervention defined by the participants as help and not as a form of conflict management at all (see Black and Baumgartner 1983:109–111; see also Horwitz 1982).

29. But social inferiors might be required to participate. For example, Roman law held that "if an owner was killed, all the slaves within earshot at the time had to be interrogated under torture and killed" (Wiedemann 1981:169). In nineteenth-century Mexico, servants were legally required to give their lives to protect their masters. Failure to do so was punishable by death (Romanucci-Ross 1986:11–12).

30. By the same logic, we could test these models by showing that social fields with completely opposite characteristics have the least conflict management predicted by each (suggested by Michael Musheno).

31. Lasswell observes that punitive child-rearing practices seem to occur in societies with punitive governments (1964:xii).

32. It may therefore be difficult or impossible to transplant a mode of conflict management between socially different settings.

33. For example, Jewish parents traditionally obey a seven-day period of mourning (*shivah*) when they disown a child for marrying a gentile. The Banyoro of Uganda may handle conflict between fellow clan members by "cutting kinship" (*obwiko*), a formal separation initiated when the aggrieved party utters a formula such as the following: "From now on, you shall not come to my place nor shall I come to yours, and your children shall not come to my place nor shall mine come to yours" (Beattie 1971:212; punctuation edited).

34. Self-similarity is a basic organizing principle of nature, as when a branch resembles a tree or a leaf a branch. Self-similar structures, known as "fractals," are recognized in such fields as physics, chemistry, geology, and astronomy (see, e.g., Gleick 1987:81–118; La Brecque 1987).

6

TOWARD A THEORY OF
THE THIRD PARTY*

with M. P. Baumgartner

Here we present a classification of the roles played by people who intervene as third parties in the conflicts of others. Such a classification, or typology, is a first step toward a general theory of the third party, since it specifies the primary range of variation that a theory of this kind must confront. Although our typology is the product of an extensive review of anthropological, sociological, and historical literature on the management of human conflict, it will undoubtedly need revision and refinement in light of future inquiry. What follows, then, should not be construed as definitive. Even so, it is intended to be comprehensive.

The theory of the third party — which necessarily refers to such a typology — seeks to understand when and how people intervene in the conflicts of others. It builds on existing formulations that specify how the social characteristics of the adversaries, including the nature of their relationship, predict and explain what happens to their case (such as whether it is taken to a court of law and, if so, who wins). We already know, for example, that the relative status of the adversaries, their intimacy with each other, and the degree of their organization are relevant to how their dispute is pursued and processed (see especially Black 1976). The theory of the third party addresses the relevance of analogous characteristics of any other parties who might participate in a conflict. Although not every conflict results in the intervention of third parties, in all societies a great many do, including most that become public.

The range of conduct embraced by our typology is very broad and departs radically from earlier efforts of a comparable nature. In particular, our concept of the third party embraces virtually all individuals or groups who intervene in any way in an on-going conflict, including those who are overtly and unabashedly partisan from the outset, such as lawyers, champions-at-arms, and witnesses. In contrast, earlier typologies have treated as third parties only those who are, or who claim to be, non-partisan, such as mediators, arbitrators, and judges (e.g., Galtung 1965; Eckhoff 1966; Koch 1974:27–31; Shapiro 1975:323–325; Sander 1976; McGillis and Mullen 1977:4–25; but see FitzGerald, Hickman, and Dickins 1980).

We include partisans as third parties because, in the first place, a distinction between partisans and nonpartisans, though useful for some purposes, is not absolute. On the one hand, many third parties who claim to be neutral in a conflict are actually biased in favor of one side or the other. This is known by every lawyer who goes to court, and it may also be the case in more informal settings, such as mediation in a tribal society, a private association, or a family. Apart from bias apparent during the settlement process itself, moreover, the whole point of resorting to a third party is often simply to determine which adversary the settlement agent will ultimately support. A modern judge chooses which side of a conflict the state will take, for example, and arbitrators frequently decide to throw their weight entirely behind one party as well.

On the other hand, people who intervene as supporters rarely if ever do so without first assessing the merits of a case. Lawyers, for instance, do not automatically accept the business brought to them by potential clients, but first evaluate the issues in question much as would a judge or arbitrator (see, e.g., Macaulay 1979). The same applies to kinfolk and friends who come to the aid of their fellows. There is a limit to the conduct they will defend, and there are people they may be reluctant to oppose. Even under the pressure of collective liability, where all members of a social category are accountable for the conduct of each, cooperation depends on an assessment of each matter at issue, and there is a point beyond which any group will refuse to be identified with one of its wayward members (see Moore 1972; Posner 1980:43–44). In short, supporters commonly relate to conflicts partly in the manner of settlement agents, and vice versa. For this reason alone, it would seem unwise to ignore partisan intervention in a theory of the third party.

Another reason for including supporters in a typology of third parties is that they may play an important role in the actual management of conflict. In some cases, they may be the deciding factor in how the issues in dispute are defined at the outset (see FitzGerald et al. 1980:14–15; Mather and Yngvesson 1981:807–810) and in whether and how they are subsequently resolved. At every stage, the social status and other characteristics of each supporter, as well as the number and organization of the supporters as a group, contribute to the structure and process of the conflict situation. Their attributes have significance for the conduct of the principals and also for that of any settlement agent who becomes involved. In fact, the relationship of a supporter to a settlement agent may prove critical in the ultimate fate of a dispute.

Because the typology that follows is so inclusive, the body of theory applicable to it is necessarily very general in scope. It predicts and explains much about what transpires during fights and feuds, in the offices of attorneys and psychiatrists, and in village moots and modern courtrooms. It thus subsumes aspects of more limited theories ordinarily viewed as complete unto themselves, such as theories about vengeance, feuding, negotiation, litigation, or adjudication. Viewed against the broad range of phenomena contemplated by the typology, every pattern of conflict is one of a spectrum of possibilities, each of which occurs under specifiable conditions. One aim of our typology, then, is to cast a theory about third parties at a universal level. The chapter concludes with several formulations that illustrate this theory.

A TYPOLOGY OF THIRD PARTIES

Our typology classifies third parties along two dimensions: the nature of their intervention (whether partisan or not) and the degree of their intervention. It identifies a total of twelve roles, including five support roles (informer, adviser, advocate, ally, and surrogate) and five settlement roles (friendly peacemaker, mediator, arbitrator, judge, and repressive peacemaker). Each is ranked according to the degree of intervention it entails, with the extent of partisan involvement featured in the case of the support roles and authoritative involvement in the case of the settlement roles (see, e.g., Gluckman 1965b:222; Sander 1976:114; compare, e.g., Abel 1974; Griffiths 1984). In addition, we include one role that combines partisan and nonpartisan elements (the negotiator) and one that lies beyond these categories entirely (the healer). The twelve roles are graphically represented in Figure 6.1.

In the remaining pages we describe the typology in further detail, illustrating each role with examples from diverse settings across time and

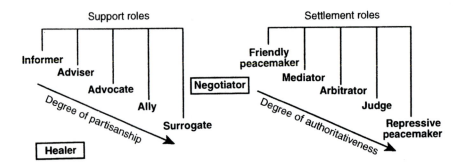

Figure 6.1 Typology of third parties.

space. As we proceed, the reader should bear in mind that the typology does not describe a set of discrete categories but rather a number of intervals along each continuum of intervention, partisan and authoritative, every role shading into the next.

SUPPORT ROLES

Although impartial arbiters come quickly to mind as examples of third parties, and although they receive a disproportionate amount of scholarly attention, most people who interpose themselves in the conflicts of others make no claim to neutrality. Instead they act entirely on behalf of one side, and are generally so recognized from the beginning by all concerned. These actors, performing support roles, are distinguished among themselves by the amount of assistance they give and by the extent of risk and hardship they assume. Put another way, they differ in the extent of their investment in the conflicts in which they participate. This section describes five major support roles: the informer, the adviser, the advocate, the ally, and the surrogate. It closes with a note on opposition, the obverse of support.

Informers

Among the various supporters of people in conflict, the smallest investment is generally made by the informer. People who assist others in this way provide information or facts but do not participate in resolving the conflict itself. Their contribution is usually restricted to an early stage of a conflict, and is more likely than other kinds of support to be provided in secret.

Informers may be recruited by a principal or by another supporter, or they may step forward on their own. Often the informer is simply a gossip. In intimate communities of all kinds, frequent chatter about the activities of others is a prominent feature of social life (see, e.g., Gluckman 1963; Merry 1984). Some individuals even become specialists in transmitting information about their fellows and are known as town or village gossips. Those who exchange information casually as well as those for whom doing so approaches an avocation may directly communicate information pertinent to conflicts. Still others may be paid for their services. In modern American police work, for example, informers are often paid, in money or other consideration, for information about narcotics offenses (see Skolnick 1966:Chapter 6; Gould, Walker, Crane, and Lidz 1974:72–76). In ancient Athens, where prior knowledge of an opponent's arguments in court was considered especially valuable, there were many successful attempts to bribe attorneys or friends into divulging confidential information of this sort (Chroust 1954a:375–376). Other informers are neither gossips nor merchants in information but step forth from a sense of moral outrage against an offender, sympathy or affection for one of the principals, or dislike of the opponent. People are occasionally coerced by threats or violence into giving information as well.

In some instances an individual may invest time and energy in the task of uncovering information relating to another's grievance or offense. This defines the role of the partisan investigator, a subtype of the informer. The prototype is the modern private detective, a professional who, for a price, invests considerable resources in discovering and reporting what a client wants to know. Partisan investigators may be amateurs as well — "snoops" and "spies" of various kinds.

An exotic variant of the informer, also worthy of brief notice here, is the diviner. In some societies aggrieved parties can bring their questions about the identity or intention of offenders to individuals skilled in the use of supernatural methods of discovery. Usually in return for material compensation, such specialists may read leaves, cards, or animal entrails; enter trances; perform rituals; or take other measures designed to uncover facts useful to their clients. Among the Azande of the Sudan, for example, witch-doctors drink potions and dance themselves into a frenzy to determine who is responsible for a person's misfortunes (see Evans-Pritchard 1937:Part 2). In seventeenth-century England, "wise women" and "cunning men" used a variety of techniques to reveal who had stolen something from their clients (Thomas 1971:212–222). Among the Qolla of Peru, skilled *maestros* are believed to be able to discover thieves (Bolton 1974).

Informers can be crucial to the conflict process by focusing the diffuse anger of a victim or enabling a party to gain decisive advantage over an opponent. Yet in comparison with other kinds of supporters, they have, as a group, only a small involvement. Having imparted their information, they leave others to use the facts they have provided.

Advisers

Advisers give opinions to a principal about how to manage a conflict. They assist in devising the strategy by which a dispute will be prosecuted, but do not participate in executing it. In many cases, in fact, their contribution is made behind the scenes and remains unknown to the opposition.

In societies where they have evolved, attorneys frequently adopt the role of adviser. Giving advice to clients occupies a great deal of the time of contemporary American lawyers, for instance (see, e.g., Carlin 1962; Smigel 1964:Chapter 6). In the Soviet Union, lawyers dispensed advice from storefront "consultation offices" or as "jurisconsults" to organizations (see Barry and Berman 1968; Giddings 1975). In ancient Greece and Rome, attorneys advised clients on what to do about their interpersonal problems (see Chroust 1954a, 1954b).

Advice may also come from those empowered to adjudicate disputes. One anthropologist who studied the Tiv of Nigeria thus notes that "the sort of advice which we in the West have come to associate with legal counsel is, in Tivland, usually given by the persons who are going to judge one's case" (Bohannan 1957:29). Many Tiv approach judges informally to ask them what course of action they recommend in a dispute, and, as a result, numerous cases are settled without further ado. It is not, however, only in traditional societies that judges perform this function. In an affluent suburb in modern America, for example, it is not uncommon for the municipal judge to dispense advice to aggrieved individuals who come to him privately for consultations (Baumgartner 1981). Some societies also have specialized individuals who, for a fee or other consideration, give legal advice in the capacity of "broker." These people have no official position or formal training, but nonetheless have influence in official circles and are experts in the operation of a legal system. Because of their unusual knowledge about how to manipulate the law, they are frequently approached for their opinions by fellow villagers. In a village of Lesotho, for example, a broker routinely helps others decide whether to initiate litigation and, if so, how best to manage cases in court (Perry 1977).

Traditional patron–client relationships are fertile ground for advice. The terms of such social arrangements generally include assistance to the client by the patron in times of difficulty — assistance that often amounts to the giving of advice about conflicts. In ancient Rome, for instance, a powerful *patronus* might give his *cliens* legal advice as a way of discharging his obligations (Kelly 1966:27). Local gentry are frequently approached for advice as well.

Family members, friends, and other associates often assume the role of adviser when one of their number becomes involved in a conflict. Surveys of the contemporary American public, for example, reveal that intimates are especially likely to be called upon for advice and moral support when trouble arises (see, e.g., Schulman 1979). One student of consumer problems in the United States comments that "the complainants' sense of outrage and injustice is often validated by friends, colleagues, and even supervisors who empathize with and may urge them to complain" (Addiss 1980:172). In other societies as well, intimates appear to play a crucial role in determining how offenses will be dealt with and peace restored (see, e.g., Ekvall 1954; Jones 1974:67–68). Often such advice is situational and spontaneous. Among the Yanomamö of Venezuela and Brazil, for instance, fellow villagers give their opinions freely about quarrels in progress (Chagnon 1977:92), and the same is true of the Kapauku of highland New Guinea (Pospisil 1958:254–255).

Advisers may shape the character of a conflict considerably by urging moderation or by agitating for a forceful response to a grievance. At the same time, some simply help plan the execution of a strategy, as was true of the ancient Greek specialists known as "logographers" who, for a fee, served as ghostwriters of the impassioned speeches litigants made before the courts (Chroust 1954a:345–350). Regardless of the substance of their opinions, however, advisers invest and risk comparatively little. More active support is found in several other roles.

Advocates

Advocates step forward publicly and plead the cause of the people they support. They range from representatives who merely state a principal's position to sponsors who invoke their own reputation and social standing for the benefit of someone else. As is true of informers and advisers, they may voluntarily give assistance, or they may be paid for their services. In some tribal societies, an advocate might step forth on behalf of an aggrieved individual simply to publicize the complaint for all to hear. Among the Hopi Indians of the American Southwest, for example, an elder esteemed for his oratorical abilities may air a villager's complaint by climbing to a rooftop and giving a stylized chant in which he pleads with an alleged offender to desist from wrongful activity or to make amends for a misdeed. This is known as a "grievance chant" (Black 1967). The Cheyenne Indians of the American Plains have a "camp crier" who presents complaints when the offender is unknown, hoping to end the offensive behavior or possibly gain other satisfaction for the complainant, such as the return of a stolen article:

> *Appropriation of another's property seems not to have been too uncommon. Calf Woman says that lots of times she heard the crier haranguing about the loss of an article by somebody. . . . As an example, Deaf Ear lost his entire buckskin suit. A crier made the announcement. Still, no suit. A second crier offered a horse [as a reward]. "It is a well-marked suit. Any member of the family will know it. You'll feel badly [sic] if you are caught with it on," he warned. The suit was returned. (Llewellyn and Hoebel 1941:226)*

Advocacy is one of the primary functions of modern attorneys and is also undertaken by various other participants in legal life. Character witnesses, for instance, vouch for the integrity of a disputant as a human being. In the Soviet Union, organizations of citizens were once encouraged to appoint a member to appear in court as a "social defender" if, in their experience with a defendant as a neighbor or co-worker, they found the individual to be a worthy associate (see Feifer 1964:Chapter 4). One of the most ritualized forms of advocacy, compurgation, was prominent in the trials of early Germanic and Celtic societies. The compurgator was an individual who swore a supporting oath to substantiate the claims of a principal; in sufficient numbers (as determined by the circumstances of a case), along with a perfect recitation of the required formulas, their combined backing was decisive (see Lea 1892:13–99; Pollock and Maitland 1898: Volume 2, 634–637; Berman 1978:561–562). Early Roman courts had advocates of several kinds:

> *Hearsay evidence was permitted and any number of prominent persons might be heard on their opinions. The social prominence of such "witnesses," who went by the significant name of* laudatores *(praisers), in itself was considered an adequate substitute for real knowledge of the facts on their part. To have less than ten such* laudatores *was considered an outright disgrace. (Chroust 1954b:131)*

During the same period, Romans might hire claques to appear in court during their trials and, at appropriate moments, support their testimony with applause and cheers or assail that of their opponents with hoots and whistles (Chroust 1954b:132–133).

Advocacy is also one of the principal kinds of support provided by patrons to their clients. Thus, in Japan,

> *If a* kobun *[client] got in trouble with the police—caught for gambling, say, or fighting—his family would turn to the* oyabun *[patron] as the*

obvious one to go and moraisageru *him — a curious word meaning "to*
secure release from custody on the informal guarantee of a social superior,"
literally, "to get back down." (Dore 1978:291)

Patrons in Latin America (Tumin 1952:126) and Thailand (Engel 1978:22) similarly engage in advocacy on behalf of their clients. Among the Tiv of Nigeria, however, advocates for someone whose case is being aired in a moot are likely to be peers (Bohannan 1957:168). This pattern appears to be widespread: Siblings speak up for siblings, co-workers for co-workers, and friends for friends. While less dramatic than other forms of advocacy, informal support of this kind seems to be more common.

The investment made by advocates on behalf of those they support is generally greater than that made by informers or advisers. Advocates are directly involved in the process of conflict management and, especially as they move toward active personal sponsorship, may come to stake their own reputations for the benefit of the principals they support. Even so, their role does not often require significant material contributions or risks. For a higher degree of commitment, an ally or a surrogate is needed.

Allies

Of all who give support, the ally is perhaps the most celebrated. Allies accept personal burdens for the good of others. They may render themselves vulnerable to physical injury, for instance, or contribute from their own resources to help secure an advantageous outcome for the person or group whose cause they espouse. Although they share the jeopardy of a party in conflict, they do not take wholly upon themselves all of the risks involved. Their support stops short of the maximum.

In tribal societies, alliance usually arises from kinship. In the typical scenario described in many accounts, a group of relatives assembles upon learning of a conflict involving one of their number. After discussing the matter, they decide on a course of action and approach the opponent, who is likely to be buttressed by supporters of a similar kind. In the ensuing confrontation, the family members may be prepared, if necessary, to exert force against the opponent. If, on the other hand, a peaceful settlement emerges as a possibility, they may contribute goods — livestock, shells, or whatever — to conclude the affair. At the same time, they stand to benefit materially should the ultimate settlement be in favor of their side. This widespread pattern of kin alliance has been noted among the ancient Germans (Berman 1978) and their descendants in feudal times (Bloch 1939:Chapter 9), the Jalé of highland New Guinea (Koch 1974), the Ifugao of the Philippines (Barton 1919), the Nuristani of Afghanistan (Jones 1974), the nomads of Tibet (Ekvall 1954), the Nuer of the Sudan (Evans-Pritchard 1940), the Ndendeuli of Tanzania (Gulliver 1969), the Yanomamö of Venezuela and Brazil (Chagnon 1977), the Bedouin of Libya (Peters 1967), the Sards of Sardinia (Ruffini 1978), and many others. A particularly well-developed alliance system is found among the nomads of northern Somalia, who maintain organizations called "*dia*-paying groups" (literally, bloodwealth-paying groups) expressly designed to handle complaints by or against their members. A *dia*-paying group is composed of men who are genealogically related and involves a contract specifying how much compensation the group will demand in case of a homicide, injury, or insult against a member by an outsider; the proportion to be kept by the organization; the proportion that the organization will pay if a member commits an offense against an outsider; and so on (Lewis 1959, 1961).

Allies are also frequently found beyond the family circle. In feudal Europe, for instance, vassals were obligated to assist their lords in times of conflict (Bloch 1939:Chapter 16). Circles of friends often act as allies for one another, too. Among the Pokot of Kenya, an aggrieved wife may call upon her female friends and neighbors to form a "shaming party" to humiliate her husband publicly by, for example, tying him nude to a tree, beating him with sticks, and urinating on him (Edgerton and Conant 1964). In modern America, an observer of the Hell's Angels motorcycle club notes that in conflicts between an Angel and an outsider, club members "have a very simple rule of thumb . . . a fellow Angel is *always right*. To disagree with a Hell's Angel is to be *wrong* — and to persist in being wrong is an open challenge" (Thompson 1966:71). In support of their fellows, moreover, Hell's Angels are quite willing to resort to violence (Thompson 1966: Chapter 6). In ancient Athens, men of consequence usually belonged to a club or fraternity expressly designed to provide assistance to members in legal difficulty. One's fraternity brethren might donate from their own funds in order to hire the best professional assistance for their comrade, and might also use their personal funds to bribe the authorities on his behalf (Chroust 1954a:352–353).

Like other supporters, some allies must be paid for their services. For example, mercenary soldiers may be hired by a nation or faction to fight alongside its own members in a violent conflict with another group, or people may be bribed to hide and supply those operating against their opponents in secret, which may expose them to punishment if discovered. Allies may be recruited by coercion as well, a pattern sometimes seen when people fight for another's cause or shelter fugitives.

Regardless of how they are mobilized, however, allies — by definition — invest heavily in the conflicts in which they participate. Their contribution greatly exceeds that of informers, advisers, and advocates. Even so, their involvement remains secondary to that of the adversaries. Here they differ from the most supportive of all supporters: surrogates.

Surrogates

The surrogate substitutes for another person or group in the management of a conflict, largely or totally relieving a principal of responsibility and risk. Substitutes of this kind comprise a significant portion of all third parties, though they may be the least common of the several supporters in our typology. Surrogates may be distinguished by the precise nature of their conduct and liability, and by the circumstances surrounding their mobilization, whether voluntary or not.

One variety is the avenger or champion who prosecutes another's grievance as if it were his own. In many societies, relatives of murdered or incapacitated victims of violence assume this role. Among the Cherokee Indians of southeastern America, for example, the nearest relative of a person slain was expected to kill a member of the slayer's clan (Reid 1970:90–91). Among the Ifugao of the Philippines, a close male relative of a murder victim is expected to kill the murderer or someone in the murderer's family, and until this is accomplished the would-be avenger must wear his hair long as a visible symbol of his unfulfilled mission (Barton 1919:68–76, plate 11). Not infrequently, vengeance follows vengeance in a continuing exchange of violence known as a feud (see, e.g., Thoden van Velzen and van Wetering 1960; Otterbein and Otterbein 1965).

People who are not physically incapacitated also occasionally seek a champion better able than themselves to deal with an opponent. Among the Comanche Indians of the American Plains, for instance, an aggrieved party might approach a renowned warrior for these purposes, and the warrior could not easily refuse: "A war leader who refused to accept the request for aid in prosecution was to be deemed unworthy of his rank, for it was imputed that he feared the defendant. No war leader could admit fear" (Hoebel 1940:64). Similarly, in feudal Europe, the code of chivalry dictated that ablebodied knights should not refuse to take up arms on behalf of any weak and needy person (Bloch 1940:Chapter 23). More prosperous citizens could have recourse to professional champions who would fight battles for a price (Lea 1892:179–198). In modern societies, the state acts as a champion when it prosecutes a citizen's grievance as a crime (see below).

Another variety of surrogate makes an advance commitment (or is committed involuntarily) to satisfy any claims that might arise from the misconduct of someone else. Hostages, for instance, perform this function in many societies. Among the ancient Germans and Celts, one or both parties might give up hostages when forging an important agreement (such as the terms by which to settle a dispute through a payment of compensation). Until the agreement was fully honored, each principal was expected to provide for any hostages held in a manner befitting their rank. Should a party renege, the hostages might be injured or enslaved (see Berger 1940a, 1940b). A related practice, still seen in commercial life, is the institution of suretyship, whereby a third party pledges to repay a debt if the original debtor fails to discharge the obligation (see Berger 1940a, 1940b).

Yet another surrogate is the scapegoat, an individual or group who, without being appointed in advance, is compelled to bear punishment for the offense of someone else. Where collective liability prevails, any member of a wrongdoer's group — such as a close or distant relative — may become the target of revenge. Scapegoats may also be selected along ethnic, national, or racial lines. During the Nazi occupation of Poland in the 1940s, for example, it was Nazi policy to punish randomly selected Poles whenever a Polish national committed an offense against the Nazi regime (Gross 1979:Chapter 9). Scapegoats are not always selected because of their similarity to the offenders, however. Among the Suku of the Congo, a victimized clan might bypass the offender and his clan and retaliate against someone from a third clan altogether. This new victim may then seek satisfaction by taking revenge against someone from a fourth clan, and so on (Kopytoff 1961). The Tlingit Indians of the American Northwest Coast punished a scapegoat when a member of the nobility was discovered in the act of theft, since it was believed that any aristocratic thief must have been bewitched. The accused witch, typically a slave, was thereupon executed and the matter closed (Oberg 1934:149, 155).

Other scapegoats volunteer for punishment on behalf of an offender. In modern America, for example, it is widely alleged that some individuals (known as "fall guys") are serving time in prison for falsely confessing to misdeeds committed by higher-ranking associates in organized crime. In traditional Thailand, men often accept the blame for the misconduct of their higher-status patrons (Engel 1978:74). In Manchu China, where witnesses were commonly hired to testify to one party's innocence or another's guilt, surrogation was available as well:

> There were . . . some who made a living by confessing guilt and submitting on behalf of real offenders to corporal punishment, and we hear of "a band of devoted men" in the neighborhood of Canton prepared to risk transportation and even death for the sake of payment to their families. (van der Sprenkel 1962:71)

And in a famous fictional account of revolutionary France, Sydney Carton substituted himself for Charles Darnay on the guillotine and lost his head (Dickens 1859).

Whether voluntary or not, for payment or not, the support provided by surrogates defines the extreme of partisanship. Although the surrogate's contribution is enormous, whether it results in settlement of a conflict is another question altogether. Much of the remainder of this chapter pertains to third parties who strive to end — superficially, at least — the conflicts in which they become involved. But first we comment briefly on the negative dimension of support: opposition.

Opposition Roles

In any conflict, one side's supporter is the other side's opponent. All support roles, seen from the perspective of the principal on the other side, are opposition roles. Opponents act to force concessions from a party to a dispute, to inflict injury, or to thwart efforts to obtain satisfaction from an adversary. Their conduct may help ultimately to make one party lose.

Folk concepts sometimes refer to the reverse of a support role, as when informers are labeled "stool pigeons," "rats," or "tattletales." In the Soviet Union, citizens known as "social accusers" denounced a defendant during a trial; "social defenders" provided support (see Feifer 1964:104–106). Although no special vocabulary may distinguish support from opposition, in on-going disputes the distinction is usually obvious.

Often a third party is primarily a supporter or an opponent. The former are normally drawn into conflicts through their relationship with the principal whose cause they seek to advance, the latter through their relationship with the principal whom they seek to undermine. Enemies of one principal may assist the other to advance their own interests. In ancient Athens, for example, where paid advocates were despised and the usual excuse for assisting a litigant was a bond of intimacy, a lawyer might openly declare a hostile interest in the case:

> As an additional justification for his appearance the lawyer could always make the unusual plea that he did so because he was an enemy of the opposing side or the opposing lawyer and therefore had a personal interest in the outcome of the case. (Chroust 1954a:359)

The best chance poor and powerless people may have in conflicts with more influential antagonists is to seek the support of any peers of the latter who are also their enemies. In at least one part of traditional India, for instance, one "means of redress for an aggrieved lower-caste person, if his dispute was with his own patron, was to seek the help of his patron's enemies within the dominant caste" (Cohn 1965:92). In seventeenth-century France, a royal edict of Louis XIV accused social inferiors of fomenting discord between aristocrats for similar reasons:

> *It does appear that there are persons of ignoble birth . . . who have never borne arms, yet are insolent enough to call out gentlemen who refuse to give them satisfaction, justly grounding their refusal on the inequality of the conditions; in consequence of which these persons excite and oppose to them other gentlemen of like degree, whence arise not infrequently murders [i.e., duelling fatalities], the more detestable since they originate from abject sources. (quoted in Baldick 1965:60)*

In political and international arenas as well, opponents frequently ally themselves with their enemy's enemies. "Politics makes strange bedfellows" is a colloquial expression that speaks to the unlikely associations often based on common opposition.

SETTLEMENT ROLES

Although most conflicts in all societies have a bilateral character — one side opposing another and any third parties assuming the role of supporters — all societies also seem to have at least occasional conflicts in which third parties intervene without taking sides and give the matter a trilateral character. When third parties intervene in a predominantly nonpartisan fashion, their behavior may be classified with the settlement roles in our typology (see Figure 6.1 above). We discuss these roles in order of the degree of intervention each entails.

Friendly Peacemakers

Peacemakers simply try to influence the parties in conflict to abandon their hostilities. They are distinctive among settlement agents in one major respect: Unlike other third parties who relate to both sides of a conflict, peacemakers do so without in any way addressing the matter at issue between those involved. They strive merely to end the dispute, outwardly at least, regardless of its causes or content. There are, however, two radically different kinds of pacification — one friendly, the other repressive. The first entails the least intervention of any settlement role, the second the most. Here we describe the friendly variety, returning to the repressive variety after surveying the roles that lie between them on the continuum of authoritative intervention.

A friendly peacemaker acts in the interests of both sides of a conflict and is, in effect, supportive of both without taking the side of either. This may entail an effort to separate the antagonists from one another, by physical restraint if necessary, or simply to distract them from their hostilities. In either case, the peacemaker may seek to convince the parties that their conflict is doing more harm than good for all concerned: that it is foolish, futile, or even funny, and that it should be ended without further ado. Among the Cheyenne, for example, who stigmatize murderers as "putrid" and believe they bring misfortune to the entire tribe until a purification ritual is performed, bystanders commonly try to persuade angry people to restrain themselves: "People intervened when men quarreled violently. What they said was 'You must not.' 'You must not be a murderer.' 'You will disgrace yourself.' 'It is not worth it' " (Llewellyn and Hoebel 1941:134; also see 133). The Shavante of central Brazil consider only disputes between men to be worthy of a hearing in their informal court (the "men's council"), whereas those between women are viewed as "laughable and unworthy of serious attention" (Maybury-Lewis 1967:179). But when women become violent to the point of seriously endangering each other, the men will pull them apart (see, e.g., Maybury-Lewis 1967:180). Among the Yanomamö of Venezuela and Brazil, women often throw the leaves of a magical plant on men who threaten to use their war clubs, since this allegedly "keeps their tempers under control and prevents the fight from escalating to shooting" (Chagnon 1977:37).

The Mbuti Pygmies of Zaire have an unusually well-developed system of friendly pacification, specialized in the "camp clown":

> The only individual who might be recognized as occupying a special political position in the life of the hunting band, on any ground other than age, is the camp clown. . . . His function is to act as a buffer between disputants, deflecting the more serious disputes away from their original sources, absolving other individuals of blame by accepting it himself. . . . The clown, however, never passes judgment or exerts authority (except through ridicule). (Turnbull 1965:182–183)

The camp clown is not unlike the court jester of the European Middle Ages. In northern Somalia, friendly pacification is provided by religious leaders (*sheikhs* and *wadaads*) who resolve many disputes simply by insisting that each party swear an oath to be peaceful toward the other (Lewis 1961:217). In modern societies, friendly peacemakers include bartenders, lifeguards at public beaches (see Edgerton 1979:47–49), and the friends, relatives, and peers of adversaries from all walks of life. Indeed, in some situations peacemakers are so near at hand and so quick to intervene when trouble occurs that those with complaints can hurl themselves at their opponents without fear of retaliation, knowing full well that they will be restrained before any harm can be done. This pattern has been observed in Japan:

> It's amazing, really, how some people change when they're drunk and surrounded by a lot of people. They seem to go out of their mind, some- times, but they know really that they're safe, because if they provoke the other chap to violence there are enough people there to keep them apart. And the next morning they'll all be smiles and greet each other as if nothing happened. But the one who spoke his mind will know the other one will remember what he said. He'll have got his point home. In fact, people — you could see it — often used to come to a party with the express intention of picking a quarrel and getting something off their chest. (quoted in Dore 1978:266)

It thus seems that friendly peacemakers not only keep hostilities from escalating but may sometimes unintentionally create a forum for the airing of grievances.

Mediators

In scholarly as well as popular thought, the roles most associated with the idea of the third party are those of the mediator, the arbitrator, and the judge (see, e.g., Eckhoff 1966; Koch 1974:27–31; Shapiro 1975:323–325). Such roles are actually found in only a limited range of social settings, however, and include some of the most developed and specialized forms of social control ever observed. Because the literature pertaining to them is extensive, the present discussion is limited to a brief overview.

On the continuum of intervention portrayed in our typology, media- tors appear one step beyond friendly peacemakers (see Figure 6.1). Like peacemakers, mediators in their pure form refuse to take sides, but they differ from peacemakers in their willingness to acknowledge and, often, to delve into the problem between those in conflict. Mediators seek a solution by encouraging the parties to reach a mutually agreeable settle- ment, typically a compromise. Because they encourage the disputants themselves to negotiate an outcome, mediation has been described as "su- pervised negotiation" (Hart and Sacks 1958:655) and, similarly, as "negoti- ation by brokerage" (Koch 1979:4). It may nevertheless include diverse modes of behavior, ranging from complete passivity — with a mediator's mere presence the only contribution made — to highly aggressive attempts to devise and promote a settlement (see Fuller 1971; Gulliver 1977). Ulti- mately, however, mediators defer to the principals in selecting the final resolution.

Social scientists, especially anthropologists, have described mediators at work in a number of societies (for overviews, see Witty 1980:Chapter 1; Merry 1982). But the scholarly literature may inadvertently overrepresent the more active forms of mediation, if only because the varied behavior of active mediators may seem more worthy of detailed description. Passive mediation — in which the principals are quietly encouraged to discuss their differences — is probably more frequent, and has a force of its own that should not be underestimated:

> *By his very presence a . . . passive mediator can encourage positive com-*
> *munication and interaction between the parties, stimulating the contin-*
> *uation or the renewal of the exchange of information. Because he is there,*
> *the parties are often constrained to observe minimal courtesy to each other,*
> *to reduce personal invective, and to listen and to respond with some*
> *relevance. . . . This has been a quite deliberate strategy on occasion, for*
> *example, by some American industrial mediators. They attend a meeting*
> *between the two parties, but sit and say nothing and seek to show no*
> *particular reaction to what is said and done. (Gulliver 1977:26–27, in-*
> *cluding note 13)*

Passive mediation is commonly used by police officers when handling interpersonal disputes (see Black 1980:Chapter 5, especially 132–133). An American officer thus made the following observation about a colleague:

> *One police officer I really admired, he'd come into a family beef with*
> *a husband and wife throwing and yelling at each other. Then he'd set*
> *[sic] down on the couch and take his hat off, and he didn't say a word.*
> *Sooner or later the couple felt kind of silly. He'd take 45 minutes in each*
> *of these situations, but he never had to come back. (quoted in Muir*
> *1977:82)*

Mediation among friends is likely to be very passive as well, as is the mediation — usually not recognized as such — sometimes performed by children when conflicts erupt between their parents (see Baumgartner 1981:Chapter 2).

Many mediators portrayed in the anthropological literature fall so far toward the other extreme that they nearly cross the line into arbitration. This applies, for instance, to the *monkalun* of the Ifugao, a tribal people of the Philippines:

> *To the end of peaceful settlement, [the* monkalun*] exhausts every art of*
> *Ifugao diplomacy. He wheedles, coaxes, flatters, threatens, drives, scolds,*
> *insinuates. He beats down the demands of the plaintiffs or prosecution,*
> *and bolsters up the proposals of the defendants until a point be reached at*

> *which the two parties may compromise. If the culprit or accused be not*
> *disposed to listen to reason and runs away or "shows fight" when ap-*
> *proached, the* monkalun *waits till the former ascends into his house,*
> *follows him, and* war-knife in hand, *sits in front of him and compels*
> *him to listen. . . . The* monkalun *has no authority. All that he can do is*
> *to act as a peacemaking go-between. His only power is in his art of*
> *persuasion, his tact, and his skillful playing on human emotions and*
> *motives. (Barton 1919:87)*

Although the *monkalun* is one of the most frequently cited examples of a
mediator in the anthropological literature, this description suggests that
he might sometimes behave as an arbitrator or even — in light of his threats
of violence — judge. Consider now the arbitrator.

Arbitrators

Arbitration lies between mediation and adjudication on the continuum
of authoritative intervention (see Figure 6.1). Unlike a mediator but like a
judge, the arbitrator pronounces a resolution to the conflict, possibly even
designating one side as totally right and the other as totally wrong. Also
like a judge, the arbitrator makes a decision without regard — outwardly at
least — to the wishes of the parties involved. Unlike a judge, however, the
arbitrator does not have the capacity to enforce a settlement if it is
subsequently violated or ignored. Arbitrators give opinions rather than
verdicts.

Opinions nevertheless operate as effectively as judicial verdicts in
many instances. Often the adversaries agree in advance to abide by whatever an arbitrator decides, as happened, for instance, when Spain and
Portugal agreed to let the Pope of the Roman Catholic Church determine
how South America would be divided between them. The arbitrator's decision may also be enforced by someone external to the arbitration process
itself, such as close associates of those in conflict or members of the community at large. Considerable pressure to accept arbitrated decisions is
commonly present, a pattern documented in tribal and other simpler societies where traditional leaders may be mobilized to resolve disputes by
arbitration. When arbitrators make a decision in northern Somalia, for
example, enforcement typically is the responsibility of the principals'
relatives:

> *If their kinsmen wish to reach a peaceful settlement, either through fear of*
> *war or pressure from the [British] Administration, and if they consider*
> *that the [arbitrators'] decision is a reasonable one, they will see that it is*

executed. If necessary, pressure will be put upon the parties directly con-
cerned to force them to accept the award. But the panel of arbitrators, in
itself, has no punitive sanctions with which it can coerce litigants into
accepting its judgments. (Lewis 1961:228)

In modern societies, an arbitrator's decision may be enforceable by a court
of law, as in the American process known as "binding arbitration" (for
overviews, see, e.g., Mentschikoff 1961; Getman 1979). On the other hand,
much arbitration occurs without any mechanism of enforcement at all,
apart from the displeasure of those making the decision or, possibly, supernatural spirits. Spiritual powers are themselves used as arbitrators in
some cases, such as when a dispute is resolved by a supernaturally con-
trolled ordeal or oracle (Koch 1979:5).

A highly developed system of arbitration arose in ancient Ireland,
where the practice came to be known, somewhat misleadingly, as *"brehon
law."* The *brehon* was among the most esteemed of men:

The brehon *was an arbitrator, umpire, expounder of the law, rather than*
a judge in the modern acceptation. . . . [His] position resembled that of
an eminent Roman jurisprudent, *whose opinion was eagerly sought and*
paid for by people in legal difficulties. He heard the case, gave it the
necessary consideration, and pronounced a decision in accordance with
law and justice. This decision, though called a judgment, and eminently
entitled to that name, was not precisely what the word judgment means
with us. It was rather a declaration of law and justice as applied to the
facts before him, . . . an award founded in each particular case on a
submission to arbitration. There was no public officer whose duty it was
to enforce the judgment when given. The successful party was left to
execute it himself. (Ginnell 1924:51)

Although the party favored by a *brehon's* decision was theoretically "left to
execute it himself," in fact the pressures of kinship and popular opinion
were usually equal to the task of gaining compliance:

These combined forces went far to render executive officers of the law, as
sheriffs, bailiffs, and police, unnecessary. They were practically irresisti-
ble, for they could go the length of outlawing a man and rendering his life
and all he possessed worthless to him if he dared to withstand the execution
of what a brehon *had declared to be the demands of law and justice. They*
were quite as effectual as is what we now call the arm of the law. (Ginnell
1924:51)

Since international tribunals normally have no capacity to enforce their
rulings, much "international law" is actually arbitration as well.

Judges

Because arbitrators do not have the capacity to enforce their decisions, they are forever dependent on someone else and have considerably less authority than judges. Judges do not merely give opinions; they give orders. They are dependent on no one, except in the limited sense in which those with authority always must depend on their subordinates for obedience (see Simmel 1908b:Part 3, Chapter 1). In short, judges address the matter separating the adversaries (like mediators), make a settlement decision (like arbitrators), and, if necessary, enforce it.

Many variants of adjudication appear in social space, each with different procedures, personnel, and jurisdictions (see Fuller 1978). Some judges, for instance, are empowered only to hear complaints brought by citizens, whereas others can initiate cases on their own. Some are called upon only to decide whether specific charges are justified, whereas others delve into the details of an allegation. Some routinely decide which of two parties is right or wrong, whereas others commonly find both sides have merit. These and other characteristics combine in a number of different ways.

Among the Tarahumara Indians of northern Mexico, for example, the *gobernador*, or mayor, holds public trials and punishes those he defines as offenders, but he has no power unless a specific complaint is brought to him. As one *gobernador* commented, "There are many bad things, but people do not complain. If they complain to me, then I must do something. If not . . . , we can only give advice and warn the people not to do these things" (Fried 1953:295). Among the Kpelle of Liberia, too, the chief's court hears only complaints brought by citizens, and it normally ascribes blame to only one side (Gibbs 1962). The same is true of most courts in modern society. The Lozi judges of Barotseland (now Zambia), however—the first tribal judges to be observed systematically by an anthropologist—also seemed to hear only complaints by citizens, but they often resolved cases by declaring both parties at fault to some degree (Gluckman 1967). Still another pattern was followed by the courts of Manchu China, where one party had to be found wrong and to suffer accordingly in virtually every case. There could be no dismissals: "The unavoidable consequence of a legal case once started was punishment for at least one person. It could end in punishment for the accused, if judged guilty; if he were not, punishment would be assigned to the unjustified accuser" (van der Sprenkel 1962:69; for a similar process among the Ashanti of Ghana, see Rattray 1927:Chapter 22).

Another variable is the number of judges. While modern trial courts in the United States and similar societies typically have only one judge (unless there is a jury), so-called popular tribunals have several (e.g., Berman 1969). The Lozi court—or *kuta*—apparently had about 20 (Gluckman 1967:9–14) and conducted an unusually elaborate mode of settlement. After the plaintiff, defendant, and their witnesses had spoken, the numerous members of the court took over:

> *The* kuta, *assisted by anyone present, proceeds to cross-examine and to pit the parties and witnesses against one another. When all the evidence has been heard, the lowest* induna *[an official] gives the first judgment. He is then followed by councillors [sitting] on the three mats (*indunas, princes, and stewards*) in ascending order of seniority across from one mat to the other, until the senior councillor-of-the-right gives the final judgment. This is then referred to the ruler of the capital, who confirms, rejects, or alters it, or refers it back to the* kuta *for further investigation and discussion. It is this final judgment by the last* induna *to speak which, subject to the ruler's approval, is binding. (Gluckman 1967:15)*

As the best known of modern third parties, judges may not need further description. Yet in the popular mind, judges are associated strictly with law — governmental social control (Black 1972:1096) — whereas in our typology the concept of the judge is somewhat broader, including any third party who resolves a conflict with an order backed by sanctions. Adjudication in this sense occurs in a wide variety of social settings, even in stateless societies that have no law on a permanent basis. The stateless nomads of northern Somalia, for example, traditionally adjudicate disputes within their lineage organizations ("*dia*-paying groups"):

> *Fighting between individual members of a* dia-paying *group, when several members are present, leads to prompt and concerted action. The disputants are separated; if necessary, they are seized by young men on the instructions of the elders and brought for trial before a* dia-paying *group council. When compensation has been determined . . . or a fine imposed, it must be paid or at least promised, or punitive action will be taken by the group as a whole. A recalcitrant member of a* dia-paying *group is bound to a tree and several of his best sheep or a coveted camel slaughtered before him until he agrees to the judgment of his elders. The slaughtered stock are eaten by the elders. (Lewis 1961: 232, punctuation edited)*

Adjudication in our broad sense also occurs in families, particularly those with a patriarchal structure, and organizations such as business firms and voluntary associations in which judgments against members may ultimately be enforced with expulsion.

Repressive Peacemakers

Repressive pacification displays the most authoritativeness by a third party that is ever seen. Paradoxically, it shares with the gentlest mode — friendly pacification — one major characteristic: an indifference to the issues dividing those in conflict. Here, however, indifference does not express a nonjudgmental and friendly concern for the well-being of the parties but rather a total lack of concern, if not contempt. Any grievance that one or both adversaries might have against the other is likely to be dismissed, if it is noticed at all. The process is negative rather than positive in spirit, hostile, and possibly even wantonly destructive toward those involved. The point is simply to end the conflict as quickly as possible, violently if necessary, without regard to the consequences for the parties. If neither side is allowed to get the better of the other, it is only because, by dint of their conflict, both are deemed wrong and possibly worthy of punishment. Indeed, the conflict itself is regarded as an offense against the third party.

In colonial settings, foreign officials often use repressive pacification to eliminate violence by the native population. Traditional modes of social control such as blood vengeance, feuding, and fighting are outlawed and subjected to penal measures. That such traditional practices entail the pursuit of justice by those involved is ignored entirely. The British, French, Germans, and other Western Europeans commonly handled conflict within colonial populations in this way, as have other conquerors. In northern Albania, repressive pacification occurred during the Turkish and Austro-Hungarian occupations:

> *Friends were not the only interveners. Occasionally the Turkish government took a hand, declaring on penalty of imprisonment, internment, and burning out that all feuds more than seven years old were to be compounded by a money payment and not reopened. When during the 1914–18 war Austria-Hungary was in occupation of all north Albania, she also ordered blood feuds to be ended with a money payment.* (Hasluck 1954:259)

In Irian Jaya (West New Guinea), first the Dutch and later the Indonesians took similar steps. In the district of Jalémó, for instance, the people learned that "a new kind of stranger who neither spoke nor understood their language would punish any form of violent behavior" (Koch 1974: 223; for the same policy by the Australians in Papua New Guinea, see Reay 1974:205, 209). During the establishment of the Soviet Union, conflict handled by traditional means among the Asian peoples was also prohibited:

The history of many peoples shows that usually, over a period of time, the vendetta is gradually replaced by a system of monetary compensation or blood money. The Soviet authorities prevented this natural evolution from taking place by making it a criminal offense to give or receive such compensation. At the same time, they set up procedures for the reconciliation of feuding families. Those who refused to be reconciled were deported. (Chalidze 1977:119)

Repressive pacification occurs in many noncolonial settings as well. Among the Tikopians of Polynesia, for example, the chief of each clan is said to own his group's land and can repress disputes between clansmen by threatening to evict them:

He says to the disputants, "Abandon your fighting that you are carrying on there. Plant food properly for the two of you in my ground." The words "my ground" are not empty of significance. For if the men persist in their quarrel the chief will send a message, "Go the pair of you to your own place wherever that may be; go away from my ground." In fact, they have no ground to resort to; their alternative is the ocean [i.e., suicide], so they capitulate. (Firth 1936:384)

In modern America, the police act as repressive peacemakers when feuds arise between juvenile gangs or between so-called organized crime families and, for that matter, whenever they encounter fighting or other violence (which is typically a mode of conflict management between those involved). Adults such as parents and teachers often relate similarly to the disputes of children. The fighting itself is treated as offensive and punishable, regardless of why it occurs. From the standpoint of a repressive peacemaker, a conflict between people is not unlike a conflict between cats or dogs.

MARGINAL ROLES

Although the major division in our typology of third parties is between supporters and settlement agents, two roles are not fully captured by either of these categories. The negotiator synthesizes both support and settlement behavior, while the healer belongs in a class of its own, entirely beyond the rest.

Negotiators

It is important, first, to distinguish between the concepts of *negotiation* and *negotiator*. Whereas the former refers to a particular process of conflict management, the latter refers to a particular role performed in such a process. More specifically, negotiation is a process of joint settlement of a dispute (see Gulliver 1979:5). The person presenting one side's case may be the principal himself or herself, or it may be a third party acting on the principal's behalf. In our typology, the role of negotiator refers to a third party who represents a disputant and works out a settlement — negotiates — with the other side. And since the principals might negotiate a settlement on their own, negotiation does not necessarily involve anyone performing the special role of negotiator (compare, e.g., Gulliver 1979:3–6).

Negotiators perform a hybrid role, mixing support and settlement behavior. Like advocates or allies they are partisan, openly taking one side, but like arbitrators or judges they also participate in the resolution of conflicts (see Eisenberg 1976:662–665). They represent only one party, and yet serve both. In modern society, for example, lawyers often act as negotiators for their clients. In fact, the vast majority of civil complaints and lawsuits in modern America are resolved by a negotiated settlement — usually worked out by lawyers — rather than by the judgment of a court, and criminal cases resulting in conviction usually are settled by the negotiation of a guilty plea (known as "plea bargaining") rather than by a trial (see, e.g., Newman 1956, 1966; Buckle and Buckle 1977; Mather 1979). Insurance adjusters are active negotiators as well. In the United States, they successfully negotiate a settlement in over 95% of all bodily injury claims against insured automobile drivers (Ross 1970:24–25, 141).

Negotiators are prominent in many societies and are sometimes virtually the only third parties available to handle conflict. Among the Yurok Indians of northern California, for example, negotiators known as *wegô*, or "crossers," apparently handled most cases involving different segments of the tribe:

> They were chosen by the parties at issue: two or three, possibly four, to a side. There were always expected to be more than one, since a single man could not properly maintain his case against several opponents. They were, however, supposed to be impartial enough to be able to reach a fair agreement with the representatives of the other side. . . . They examined the "litigants" and necessary witnesses, then went into conference and rendered a verdict. . . . Each wegô received from his client a standard fee of one large dentalium shell. This fee was called we-na'ai, "his moccasin," because it reimbursed the wegô for the walking back and forth he had to do in his commission. (Kroeber 1926:514–515)

The role of the negotiator is also highly developed in the customary law of northern Albania, where each principal in a conflict may, in effect, hire an elder to work out a settlement on his behalf. Each must first deposit a "pledge," such as a gun or watch, with the elder of his choice to assure that a proper fee will be paid at the conclusion of the case. If the principals accept the elders' decision, the fee is paid, the pledge returned, and the case closed (Hasluck 1954:Chapter 13). Settlement by negotiators is prominent in Thailand as well, where each principal commonly relies on a *phuyai*, or "big person," to work out a resolution with the other side (Engel 1978: 75–77). In tribal Europe, among the early English, Scots, French, Germans, and others, the negotiator for a kin group was known as a "forspeaker" (see Pound 1953:70). When duelling was a form of dispute settlement in Europe, the "second" (the assistant of each combatant) often served as a negotiator to end the conflict before blood was spilled. As one early commentator suggested, "There is not one cause in fifty where discreet seconds might not settle the difference and reconcile the parties before they came into the field." A famous fencing master thus observed that "it is not the sword or the pistol that kills, but the seconds" (both quoted in Baldick 1965:38).

Healers

We turn lastly to the healer, a third party who intervenes in human conflict without seeming to do so at all. This is, in modern language, the therapist. In some societies healing may be performed by an exorcist or sorcerer, in others by a psychiatrist or medical practitioner. But all healers share a distinctive approach toward people in conflict.

Perhaps the most significant characteristic of healers is that they generally proceed without any explicit recognition that a conflict is the occasion for their intervention. Rather, their involvement is defined as a kind of help, a treatment for someone suffering from an affliction beyond his or her control. The problem is to restore the afflicted individual to normality rather than — as in the other forms of intervention discussed above — to contribute to justice (see Black 1976:4–6). Healers are nevertheless actively involved in the enforcement of moral standards, in nurturing conformity in deviants, and in reconciling estranged people. Insofar as the affliction requiring their attention is a pattern of conduct viewed as undesirable, healers act on behalf of a complainant, an alleged offender, or both. To this degree they are properly understood as third parties in our sense (see, e.g., Goffman 1969; Black 1976:4–6, 118–121; Horwitz 1982). In calling upon the services of a healer, even for help with their own affliction, people may dramatize grievances, enlist support, or draw attention to someone who has offended them (see Lewis 1966; Baumgartner 1981:Chapter 2).

Many healers are skilled in the supernatural arts. In Somalia (Lewis 1966), among the Tonga of Zambia (Colson 1969), in medieval Europe (Cohn 1975), and elsewhere, people behaving inappropriately may be considered possessed by a supernatural spirit and in need of a curative ritual by a specialist. Typically the object is to propitiate, expel, or master the offending spirit. This process is illustrated by a case in a Swahili tribe of East Africa:

> *Chuma had an episode of mental disturbance. He became irrational and violent and, as his brother described it, would throw men about with the strength of an ox. . . . Chuma's brothers went to Tawalini and found out through divination that his trouble was caused by a* shetani *[spirit] that had been sent to annoy him by the outraged husband of a woman to whom he had been paying attention. . . . The deranged man was exorcised by [a religious specialist]. Seven loaves of bread and seven coconuts were arranged on a table which was held over Chuma's head by his brothers, their hands joining to form a circle around him. A cock was slaughtered . . . and the blood applied to the patient. Then parts of the Koran with special mystical meanings were read aloud. The rite accomplished its purpose; Chuma recovered completely and went back to his occupation of fishing. (Gray 1969:182)*

In much of Latin America, a religious specialist may treat abnormal behavior in a client by staging a ritual to retrieve his or her "lost soul" (see, e.g., Gillin 1948, 1956).

Medical specialists may attribute behavioral abnormalties to organic causes and treat them accordingly. In ancient Egypt and Greece, unacceptable conduct in a woman might be attributed to a "wandering uterus" (see Veith 1965). In the same vein, a sixteenth-century French surgeon made the following observations:

> *For som accidents com by suppression of the [menses], others com by corruption of the seed, but if the matter bee cold, it bringeth a drousiness . . . whereby the woman sinketh down as if shee were astonished, and lieth without motion. . . . If of a cholerick humor, it causeth the madness called* furor uterinus, *and such a pratling, that they speak all things that are to bee concealed; and a giddiness of the head, by reason that the animal spirit is suddenly shaken by the admixture of a putrefied vapour and hot spirit; but nothing is more admirable, then that diseas taketh the patient sometimes with laughing, and sometimes with weeping, for some at the first will weep and then laugh in the same diseas and state thereof. (quoted in Veith 1965:114)*

Physical remedies such as fumigations of the uterus, ingestion of herbs, and the application of ointments were prescribed to cure the organic problems responsible for these behavioral symptoms (Veith 1965). In the modern era, physicians may attribute unusual behavior to disorders of the brain and pursue treatment through the use of drugs.

Modern psychiatrists or psychologists also regard deviant behavior as the outcome of underlying emotional disturbances curable through a variety of psychotherapeutic techniques. They encourage patients to discuss their problems, analyze their dreams, and probe into details of their personal lives. They orchestrate group encounters or recommend changes in a person's way of life (including commitment to a mental hospital). Some prescribe behavior-modification therapies to help people overcome alcohol or other drug addiction, overeating, undereating, and violent tendencies.

In its own way, the role of healer combines elements of support and of settlement. Healers serve as friends to their patients, doing everything on their behalf, but at the same time they speak with authority about what is "wrong" with the patient and what is necessary to achieve a "cure" or "adjustment." In this sense, they occupy a composite role. But unlike negotiators or other third parties, healers are neither explicitly partisan nor authoritative, nor are they even explicitly identified with human conflict. We therefore place them entirely beyond the dimensions of our typology.

A NOTE ON LEGAL OFFICIALS

In the foregoing pages we have not given special attention to third parties who intervene in the name of the state, i.e., legal officials. Each mode of intervention occurs in a wide range of social settings, informal as well as formal, and it would be inaccurate to identify any single species of third party exclusively with law. But the opposite applies as well: Though none of the roles in our typology is performed by legal officials all of the time, all are performed by legal officials some of the time.

In a modern society such as the United States, legal officials occasionally perform virtually every one of the twelve roles in our classification. Police officers often simply give information or advice, prosecutors act as judges when they dismiss cases, judges mediate and arbitrate, and so on. Indeed, police officers themselves perform every role in the typology, shifting from one to another as they move from encounter to encounter (see Cumming, Cumming, and Edell 1965; Bittner 1967; Rubinstein 1973; Bard and Zacker 1976; Black 1980:Chapter 5). Their role even changes as a single case moves through the stages of the criminal process, so that an officer might handle a case in the field as, say, a healer or a friendly peacemaker, resolve it by arrest (in most instances a kind of adjudication), only to become a witness (an ally of the prosecution) when the case is heard in court. Complainants likewise lose their centrality when a legal official, the prosecutor, steps forth as a surrogate to pursue their grievance in the name of the state (compare Christie 1977). Such transformations occur in conflict management of all kinds. Conflict constantly fluctuates, and any classification of those involved should be viewed as provisional, valid only until a new episode begins (see Mather and Yngvesson 1981).

CONCLUSION

Our typology offers a vocabulary with which the many species and varieties of third parties may be classified. It serves a purpose similar to that which a handbook or field guide might serve a butterfly collector or a bird watcher. Beyond this, however, the typology describes a universe of its own, a range of variation. In so doing, it invites a theory of the third party: Why do third parties intervene in conflicts in so many different ways? Why does one conflict result in, say, mediation or arbitration while another is adjudicated or repressed? Why does one person intervene as an advocate or ally while another only gives information or advice? The typology challenges us to understand differences in conflict management across communities and societies and, for that matter, across social settings of all kinds. It challenges us to predict and explain the role of third parties from one case to the next.

We close with several formulations that address variation in settlement behavior — friendly pacification, mediation, arbitration, adjudication, and repressive pacification. These formulations specify how the authoritativeness of third parties is associated with their social characteristics. Settlement behavior reflects its location and direction in social space.

First, our review of the empirical literature suggests that the role of settlement agents varies with their social status in relation to that of the principals, i.e., their relative status (for further details on the concept of status used here, see generally Black 1976:Chapters 2–6). Rarely is a settlement agent's status lower than that of the parties in conflict, more often it is about equal, but usually it is higher. Moreover, it appears that *authoritativeness is a direct function of the settlement agent's relative status*. Recalling the rank order of the five settlement roles by their degree of authoritativeness (see Figure 6.1), this formulation implies that the status distance between a third party and the principals will be the least in friendly pacification, greater in mediation, greater still in arbitration and then in adjudication, and greatest where repressive pacification occurs. Since our purpose is merely to illustrate the theory of the third party, we shall not review the empirical evidence relating to this formulation, but turn instead to a second example.

Settlement behavior also varies with the degree of relational distance, or intimacy, between the third party and the principals (see Black 1976: 40–41, for an explication of relational distance). A settlement agent might be extremely intimate with both principals — as when a conflict begins and ends within a single household — an acquaintance somewhat removed from both, or a complete stranger. Generally the intimacy between the agent and each of the principals is about equal, so that the three parties together form an isosceles triangle of relational distance (see Simmel 1908: 149–153). But the distances involved vary considerably, and it appears that *authoritativeness is a direct function of the relational distance between the settlement agent and the principals.* Friendly pacification is thus most likely where a settlement agent is highly intimate with the parties in conflict, mediation where there is a bit less intimacy, and arbitration where there is less still. Adjudication is most likely when there is even more distance between the settlement agent and the parties — they typically share only the same community or region — whereas repressive pacification is most likely when a settlement agent is maximally distant from the parties. It seems, too, that what applies to intimacy applies as well to cultural homogeneity, so that *authoritativeness is a direct function of the cultural distance between the settlement agent and the principals.*

Support behavior is similarly subject to this strategy. It is thus possible to predict and explain each degree of partisan intervention — from the giving of information and advice to advocacy, alliance, and surrogation — with such characteristics of third parties as their relative status, their intimacy with those in conflict, and their cultural identity. It is also possible to specify how the nature of support predicts and explains settlement behavior, and vice versa, and to specify conditions under which a negotiator or healer might appear. The theory of the third party contemplates all of this and more.

It might finally be noted that a theory of the third party has practical as well as scientific significance. Since the theory specifies how conflict management varies with the social characteristics of third parties, its formulations might be used to advantage by particular segments of society or, on a case-by-case basis, by one side or the other in a conflict. What, for instance, would result from a greater degree of social heterogeneity in the largely homogeneous judiciary of modern America? What would result from an increase in the number of judges who are black, Hispanic, Asian-American, female, working-class, or who have other characteristics that have traditionally been excluded? If such characteristics yield specifiable patterns of adjudication — such as lesser severity or a greater tendency to make compromise decisions — this knowledge would be relevant to legal policymakers and reformers, not to mention practicing attorneys and their clients. The same applies to the social characteristics of juries, police officers, and other third parties in the legal process. A theory of the third party therefore offers countless opportunities for legal engineering. It may also pose a challenge to conventional conceptions of justice.

ENDNOTE

*Reprinted with permission (and minor revision) from pages 84–114 in *Empirical Theories about Courts*, edited by Keith O. Boyum and Lynn Mather. New York: Longman, 1983.

An earlier version was presented by M. P. Baumgartner to the Disputes Processing Research Program, University of Wisconsin, and by both authors to Harvard Law School's Center for Criminal Justice. We thank the participants for their helpful comments. We also thank Mark Cooney, Lynn Mather, and Sally Engle Merry for comments on an earlier draft.

7

TAKING SIDES*

A partisan takes one side of a conflict[1] and acts as an informer, adviser, advocate, ally, or surrogate of a principal party (Black and Baumgartner 1983:84–98). Partisans commonly believe their commitments reflect the merits of each adversary — who is right or wrong. Even so, their location in social space predicts whose side they choose.

Partisanship may determine how conflicts are waged and won. In the simple societies studied by anthropologists, for example, the number of partisans on each side frequently decides the winner: Might makes right. Thus, in the New Guinea highlands, "for the most part, justice itself is defined by strength, as is what is moral. It is good to be strong — physically strong and strong in numbers" (Langness 1972:180). Among the Swat Pathans of Pakistan, "an encroachment on a man's rights, or an obvious threat to them, usually leads to the mobilization of a group of his allies. . . . If there is a great discrepancy between the forces, the weaker party must give in" (Barth 1959:119). Much the same occurs in Africa (e.g., Evans-Pritchard 1940; Gulliver 1963, 1969; Stauder 1972), the Americas (e.g., Lowie 1935; Maybury-Lewis 1967; Chagnon 1977), Australia (e.g., Meggitt 1962; Hiatt 1965), the Philippines (e.g., Kiefer 1972; Frake 1980; Rosaldo 1980), and elsewhere.

Whether might makes right or not, partisanship may be fateful in any conflict — international, societal, local, organizational, or familial. Here we seek to predict partisan and nonpartisan behavior from one case to another and to outline scenarios of partisanship in diverse settings. The chapter concludes with remarks on the evolution of partisanship across history.[2]

SOCIAL GRAVITATION

Conflicts normally have two adversaries and possibly also third parties — anyone else with knowledge of them.[3] The theory of partisanship predicts when and how third parties take sides: Whom do they support? How quickly? How much support do they give?

One factor in partisanship is the social distance between the adversaries and the third parties: Are they members of the same family, friends, or strangers (relational distance[4])? Are they members of the same ethnicity or religion (cultural distance[5])? These distances predict who, if anyone, will align themselves with whom, when, and how: *Partisanship is a joint function of social closeness to one side and social remoteness from the other.*

Each adversary effectively creates a gravitational field that attracts third parties with a strength proportional to their nearness to them and their distance from the opponent.[6] Intimates attract each other, for example, and are less likely than strangers to take opposite sides of a conflict. Third parties remote from both adversaries tend to be little attracted to either, those close to both tend to be drawn to both but strongly partisan to neither, while those close to one and remote from the other tend unequivocally toward partisanship.[7] The greater the discrepancy between these distances — the closer one adversary and the further the other — the stronger partisanship will be and the more rapidly it will appear. This resembles physical gravitation, which strengthens with the nearness of one mass and the remoteness of others. The social distances among and between third parties themselves also contribute to the gravitational field and may indirectly draw them toward one or both sides. Maximal partisanship arises from a severe polarization of all the parties with knowledge of a conflict: two clusters of close people, each distant from the other.

A Note on Status Effects

This chapter primarily addresses the effects of social distance on partisan behavior. Before proceeding, however, we should note a second factor:

social status.[8] Are the adversaries and third parties equal or not? If not, who is superior to whom? By how much?

Status — or social stature — is the analogue of mass in the physical world. Like the mass of an object, status creates its own gravitational field. Wealthier or otherwise more prominent adversaries therefore attract more partisanship, especially from their inferiors.[9] The greater the differences, the greater the effects: *Partisanship is a joint function of the social superiority of one side and the social inferiority of the other.*[10] Partisans themselves add social stature to an adversary, and so each partisan increases the likelihood of more partisans in the manner of a bandwagon. Partisanship begets partisanship. And the greater the stature of their side, the more help they tend to give. Partisans of higher status are harder to recruit, but are more valuable and may be crucial to adversaries of lesser stature (see Baumgartner 1984a:318–320).

An extreme case of the attractive force of social stature is patriotism — the partisanship enjoyed by nation-states. As the saying goes, "My country, right or wrong." In time of war, thousands (if not millions) willingly risk life and limb for their country. Another example is the attraction of crowds (see, e.g., Le Bon 1895; Rudé 1964). Superordinates of all kinds also attract support. Whereas adversaries in egalitarian societies enjoy the support of kinfolk and other intimates — examined shortly — those in hierarchical societies enjoy the support of dependents and other followers. In feudal societies such as those of Europe, China, and Japan, intimacy and superiority operated simultaneously (see, e.g., Bloch 1939:124–125; Lewis 1990:80–94). In ancient Rome, upper-class men (*honestiores*) could rally a "gang" of followers to resist their legal opponents and enemies (see Garnsey 1968:4–11; Lintott 1968:Chapters 2, 6). In medieval England, where servants were widespread (even among wealthier peasants), masters had similar advantages (Given 1977:49–54). In Thailand, "patrons" of higher standing often lead an "entourage" of lesser "clients" who may voluntarily accept blame or even punishment in their place (Engel 1978:71–74).[11] And in modern America, lawyers tend to gravitate to clients of higher status and to avoid individuals with complaints against superiors such as business organizations (see, e.g., Macaulay 1979). Litigants of higher status also more easily recruit witnesses to testify — even lie — on their behalf (see Cooney 1991a:192; 1991b; e.g., Gluckman 1967:111). More evidence therefore accumulates on their side.

In sum, just as physical gravitation is a function of both distance and mass, so is social gravitation: *Partisanship is a joint function of the social closeness and superiority of one side and the social remoteness and inferiority of the other.* Those with the most intimacy and social stature attract the most support.

PARTISANSHIP IN TRIBAL SOCIETIES

Social gravitation arising from intimacy is often extremely powerful in tribal societies. In many, virtually all major conflicts between individuals crystallize into conflicts between groups. Partisanship arises almost automatically from blood, marital, and residential relationships.

Among the Arusha of Tanzania, for example, patrilineal descent determines the potential partisans of each adversary. If the adversaries belong to different moities (subtribes), their partisans are their fellow moity members; if they belong to the same moity but different clans, their partisans are their fellow clan members; if they belong to the same clan but different subclans, their partisans are their fellow subclan members; and so on through maximal lineages, inner lineages, and other genealogical units until they are separated only by different families:

> *The Arusha are readily able to determine their allegiance, or their exclusion from allegiance, in any situation of conflict and dispute between two people. The [patrilineal] group or category of smallest scale of which the two disputants are both members is divisible into its two segments, or* ilwasheta, *such that each segment contains one of the disputants, and the other members of that segment are automatically his supporters. The word "automatically" is used here because to every Arusha adult the pattern is well known; it is relatively uncomplicated, and precise alignments of supporters can easily be determined in any particular case as it occurs. (Gulliver 1963:118)*

The individuals first lending support in any instance are those with additional ties to the adversaries, such as neighbors, in-laws, maternal kinsmen, and age-mates (Gulliver 1963:118–120). The longer the conflict endures, the wider the genealogical net is cast, so that over time the last to take sides are the furthest from each adversary in all respects (Gulliver 1963:124–125). Rarely, however, do adversaries seek the support of anyone near the opposing side:

> *He does not . . . seek the assistance of anyone who is closely linked with his opponent because, ideally and largely in practice too, he wants a body of supporters who are undivided in their loyalty and wholly on his side. (Gulliver 1963:127, punctuation edited)*

Hence, every conflict tends to evolve into two clusters divided by a social chasm.

The Nuristani of Afghanistan also rely overwhelmingly on blood ties: "A man normally supports and is supported by members of his extended family, lineage segment, lineage, and clan, in that order, these considerations outweighing all others" (Jones 1974:62–63, Nuristani terms omitted). The same applies to the Yakan of the Philippines: "In theory, a disputant draws his support from his circle of consanguinial kin, the obligation to give support being inversely proportional to the genealogical distance from the disputant" (Frake 1980:203, punctuation edited).[12] And the Ifugao of the Philippines: "Those who are related to both take sides with him to whom they are more closely related" (Barton 1919:86).

Partisans frequently recruit their own intimates to their side, even when these individuals have no direct ties to the one who benefits. Each side may thereby accumulate a chain of partisans from various social locations, each linked to one or more of the others. Among the Ndendeuli of Tanzania, for example,

> In a dispute between neighbors A and E (who are not directly linked and do not regard each other as kin), A expects the support of his kin-neighbor B; and B may seek the support of his own kin-neighbor C (who is not kin to A) to the side of A. (Gulliver 1971:134; see also Gulliver 1969:32–33)

But partisanship is not merely a matter of individual support. Groups also participate. They may incorporate conflicts as their own in a pattern known as "collective liability" or "collective responsibility" (see Moore 1972; Koch 1984). When a killing occurs among feuding peoples such as the Bedouin of north Africa or the tribes of Montenegro, the descent groups of the original parties seek to "even the score" by reciprocating death with death, often for months or years on end (e.g., Peters 1967; Boehm 1984). The nomads of northern Somalia have lineage-based organizations whose sole function is to handle their members' conflicts, usually by demanding or paying compensatory damages (Lewis 1959, 1961). The Shavante of Brazil have lineage-based "factions" that perform the same function (Maybury-Lewis 1967:Chapter 5, especially 179–189). The early Anglo-Saxons of Europe collectivized conflict as well: "Personal injury is in the first place a cause of feud between the kindreds of the wrong-doer and of the person wronged" (Pollock and Maitland 1898:Volume 1, 46). The same applied to the early Chinese (Lamley 1990).

At the other extreme are highly individualized societies in which hardly anyone automatically supports anyone else and partisans must be carefully cultivated. Among the Tausug of the Philippines, for instance, those embroiled in conflict actively seek new friends: "The number of friends a man has outside his own community is usually directly proportional to the degree to which he is actively involved in armed conflict and feuding" (Kiefer 1972:61). A man without friends typically says it is "because I have no enemies" (59).

Women may similarly rely on friends to handle troublesome men. In Kenya, Pokot women will band together as a "shaming party" to punish and humiliate a man who mistreats his wife (Edgerton and Conant 1964). And when quarreling among themselves, otherwise friendly women of the Walbiri Aborigines of Australia "sink their differences and join forces to attack any man who intervenes" (Meggitt 1962:95).[13] Walbiri women also rush to the aid of their husbands, possibly attracting their own allies and igniting a chain reaction of larger proportions: "In a matter of minutes they may transform a half-hearted altercation between two men into a wild brawl that involves half the camp" (94). Among the !Kung San Bushmen of Botswana, two-person fights nearly always occur in the midst of intimates, and camp-wide melees commonly explode almost immediately (Lee 1979:376–387).

Partisanship may also lead to collective avoidance. For instance, !Kung disputes about laziness and stinginess often end with a "group split" — a physical separation of the adversaries and their close relatives (Lee 1979:372). The Netsilik Eskimos and their partisans move their dwellings locally in rhythm with their squabbles:

> As old quarrels are mended and new hostilities arise, fresh alignments emerge. It is by no means an uncommon sign to see a family pack its belongings and move from one part of the camp to another to adjust to its friendship alignments. (Balikci 1970:193)

After killings, the Majangir of Ethiopia first rally their intimates for a feud, but peace typically returns only with avoidance:

> The killer will appeal to close friends and neighbors, as well as kinsmen and affines of every kind, to help in his defense. Similarly, the close relatives of the man killed will try to mobilize their close friends and neighbors to help obtain vengeance. . . . The usual outcome of a feud is the separation of the hostile parties. One or both of the parties move so that they do not remain within the same community but reside at great enough distance to make it unlikely that they will encounter each other. Generally, the persons who are in the numerically weaker position in regard to support will choose to move. (Stauder 1972:166)

Tribal societies illustrate the dynamics of partisanship when people are surrounded by throngs of intimates. Similar scenarios also occur in more differentiated societies. In medieval England, for example,

> The strength of the bonds that united individuals to one another inevitably drew groups of people into violent conflict. One man's, or one woman's, quarrel easily became his kinsmen's, his friends', and his neighbors' quarrel also. Whether people cold-bloodedly joined together with their friends

or relations to carry out a premeditated assault or automatically and unreflectingly came to the aid of one of their own who had become involved in a brawl, large numbers of people often became involved in violent conflict. (Given 1977:43–44)

But now compare American suburbs, where the inhabitants have few if any close relationships beyond their households:

When tensions erupt, individuals are generally left to their own devices. Extended family members, who might otherwise be expected to lend assistance, are usually living some distance away and are, in any case, caught up in their own networks and concerns. . . . Friends, neighbors, and other associates are near at hand but are rarely intimate enough to be relied upon. Even advice is difficult to obtain from those who know little or nothing about a problem, and many people are reluctant to give it under any circumstances (believing it preferable not to get involved in others' conflicts at all). (Baumgartner 1988:97)

Suburban conflict is distinctively modern. Rarely have so many adversaries been so isolated and bereft of partisans. Conflict in modern cities is equally individualized, or more so, since people are often entirely alone day and night. Consider the famous case of Kitty Genovese, a New Yorker whose cries for help were ignored by 38 of her neighbors, many watching from their apartments as she was raped and fatally stabbed. Her attacker was socially remote from everyone there, but so was she.[14]

MODELS OF PARTISANSHIP

Next we turn to several scenarios of partisan and nonpartisan behavior: strong partisanship, weak partisanship, cold nonpartisanship, and warm nonpartisanship. Each has its own social structure and tends to exhibit a distinctive pattern of conflict.

Strong Partisanship

Strong partisanship on each side is most likely to arise when third parties are socially close to one adversary (A) but remote from the other (B), and vice versa (see Figure 7.1).

Strong partisanship not only arises from social polarization—every third party close to one adversary and distant from the other—but also produces moral polarization.[15] Each side commonly regards itself as totally right and the other as totally wrong. Compromise is difficult. Conflict is

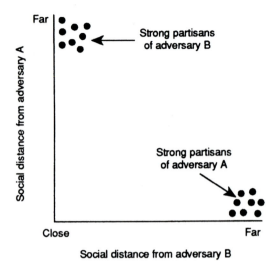

Figure 7.1   Social structure of strong partisanship.

likely to be protracted, prone to escalation, and possibly violent. Illustrations include feuding, rioting, and warfare (see, e.g., Thoden van Velzen and van Wetering 1960; Baumgartner 1988:97–98; Black 1990:44–47; Senechal de la Roche 1990:Chapter 4).

Weak Partisanship

Weak partisanship is most likely when third parties are only slightly closer to one adversary (A) than the other (B). This occurs at various social distances, and these determine the social climate of each conflict. Social closeness among all the participants creates a "warm" social climate, whereas social remoteness creates a "cold" social climate (see Figures 7.2 and 7.3).

When third parties are socially close to both adversaries (though closer to one, as in Figure 7.2), they are likely to show concern ("warmth") for both, even if ultimately they take sides. The pattern of conflict may be ambivalent and unstable. If physically close, the participants often become agitated, noisy, and even violent, as illustrated by the melees that sometimes erupt among hunters and gatherers such as !Kung Bushmen or Walbiri Aborigines. Third parties pulled in opposite directions may also display indecisiveness and a lack of commitment. Conflict tends to be dissipative, losing its momentum almost as soon as it begins. For example,

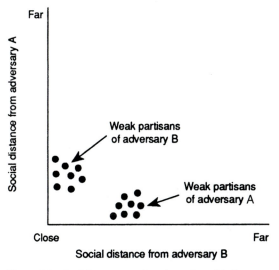

Figure 7.2   Social structure of weak partisanship in a warm climate.

fights among the !Kung usually end within seconds or minutes, everyone laughing at their own behavior (Lee 1979:372; see also Marshall
1961:246; Knauft 1987a:476–477). Right and wrong lose their clarity and
importance.

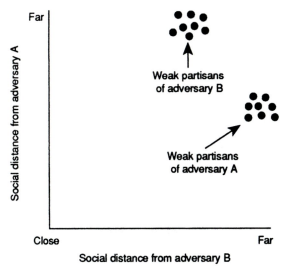

Figure 7.3   Social structure of weak partisanship in a cold climate.

Third parties socially distant from the adversaries (though closer to one, as in Figure 7.3) frequently show indifference ("coldness") toward both, even if weakly favoring one while ignoring the other. Here too conflict tends to dissipate rapidly. Near strangers may avoid direct involvement by removing themselves physically, or make only superficial commitments which they readily abandon. Adversaries with little support are likely to lose heart and to separate or otherwise make peace. Violence, especially collective violence, is uncommon.

Cold Nonpartisanship

Nonpartisanship with indifferent behavior ("coldness") toward the adversaries is most likely when third parties are socially remote, and equally so, from both (see Figure 7.4).

Cold nonpartisans tend to become bystanders, leaving the adversaries to fend for themselves. And without partisans, a conflict is less likely to escalate. Lone adversaries are more inclined to indirect and nonviolent tactics such as avoidance and gossip, or to total inaction (Baumgartner 1988:97). Conflict tends to be minimalistic, as seen in American suburbs (on "moral minimalism," see Baumgartner 1988:Chapters 3–6). But cold nonpartisans may also allow a conflict to get worse.

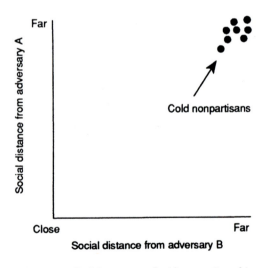

Figure 7.4 Social structure of cold nonpartisanship.

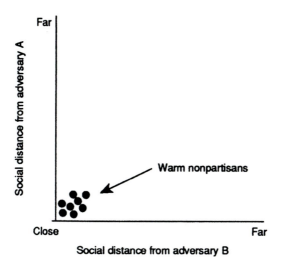

Figure 7.5   Social structure of warm nonpartisanship.

Warm Nonpartisanship

Still another social structure generates supportive behavior ("warmth") toward both adversaries: when the third parties are equally close to both (see Figure 7.5).

Warm nonpartisans are remedial. They encourage everyone to end hostilities. If fighting begins, they may literally pull the adversaries apart or stand between them until tranquility returns. They may also act as mediators or go-betweens to facilitate a settlement or an agreement to drop the matter altogether. The adversaries are likely to comply.

Simple societies such as hunters and gatherers tend to alternate between the remedial and dissipative patterns of conflict characteristic of warm nonpartisanship and weak partisanship in a warm climate. So do families, gangs, and other intimates. Each episode reflects the distribution of third parties in social space.

In sum, partisanship is a form of social attraction that varies with the social distances between adversaries and third parties, and each alignment tends to produce its own pattern of conflict. Conflict is likely to be protracted when partisanship is strong, dissipative when it is weak; minimalistic when nonpartisanship is cold, and remedial when it is warm. But reality is not always so simple.

Variations

Adversaries often attract partisans with differing involvements, drawn from various locations in social space. One may attract a few strong partisans while the other attracts many, or one attracts many strong and weak partisans while the other attracts only a few weak ones or none at all. Add nonpartisans with diverse orientations (reflecting their social locations), and the combinations multiply still more. Since a conflict may range from two people by themselves to nearly the whole world, the possibilities are almost infinite. Even so, a number of patterns recur.

Feuds, for example, closely resemble our model of strong partisanship (see, e.g., Hasluck 1954; Peters 1967; Boehm 1984; Rieder 1985:171–202), and tribal brawls closely resemble our model of weak partisanship in a warm climate (see, e.g., Meggitt 1962:94; Lee 1979:372). Nonpartisanship occurs when people are drawn toward both sides by "cross-cutting ties," such as blood ties to one adversary and marital or neighborly ties to the other (Colson 1953; see also Gluckman 1956:Chapter 1).

One possible consequence of cross-cutting ties is a seeming inability to participate at all. For example, an Ndendeuli man "more or less equally related in the kinship network to both principals" may "avoid embarrassing participation by deliberately absenting himself from the community temporarily and thus remaining inactively neutral" (Gulliver 1971:136–137). When a moot is airing a dispute, such individuals may sit between the two sides or on the periphery to avoid being identified with either (135). Similarly, in the Philippines, Ilongots tied to both sides of a feud meticulously avoid any appearance of involvement (Rosaldo 1980:Chapter 2). The Mundurucú of Brazil are interlinked so thoroughly that they rarely even publicly acknowledge the existence of local conflicts (Murphy 1957:1032).

Others with cross-cutting and close ties may behave as warm nonpartisans and seek to dampen or resolve conflicts. The Gebusi of lowland New Guinea, who mostly live communally in longhouses, tend to respond nonjudgmentally and to encourage peacefulness no matter how violent a tribesman becomes:

> *In the rare cases where anger boils into overt antagonism, the altercation is restricted to the two principal antagonists; there is little taking of sides. . . . The goal is simply to separate the angry parties and give them time to defuse their anger. Good company must be restored as soon as possible, even if superficially or through avoidance. With time, the social wounds will also heal. (Knauft 1985:75)*

Even a "wild man" who attacks fellow villagers indiscriminately with a club, ax, or bow and arrow — possibly fatally — is regarded nonjudgmentally and accepted back into the group (Knauft 1985:75–77). Among the Ifugao, a man close to both sides and unable to choose either tends to become "a strong advocate of compromise and peaceful settlement" (Barton 1919:86). An Ndendeuli might become a mediator: "Primarily a mediator attempted to act as a broker between the principals, and he played on his links with each as demonstration of his goodwill to both" (Gulliver 1971:137). Cross-cutting ties also reduce violence (Colson 1953; see also Evans-Pritchard 1940:156; Turney-High 1971:230–231; Cooney 1988:56–60; Senechal de la Roche 1990:Chapter 4; 1992).

Another scenario arises with conflict between a member of a tightly-knit community, organization, or informal group and a stranger, outsider, or isolate. The former normally enjoys strong partisanship while the latter is left alone, with little chance of victory or even a stalemate. A lack of blood relatives in a tribal society, for example, is equivalent to moral inferiority. Among the Crow Indians of the American Plains, "No worse insult could be hurled . . . than to say, 'You are without relatives'; it meant that he was a person of no account" (Lowie 1935:11). And among the Yakan of the Philippines,

> It is seemingly impossible to muster a reliable support group with no reliance on kin ties. Persons without consanguinial kin ties in their community, such as spouses, teachers, or visitors from distant areas or different ethnic groups, are in a very precarious position if they become involved in local disputes. (Frake 1980:207)

The Jalé of New Guinea favor those without partisans as targets of vengeance: "A foreign resident tends to be a preferred victim . . . because his death involves a diminished risk of revenge" (Koch 1974:135; see also Rosaldo 1980:55). Similarly, women isolated by marriage from their own family but surrounded by in-laws are more vulnerable to domestic violence (Baumgartner 1992a). Where compensation for injuries is required, those without partisans may be unable to pay and must suffer the consequences (see Black 1989:44–45). In Zambia, a "friendless" Ndola man unable to pay damages for adultery might be forced into slavery (Chanock 1985:195; see also Kroeber 1925:32–33). In court, an isolated individual is deprived of the friendly testimony — possibly false — that might be provided by intimates, and is all the worse off if opposed by someone rich in friends and relatives (see Cooney 1991b:18–22). Partisanless people are also more likely to be accused of misconduct in the first place. For instance, they are more likely to be accused of witchcraft (e.g., Whiting 1950:64–65; Thomas 1970:64). Isolated leaders are more likely to be opposed, overthrown, or assassinated (see, e.g., Westermeyer 1973:741–742). Isolates are even more likely to turn against themselves and commit suicide (see Durkheim 1897:Book 2, Chapters 2–3; Black 1990:53; 1992:40).[16]

LATENT PARTISANSHIP

All of our models and illustrations take the presence of third parties for granted. Recall, however, that third parties are those with knowledge of a conflict. The participation of third parties therefore partly depends on how much information about a conflict (conflict information) radiates into its social environment. Some conflicts are entirely private, unknown to anyone but the adversaries, making the participation of third parties impossible. Marital conflicts are often private in this sense, though children or other family members may become knowledgeable by dint of their physical presence. Other conflicts are highly public. The "world wars" of the twentieth century were known to most of humanity, and millions actively took sides. In any event, because conflict is frequently unknown beyond the principals, or at least unknown to those who might otherwise intervene, much if not most partisanship remains latent.

An absence of partisanship may indicate a particular arrangement of people in social space, such as a lack of close relationships, or it may reflect a high degree of privacy. The paucity of partisanship in American suburbs apparently results from both:

> *Practically no one knows what offenses occur or what responses they meet. Cut off from others, living lives of extreme privacy and free of the social pressure that a cohesive group of associates might provide, people . . . handle their problems without regard to public opinion. (Baumgartner 1988:95)*

Where conflict information is rich and circulates widely, such as tribal villages and camps, latent partisanship quickly becomes active, and discord may escalate. Hence, privacy is one condition conducive to a peaceful way of life (Baumgartner 1988:Chapter 6). Like a tribal village, the international community is greatly disadvantaged in this respect, as are many organizations (see, e.g., Morrill 1992). Electronic communications create village-like conditions (McLuhan 1964:47), facilitating the flow of conflict information and encouraging behavior normally associated with tribal societies, such as feuding and vengeance.[17]

SLOW PARTISANSHIP

Social gravitation not only explains the direction of partisanship but also its velocity. Is the moral alignment of third parties instantaneous, or does it emerge more slowly?

Third parties very close to one adversary and very far from the other commit themselves more quickly than those located elsewhere. The close relatives of an adversary typically leap at once against a stranger, but move more slowly (if at all) against another relative. Third parties merely acquainted with both sides tend to move slowly, too, even if closer to one than the other. Conflicts lack urgency for those who are socially remote.

Now consider settlement behavior such as mediation, arbitration, and adjudication. Because settlement agents usually remain uncommitted to either side of a conflict during a significant portion of their participation, we ordinarily classify them as nonpartisan rather than partisan (see, e.g., Black and Baumgartner 1983). Peacemakers (who seek to terminate conflicts without addressing the issues) and mediators (who help the adversaries negotiate a settlement) in their pure form behave neutrally from beginning to end. But arbitrators and judges nearly always abandon their neutrality in the end and declare one side totally or partially right and the other totally or partially wrong. In this sense, their intervention shifts from nonpartisan to partisan, no matter what they or anyone else might claim. Their usual behavior (hearings and deliberations followed by one-sided decisions) is a form of slow partisanship. Months or longer may pass before a case reaches trial, and a judge may examine testimony for weeks or longer before reaching a decision, but the ultimate question remains the same: Whose side will the state take?

Slow partisanship reflects the principle of social gravitation. First, because slow partisans such as arbitrators and judges tend to be equally distant from the adversaries (Simmel 1908b:149–153; Black and Baumgartner 1983:113; see also Black 1984b:22), they are likely to be pulled in both directions at once. Second, because they tend to be socially remote from both adversaries (Black and Baumgartner 1983:113–114), the attraction of either is likely to be weak. Even so, in most cases they eventually gravitate to one side.

The neutrality of law — an ideal of modern jurisprudence — has limited value as a description of legal behavior. Law takes sides.[18]

LEGAL PARTISANSHIP

But which side do slow partisans take? Consider judges.

Which side judges will favor also reflects social gravitation. Although they tend to be socially equidistant and remote from both sides, their actual location deviates from this model in many cases. Disqualifications remove some of these deviations — such as when the judge is a spouse, blood relative, in-law, or business partner of one adversary — but other imbalances in social proximity often remain. For example, only one adversary may be an acquaintance of the judge; only one may share the same race, ethnicity, or gender; or only one may be a resident of the locality in which the case is tried. All such imbalances may tip the scales of justice. In societies still partially tribal, for instance, a member of tribe A involved in a lawsuit with a member of tribe B has a disadvantage when the judge belongs to tribe B (see, e.g., Beidelman 1967:32–34). In colonial Africa, a black African involved in a lawsuit with a European had a disadvantage before a European judge (Chanock 1985:131–132). In a small-town American court, an out-of-towner suing a local resident has a disadvantage (see Engel 1984). In modern criminal cases, where one side is prosecuted in the state's name by a state employee and the judge is a fellow employee (often acquainted with the prosecutor), the defendant has a disadvantage.[19]

Earlier stages of the criminal process, such as arrest and charging, are subject to social gravitation as well. The handling of complaints against police officers provides one example: Their colleagues typically side with them from the beginning (see, e.g., Chevigny 1969; Black 1980:174). Relatives, friends, and neighbors of police officers have an advantage, too (see, e.g., Black 1980:34, 174). At the other extreme are strangers accused of killing or injuring a police officer (see, e.g., Black 1980:36–40). And social gravitation influences who calls the police in the first place. For example, citizens are more likely to report a crime committed by a stranger than by a relative or friend (see, e.g., Block 1974:560–561; Williams 1984:463). Legal partisanship resembles all partisanship.[20]

THE EVOLUTION OF PARTISANSHIP

Over the centuries, partisanship has changed enormously. On the one hand, it has weakened and declined with the primordial forms of intimacy that long provided its nourishment. On the other, like so much else, it has become a commodity and a government service.

Much partisanship withered away with the extended family, the tightly-knit community, the patron–client relationship, and more generally with intimacy beyond the household. The web of support has loosened, and self-reliance has proliferated. People are ever more rarely drawn wholeheartedly into the conflicts of their associates.[21] Here and there alliances form and fight,[22] but daily life increasingly resembles American suburbs: "People move about freely, families scatter, and individuals are on their own, able to withdraw from others at will, without either the support or the constraint that strong ties entail" (Baumgartner 1988:135). Conflict has individualized and privatized. The best illustrations of strong partisanship must therefore come from anthropology and history.

But here we have examined only partisanship arising from social gravitation. With the decay and destruction of primordial intimacy, however, a new wave of partisans appears: lawyers.[23] These professional partisans come into being with social complexity (Schwartz and Miller 1964). Wealth — a form of status — replaces social proximity as an attractive force, and money replaces intimates as an advantage. Lawyers become available as hired friends. Partisanship becomes a commodity.

Also relevant has been the growth of the state.[24] Partisanship becomes a public service. People increasingly turn to law when they have no one else, and the state itself becomes a friend (see, e.g., Cumming, Cumming, and Edell 1965). A massive system of social machinery — police, prosecutors, judges, officials of all kinds — determines when and how the state enters conflicts, whose side it takes, and what consequences follow.[25] Now the state, not kith and kin, decides when an injury deserves payment and when a person deserves violence or deprivation. Even the weakest state is the most valuable partisan, and its support is fateful: It overwhelms all opponents, primordial or professional, and pacifies societies. It alters the balance of power. Once those without intimates were the great losers, but now it is those without the state.

ENDNOTES

*The following individuals commented on an earlier draft: M. P. Baumgartner, Albert Bergesen, Theodore Caplow, Mark Cooney, John Herrmann, Allan V. Horwitz, Calvin Morrill, Roberta Senechal de la Roche, and James Tucker.

1. This chapter deals mainly with partisanship that is voluntary (rather than paid, obligatory, or coerced) and moral (rather than political, religious, or intellectual).

2. Earlier theoretical work on partisanship includes Simmel (1908a:Chapter 3), Colson (1953), Coser (1956:Chapter 8), Gluckman (1956:Chapter 1), Thoden van Velzen and van Wetering (1960), Caplow (1968), Bailey (1969), Black and Baumgartner (1983), and Baumgartner (1988).

3. The concept of third parties is usually limited to those who actively intervene in a conflict and who claim to be neutral, such as mediators, arbitrators, and judges (see, e.g., Galtung 1965; Eckhoff 1966; Koch 1974:27–31). A broader concept includes active partisans such as advocates and allies (e.g., Black and Baumgartner 1983). Here our concept is still broader and includes those such as bystanders who know about a conflict but do not participate in it.

4. We can measure relational distance, or intimacy, with the degree to which people participate in one another's lives (see Black 1976:40–41).

5. Cultural distance, or diversity, refers to differences in the content of culture (see Black 1976:73–74).

6. Helping behavior of all kinds varies inversely with social distance (Black and Baumgartner 1980:200; see also Bar-Tal 1976:79). Experimental studies indicate that even a very small reduction of social distance such as prior visual exposure of one person to another, eye contact, or a brief conversation increases the propensity of a stranger to help a fellow stranger in distress (see, e.g., Darley 1967, quoted in Hackler, Ho, and Urquhart-Ross 1974:332; Piliavin, Rodin, and Piliavin 1969; Ellsworth and Langer 1976).

7. For related observations on the effects of intimacy on partisanship, see Cooney (1988:56–60).

8. Social status is an ordinal location in social space such as a level of wealth, respectability, integration, organization, or conventionality (see Black 1976:Chapters 2–6).

9. Experimental evidence suggests that social superiors attract more help of all kinds, and that equals attract more than inferiors. For example, American white men and women were more likely to help a white man than a black man posing as a motorist in distress, and so were black women, though black men helped whites and blacks about equally (Gaertner and Bickerman 1971). Also, American whites were more likely to give money to a white woman than to a black woman posing as a Salvation Army worker ringing a bell by a kettle (Bryan and Test 1967). But since racial similarity is also associated with cultural similarity, and cultural similarity increases the propensity to help, race comparisons do not provide a clear demonstration of status effects (see, e.g., Piliavin, Rodin, and Piliavin 1969; compare Wispe and Freshley 1971).

10. Social superiority and inferiority here refer to the social status of the adversaries relative to each other and to any third parties who might be available.

11. Patrons loan money and provide other services — including support in conflicts — to their clients (Engel 1978:72–74). Feudal relationships are similarly reciprocal (see, e.g., Bloch 1939:145–151). In medieval Iceland, farmers and chieftains formed relationships of mutual aid, but powerful allies might also be recruited on the basis of kinship, a fee, or a promise of future service (Byock 1982:Chapters 2, 5, and Appendix C).

12. In practice, Yakan adversaries turn first to kinsmen with whom they have frequent contact. Kinsmen rarely seen are hardly regarded as kinsmen at all: "When in view, a kinsman; out of sight, discarded trash" (Frake 1980:204).

13. A comparable transformation may occur when police officers intervene in conflicts between intimates, especially marital couples or lovers. Most such cases arise when a woman requests police help, but if the officers use coercion or try to make an arrest she may protest and join forces with the man (Parnas 1967:921; Black 1980:162).

14. This occurred in 1964 and continues to be a symbol of moral breakdown in modern life. For further remarks on the case, including its practical implications, see Black and Baumgartner (1980:especially 196, note 7) and Black (1989:Chapter 5, especially 79–80).

Even in urban neighborhoods, however, individuals typically have "a small set of close friends, kinsmen, and people known personally and well . . . from whom allies and supporters are mobilized in times of crisis and conflict" (Merry 1981:94; also see generally Chapter 5 of the same volume).

15. The strongest partisans are not only very close to one adversary and very distant from the other but also very distant from everyone else in the social universe.

16. Despite their great intimacy with themselves, people are not always their own strongest partisans. When socially close to an adversary, for example, they may pursue their own interests less aggressively than would an intimate (such as their spouse or parent) who is more distant from their adversary (compare Cooney 1988:42–43).

17. So-called terrorists depend on electronic communications to broadcast their activities and demands throughout the modern world, creating millions of third parties, and governments converse with them in the same fashion.

In the 1960s, American protest groups often chanted "the whole world is watching" during public demonstrations.

18. In simple societies where primordial systems of partisanship are still intact, legal officials may find it difficult to claim neutrality. Among the Chatino Indians of Mexico, for example, homicide cases often divide an entire community, and legal authorities tend to avoid involvement of any kind:

> A homicide in which one villager kills another creates a deep schism in the community. Any action would constitute taking sides and would invite reprisals. Given the constant threat of violence, the understandable attitude of Indian authorities is that "Only God can punish a murderer." (Greenberg 1989:196; see also 152; punctuation edited)

19. In modern America, it appears that about 95% of criminal cases result in a conviction — most by guilty pleas — whereas plaintiffs win only about half of the civil cases (see, e.g., Kalven and Zeisel 1966:Chapter 5; Wanner 1975:297). Also relevant to this difference is the simple fact that every criminal case is brought by a powerful organization — the state — whereas most civil cases are brought by private organizations and individuals (Black 1989:42–43).

20. The social structure of the complaint — such as the relational, cultural, and status distance separating the adversaries — also predicts which side the state will take (see generally Black 1976).

21. During the transition from tribal to more complex patterns of social organization, intermediate forms of legal settlement may allow the intimates of one or both sides to play a major role. For example, an adversary's close associates may be permitted to determine the result by swearing an oath. In medieval England, oath-takers for a defendant (known as "compurgators") were originally kinsmen but later might include neighbors. The plaintiff could also call a "suit" of witnesses to swear an oath supporting his claim (see Pollock and Maitland 1898: Volume 2,600–610; see also Bloch 1939:124–125). Traditional Islamic law has similar practices (see Rosen 1984:125; Black 1987b:48–49). In the early Germanic kingdoms,

> The man without a family had no one to help him bring an offending party before the courts, no one to help support his oath, no one to help him pay the compositions imposed by law on those found guilty of a crime. (Drew 1973:11)

Moreover, as noted earlier, isolated people have disadvantages in modern courts of law.

22. This happens among nation-states, in rural areas still pre-modern, and in some organizations and gangs. In modern America, for instance, an observer of the Hell's Angels motorcycle club reports that in conflicts between an Angel and an outsider, "a fellow Angel is always right" (Thompson 1966:71).

23. Historically, lawyers often encountered resistance from people accustomed to primordial partisanship. Paid advocates were viewed with contempt in ancient Athens, for example, and those assisting litigants usually claimed it was because of a pre-existing bond of intimacy or because of their own enmity toward the opposing side (Chroust 1954a:359).

Accepting payment for advocacy in court was a criminal offense in colonial Massachusetts until 1673 (Botein 1981:131). Even now, American lawyers are disparaged as "hired guns."

Mercenary soldiers are similarly despised.

24. Simmel notes that states themselves have sometimes come into being as alliances against a common enemy, as did France against the English or Spain against the Moors (1908a:100).

25. In the impersonal society of the modern world, social status is a major factor in the partisanship of the state. Law favors social superiors against inferiors, for example, and is relatively indifferent when those of lower status have conflicts with each other (see generally Black 1976:Chapters 2–6).

8

MAKING ENEMIES*

Moralism is a tendency to treat people as enemies. The worst are killed: Witches are burned, rapists lynched, adulterers stoned, traitors shot, murderers electrocuted. Some attribute moralism to particular individuals ("moralistic personalities"), philosophies ("moral absolutism"), or conduct ("immorality"), but it also arises in particular locations and directions in social space. Moralism is a product of its social environment.

Here we offer a formulation to predict and explain moralism — a principle of social repulsion — and illustrate it with the behavior of third parties and of people who handle their own grievances. The chapter concludes with a comment on the history of enemies in human societies.

SOCIAL REPULSION

Moralism is the opposite of partisanship ("taking sides") and occurs under opposite conditions. Whereas partisanship is a direct function of social closeness and inferiority (see Chapter 7), *moralism is a direct function of social remoteness and superiority.* Those with the strongest partisans tend to be socially close and superior, while those with the greatest enemies tend to be socially remote and inferior. Whereas partisanship resembles gravitation in the physical universe, moralism resembles the repulsion of opposing fields of electricity or magnetism. But physical repulsion — like gravitation — normally diminishes with physical distance, while social repulsion grows stronger as social distance increases.[1] And social repulsion is not necessarily reciprocal.[2]

First consider the behavior of third parties such as judges and mediators. When do they invoke rules? Declare winners and losers? Use force and violence?

THIRD-PARTY MORALISM[3]

At one extreme are wrathful judges who condemn people to suffer and die; at the other, friendly peacemakers who seek to restore social harmony as gently as possible (see Black and Baumgartner 1983). These tendencies appear under radically different conditions: the first when third parties are socially remote and superior, the second when they are socially close and equal or inferior.[4] Third-party behavior varies on several dimensions — its formalism, decisiveness, coerciveness, and punitiveness — and all obey the same principle.

Formalism

Formalism is the tendency to create and apply explicit rules. Highly formalistic third parties handle only alleged violations of rules and justify their decisions accordingly. Others do not refer to rules at all.

Among the Zinacanteco Indians of Mexico, for example, elders acting as third parties normally devote little or no effort to uncovering the precise facts involved, much less whether any rules were violated, but seek only to placate the aggrieved individual (Collier 1973:60). Typically they encourage the alleged offender simply to "beg the pardon" of the complainant by offering him a bottle of rum; acceptance means "the anger in his heart is ended" and the matter resolved (59–60). Or they may propose a compromise, also validated by the sharing of rum (26–28). These practices, however, occur only when grievances are handled by Zinacantecos who are socially close to the principals. Non-Zinacanteco officials merely decide whether any rules were violated and, if so, apply remedies specified in the written law (39–46). But they are less formalistic toward fellow non-Indians (Hunt and Hunt 1969:137).

Third parties in simpler societies throughout the world are highly informal. Some invoke no rules or precedents at all (see, e.g., Gillin 1934:334; Hoebel 1940:6). Others use rules that are highly elastic. Judges among the Basoga of Uganda proceed almost entirely by intuition:

> *There is a real sense in which Basoga [judges] do not know what to think about a case until they have heard what they [themselves] have to say about it. . . . Basoga in court very seldom talk about the law — about the reach of the concepts of wrong. They talk instead about the "facts" — about what happened — without articulating the legal significance of these events. (Fallers 1969:314, 320)*

Compare the courts of modern America or Europe, where every lawsuit and decision is supposed to refer to specific doctrines and precedents.[5] Nowadays, indeed, law *means* rules (see, e.g., Hart 1961; Fuller 1964). But juries, who are socially closer to the litigants, are less rule-oriented than judges (see, e.g., Hastie, Penrod, and Pennington 1983:135–142). And judges on appellate courts, the most distant from the litigants, are more rule-oriented than anyone.

Separate third parties from the adversaries — choose social superiors, cultural aliens, and complete strangers — and rules will dominate the proceedings.[6]

Decisiveness

Moralism is uncompromising. One does not bargain with the devil. Every case has a winner and a loser, one totally right and one totally wrong. In this sense, moralistic third parties are decisive. At another extreme are those who meticulously avoid taking sides and encourage the adversaries to find their own resolution. Each adversary may want something from the other — an acceptance of blame, a resumption of normal relations, an agreement about the future — and a compromise is possible. Third parties may also impose compromises to avoid one-sided outcomes.

Social distance clarifies right and wrong. Social proximity blurs the distinction or otherwise discourages its application. Third parties remote from both adversaries (like most modern judges) thus find one side completely right and the other completely wrong in most cases (see Gulliver 1979:13). Those close to both (like most tribal elders) prefer compromises (see, e.g., Frake 1963; Gibbs 1963; Gulliver 1963; Gluckman 1967; Nader 1969). Third parties among the Subanun of the Philippines, for example, are no wealthier, older, or otherwise superior to anyone else, and are usually well-acquainted with all concerned (Frake 1963:218–219). They are distinguished only by a recognized prowess in handling disputes, including an ability to drink and sing (elements of every hearing). Hence, not surprisingly, they seldom find either side totally right or totally wrong, but nearly always declare both to be partly at fault (220).

The Zinacantecos of Mexico are similarly reluctant to declare a single winner:

Zinacantecos do not have elaborate procedures for verifying the facts of a case, because the facts are not of crucial importance. Zinacanteco outcomes are compromises, and an important part of the procedure of a hearing is the compromising of the facts. . . . Frequently the facts are distorted beyond recognition. . . . Or compromise may be based on outright lies, which everyone knows are lies but which offer the only possible route to agreement. (Collier 1973:96, 97)

Non-Zinacanteco officials are just the opposite:

Litigants before the Mexican authorities . . . answer questions designed by the official to uncover the 'facts' of the case. Solutions follow from these 'facts' and tend to place all the blame on one side. (Collier 1973:60–61; see also Greenberg 1989:152, 227)

The Indians say that taking a case to a Mexican court is "like putting it in the hands of the gods" (Collier 1973:56). But with non-Indians like themselves, the Mexican officials are more flexible and often arrange settlements agreeable to all (see Hunt and Hunt 1969:122–125; Collier 1973:253–254).

The same principle operated in a natural experiment in the American West: After confining the Indians to reservations, the United States government established "Courts of Indian Offenses" in the late nineteenth century, hoping to achieve American-style justice with Indian judges. But the Indians were too close to the litigants to behave like whites: "The judges, who sought to compromise and conciliate rather than rule according to rigid points of law, were reminiscent of the tribal elders" (Hagan 1966:174). Judges and juries in modern America display the same pattern: Juries, closer to the litigants, are more likely to make "compromise decisions" (see, e.g., Frank 1930:Chapter 16; Kalven and Zeisel 1966:Chapter 1).[7]

Coerciveness

Another feature of moralism is a propensity to use force. Whereas some third parties handle cases only when asked, withdraw on request, and make no effort to enforce any resolution, others hale people before them (using arrest and incarceration if necessary), make them answer questions (by torture if necessary), and enforce their decisions (with violence if necessary). And, like formalism or decisiveness, coerciveness is a direct function of social remoteness and superiority.

Zinacanteco elders, for example, nearly always rely on persuasion (Collier 1973:27–29), whereas Mexican officials use coercion and regard the preferences of the litigants as "completely irrelevant" (60). Subanun third parties superficially resemble judges, but they are socially similar and close to the litigants and never use coercion: "If sanctioned physical force is accepted as the essential criterion of law, then there is no true law in Subanun society" (Frake 1963:221). Everyone nevertheless cooperates: "Anyone who refused to comply . . . would suffer no threat of being confined, beaten, or executed. Yet compliance is invariable" (220).

In fact, voluntary compliance everywhere increases with the social proximity of the third party. Among the Chatino Indians of Mexico, for instance, "the more closely mediators are related to the parties concerned, the more likely their efforts as peacemakers are to succeed" (Greenberg 1989:226). Similarly, American Indians prosecuted in the Courts of Indian Offenses were more cooperative than those prosecuted in courts administered by whites. Efforts to escape Indian jails were virtually unknown, and resistance to a valid charge was viewed as cowardly and rarely occurred (Hagan 1966:121). But death might be preferred to a trial by whites (165–167).

People tend to avoid third parties who are socially remote. Law, for example, is nearly always located in outer social space, even when physically close, and is nearly always a last resort. Indians thus avoid Mexican courts as much as possible (Collier 1973:40–41; Greenberg 1989:197), whereas the Subanun, whose third parties are socially close in all respects, are extremely litigious (Frake 1963:218). Tribal societies in traditional Africa were also litigious, but this changed after the establishment of government courts (Abel 1979). And societies with juries — nearly always closer to the litigants than judges — have higher litigation rates than those without: The United States, Canada, England, Australia, and New Zealand, for example — all jury societies — have higher rates than the non-jury societies of Europe (see Galanter 1983:52). Moralism is unpopular.

Punitiveness

The classic response to immorality is punishment — the infliction of pain and deprivation. But conduct alone does not explain punishment. Even homicide was handled nonpunitively in many societies of the past (see Cooney 1988). Some third parties never punish anyone for anything, whereas others constantly do. In Manchu China, judges punished someone in nearly every case: the accused if found guilty, otherwise the "unjustified accuser" (van der Sprenkel 1962:69). Under the Mongols, a Chinese policeman who failed to apprehend a thief or robber within a month was himself punished with a beating (Ch'en 1979:72).

The most formalistic, decisive, and coercive third parties are also the most punitive. All these tendencies increase with their distance — vertical, relational, and cultural — from the adversaries (see Horwitz 1990:

Chapter 2). Where the distance is small, as between Zinacanteco elders and their neighbors, conciliation takes priority. Widen the distance by using Zinacanteco officials at the town hall, and compensation is favored. Widen it more with Mexican officials who do not even speak the same language, and punishment looms to importance (Collier 1973:Chapter 1). During the colonial period, Spanish judges were still more distant and more punitive, often sentencing Indians to be whipped for conduct now ignored or treated more leniently (Taylor 1979:99). In Surinam, the elders of the Djuka ("Bush Negroes") are less punitive than government judges. In rape cases, for instance, elders typically order a payment of compensation (about $30), whereas judges use imprisonment (Köbben 1969:129). In nineteenth-century America, rape might be compensated in the Courts of Indian Offenses, though offenders were more often ordered to work on the public roads (Hagan 1966:121–123).

The frequency and severity of punishment by third parties increases with social inequality and the breakdown of intimacy (see Spitzer 1975; Grabosky 1984). Almost unknown in egalitarian tribes,[8] it comes when strangers invade everyday life and resources concentrate. And it comes with the state (see Durkheim 1900:32–43; Black 1976:Chapter 5; Horwitz 1990:Chapter 2). Punishment had its golden age in ancient empires such as those of Mesopotamia, Egypt, China, and Rome (see Collins 1974:421). Penalties included the amputation of hands, feet, and testicles, blinding, branding, burning, burying alive, crucifying, impaling, slicing, flaying, boiling, pouring of hot oil into the ears or mouth, and exposing to wild beasts or vicious dogs (see generally Durkheim 1900:37–40; Collins 1974:419–428).

Punishment was also extremely severe in Europe from the late Middle Ages until the late eighteenth century: Lips and tongues were amputated, flesh torn away with hot pincers, bodies broken on the wheel, sawed in half, drawn, and quartered (see Durkheim 1900:41–43; Foucault 1975: Chapter 1). Witches, heretics, traitors, and homosexuals were burned at the stake (see, e.g., Midelfort 1972; Greenberg 1988:302–323). These practices declined as inequality and the social remoteness of third parties attenuated.

UNILATERAL MORALISM

But moralism is not monopolized by third parties. Far from it. Although public humiliation, mutilation, torture, and the harsher forms of execution administered by judicial authorities may be highly visible and dramatic, they are rare. Most moralism arises between the adversaries themselves, occasionally assisted by close associates. Here, too, the principle of social repulsion implies where moralism achieves its fullest development: across great distances and from higher to lower elevations in social space.

Compared to equals or inferiors, for example, superior adversaries are more formalistic, decisive, coercive, and punitive. And adversaries who are socially distant are more so than those who are socially close (see Black 1990:48–49). Historically, the greatest distances in social space have been those separating different societies, and nowhere has social repulsion been stronger. Often members of different societies — especially tribal societies — are enemies by definition. Conduct is irrelevant. The Mundurucú of Brazil, for instance, attack foreign tribes entirely because they are foreign: "It might be said that enemy tribes caused the Mundurucú to go to war simply by existing, and the word for enemy meant merely any group that was not Mundurucú" (Murphy 1957:1026).[9] Similarly, many headhunting and cannibalistic tribes of coastal Melanesia "extended the treatment for enemies to any stranger who was sighted unarmed or unprotected, a practice which boded particularly ill for shipwrecked sailors or for Westerners who found themselves too far away from their ship or unarmed away from their compatriots" (Knauft 1990:256).[10] In any event, moralistic behavior is a matter of degree and has its own peculiarities in each location and direction in social space. We turn now to some of this variation.

Although extremes of moralism (emphasized above) typically emanate from socially elevated and remote locations, moralism itself does not completely disappear when these conditions are reduced or eliminated. Instead it moderates, growing softer with social equality and warmer with social closeness (see Figure 8.1).

		Social distance	
		Close (warm)	Far (cold)
Vertical direction	Downward (hard)	Paternalistic	Rigid
	Lateral (soft)	Passionate	Reciprocal
	Upward (fluid)	Explosive	Covert

Figure 8.1   Varieties of moralistic behavior.

Social distance influences the warmth of behavior, moralistic or otherwise. The greater the distance, the cooler — less emotional and less positive — it will be ("cold-hearted" vs. "warm-hearted," "cold-blooded" vs. "hot-blooded"). People may be treated as objects, without regard to their well-being, or more personally and supportively. And because it warms the social atmosphere, intimacy reduces the severity of moralism.

The vertical direction of behavior influences its texture. Downward moralism (from a higher to a lower status) is harder — less flexible and less tolerant — than lateral moralism (between equals) or upward moralism (from a lower to a higher status). The greater the inequality between the parties, the harder moralism becomes. The hardest is extremely punitive and makes no exceptions ("hard-hearted" vs. "soft-hearted").[11]

Cold and Hard

The immense distance — vertical and otherwise — between an organization such as a state and a single individual provides ideal conditions for the cooling and hardening of morality (see Bergesen 1977, 1984; Cooney 1988:209–210). When a state acts unilaterally, without courts or trials — and especially when socially and culturally alien officials do so — moralism reaches stupendous levels. Modern governments in parts of Latin America, Africa, and elsewhere kidnap, imprison, torture, rape, mutilate, and kill their enemies (see, e.g., Peters 1985:Chapter 5). After a group of military officers seized power in Argentina, for instance, thousands "disappeared," some covered with cement and thrown into rivers, others pushed from helicopters into the sea (Timerman 1980:50; see also 94–103). Thousands more were imprisoned without trial, beaten, stripped, tortured with electrical devices, and sexually violated — sometimes while close relatives were forced to watch (148). In modern America, police officers may beat, kick, or otherwise humiliate homeless men — those who are socially "down and out" (Reiss 1968; Black 1980:29–32).

Informal organization also heightens the level of moralism. Crowds are known for their ferocious behavior, especially toward lone individuals (see, e.g., Le Bon 1895). In the American South, for example, lynchings were "group dramas in which evil was defeated, good was reinstated" (Wyatt-Brown 1982:458). The person lynched, usually a black, might be tortured and mutilated as well as killed. Consider one Kentucky case in which a crowd seized a black man accused of killing his employer's wife:

Tied to a tree and surrounded by a pile of dry brush, the victim screamed for mercy. His pleas only increased the will of the mob that he should die as painfully and slowly as possible. . . . His eyes had already been burned when an onlooker threw acid in an eggshell into them. Somehow he lived through these ordeals for at least three hours, while the fire, deliberately made to burn slowly, consumed him. (Wyatt-Brown 1982:457)

In Renaissance Europe, peasants might lynch a werewolf — someone thought capable of changing into a wolf and harming innocent people (see Oates 1989).[12] Throughout history, angry crowds have blamed and killed outsiders for misfortunes such as epidemics and accidents (see Girard 1987). Riots illustrate the same tendencies (see, e.g., Rudé 1964; Senechal de la Roche 1990, 1992).[13]

A high degree of social superiority and distance may have similar consequences among individuals. American slaves, for example, were routinely whipped and occasionally mutilated or killed (Fogel and Engerman 1974:144–147; Oakes 1982:159–160; Spindel 1989:133–135). Experts recommended that slaves be whipped "in a coolly calculated manner" and "not . . . in a passion" (Fogel and Engerman 1974:146). For serious infractions, one or two ears might also be nailed to a post and amputated (e.g., Mullin 1972:62; Spindel 1989:134–135). In Brazil, an Achilles tendon might be severed (Patterson 1982:59). Slaves were valuable property and probably were not often executed (Fogel and Engerman 1974:55; Schwarz 1988:15).[14] But runaways might be "outlawed" and subsequently killed:

Outlawing a slave was a legal action, placing the runaway beyond the law, making him a public liability, and encouraging his destruction by any citizen. Those who killed outlaws . . . collected a fee from the public treasury and a reward from the slave's owner. (Mullin 1972:57)

In eighteenth-century Virginia and South Carolina, the written law authorized slaveowners to castrate or otherwise mutilate slaves who repeatedly ran away (Kolchin 1987:285). In ancient Rome, a proverb summarized the nature of the relationship between master and slave: "As many slaves, so many enemies" (quoted in Patterson 1982:339).

Serfs attract cold and hard moralism as well. On nineteenth-century Russian estates, for instance, male serfs were flogged with a birch rod, and half their heads and beards might be shaved as an additional humiliation (Hoch 1986:162, 164; see also Kolchin 1987:Chapter 5). Group floggings were conducted in the fields:

One day in May 1829 one elder, seven drivers, and seventy field peasants were whipped for poor plowing of estate fields. The next month fifty-three serfs were beaten for tilling the buckwheat fields improperly. And on a day in late July four drivers, twenty-eight field peasants with their wives, and twenty-two other males were whipped "for carelessness in the harvest of estate rye." (Hoch 1986:175–176)

Social superiority and distance make enemies, regardless of conduct. Argentina's officers tortured and killed numerous intellectuals — journalists, psychiatrists, sociologists — regardless of the evidence against them (Timerman 1981:98). The Soviets exterminated thousands for having the wrong nationality, religion, or occupation (Solzhenitsyn 1973:Chapter 2). Little evidence supported many American lynchings (Wyatt-Brown 1982:453–454). And, in Europe, werewolves were simply in the wrong place — socially — at the wrong time: Most were vagrants and strangers (Oates 1989). When social conditions are right, enemies will be found.

Now briefly consider unilateral moralism when its social location and direction counteract its fullest development.

Warm and Hard

Intimacy makes moralistic behavior more emotional and forgiving — warmer. Against inferiors, however, it can be firm. Rules are rules, and violations must be punished. Even so, those dealing with intimate inferiors commonly behave paternalistically and ambivalently. Often they are sympathetic ("This hurts me as much as you") and avoid the most severe punishments. Patriarchs, for example, rarely kill their wives or children.

Warm and Soft

Equality encourages flexibility. Intimate equals are unlikely to dictate each other's conduct with explicit rules (see Toulmin 1982). Compromise is common, coercion and punishment rare. They nonetheless behave moralistically from time to time, even to a point of violence. People in the simplest societies — highly egalitarian and intimate among themselves — are notably nonviolent in everyday life, for example, but they occasionally kill each other (Knauft 1987b:1–3; see, e.g., Balikci 1970:Chapter 9; Woodburn 1979; Knauft 1985). So do friends and relatives in modern America (see, e.g., Wolfgang 1958; Lundsgaarde 1977). Most kill "in the heat of passion." Remorseful, some turn the weapon on themselves — an action nearly inconceivable when superiors or strangers eliminate their enemies.

Warm and Fluid

Intimate inferiors such as children, old people, and women in patriarchal households tend to be outwardly tolerant of those on whom they depend for food and shelter. In no position to bargain or negotiate, much less proclaim rules or inflict punishments, these individuals may be the least moralistic of anyone. Yet they sometimes explode with temper tantrums, weeping, and related forms of protest. They may run away, commit suicide, or occasionally even use violence against a superior as well (see, e.g., Jeffreys 1952; Baumgartner 1984:306).

Cold and Fluid

The moralistic behavior of distant inferiors such as slaves and serfs is secretive, often ambiguous or invisible, and difficult to link to those responsible. Foodstuffs and other valuables mysteriously disappear, tools break, fires erupt, tasks take longer than expected, workmanship is poor, and illnesses without external symptoms disable individuals so that they cannot work (Baumgartner 1984a:308–316; see, e.g., Mullin 1972:53–55, 60–61; Owens 1976:Chapter 4; Scott 1985:265–273; Morrill 1989:397–398; Tucker 1989, 1993). Distant inferiors also gossip and grumble (see Merry 1984; Herrmann 1992), make anonymous threats and complaints (see, e.g., Thompson 1975), and run away (Baumgartner 1984a:320–324; see, e.g., Mullin 1972; Blassingame 1979:Chapter 5; Kolchin 1987:278–291). Open and violent rebellion is rare (see, e.g., Owens 1976:Chapter 4; Blassingame 1979:Chapter 5; Kolchin 1987:Chapter 5).[15] But organized inferiors may strike, riot, or otherwise rise up with violence.[16]

Cold and Soft

Equality balances right and wrong. Distant equals are mutually respectful, but also mutually fearful and touchy. This is the realm of vengeance, honor, feuds, and fights (see, e.g., Baldick 1965; Peristiany 1966; Boehm 1984; McGrath 1984; Rieder 1984, 1985:Chapter 6). Here moralistic behavior is reciprocated: Tit meets tat (see Axelrod 1984). And greater social distances bring greater amounts of violence.[17] Weapons vary accordingly. Among the Nuer of the Sudan, for instance, those of the same village fight with clubs, those of different villages with spears (Evans-Pritchard 1940:151; see also Peters 1967:269). Likewise, in the modern world, nuclear weapons are reserved for the longest distances in social space.

MORAL EVOLUTION

Social remoteness and inferiority are repulsive. They attract moralism and make enemies. Whether the behavior of a court, a mob in the street, a slavemaster, or a nation-state, the principle is the same. And moralism is lethal, its highest degree homicidal. Most killings obey its logic: the punishment of evil and the advancement of justice. The same applies to violence and destruction of all kinds, from the beating of children to the bombing of cities.

Moralism arises everywhere — between intimates and strangers, against superiors and subordinates — but social remoteness and inferiority together produce its purest and strongest expressions: the strict enforcement of rules, impersonal and mechanical, cold and hard. Classic moralism thrives on vertical and horizontal distance, the subordination of strangers, a combination only rarely seen in the history of humanity.

The primary mode of human life from the beginning — hunting and gathering — includes no distant inferiors at all (see, e.g., Service 1971). Great relational and cultural distances separate the simplest societies, but without subordination, and they are egalitarian within (see, e.g., Leacock and Lee 1982:Part 1). The subordination of strangers is recent (10 or 15 centuries old) and followed the invention of agriculture, slavery, and states. Moralism is cold and hard when close-knit villagers encounter impoverished strangers such as those identified as werewolves and witches in Europe, and when close-knit elites exert authority over atomized masses (see, e.g., Collins 1974; Gross 1979).

But werewolves and witches have disappeared. The devil has retreated. Classic moralism now flourishes best in non-Western societies dominated by military juntas and religious fundamentalists. The West is softer and warmer.

Western moralism still survives in criminal courts, where inferior strangers face prison or death. But elsewhere the conditions for punishment are waning: Subordination continues in the family and workplace, but it is weakening. Inequality of wealth is moderating. Society is flattening. Evolutionary developments — electronic communications, rapid transportation, social fluidity — are narrowing the distances between everyone (see McLuhan 1964). People are more accessible, culturally and otherwise. The social universe is shrinking.

As all of this occurs, moralism is softening and toleration increasing (see Baumgartner 1988: Chapter 6). Relativism and uncertainty about right and wrong are becoming socially acceptable, even admirable. The population of enemies is declining.

Between societies, however, the social structure of moralism is stronger. Inequality and social distance still divide the international community. Moralistic violence, including mass homicide, continues. Yet the world is evolving into one great society, a culturally homogeneous organism, and cold and hard moralism is losing its foundations. Old hatreds are more difficult to sustain. Enemies are becoming obsolete.

ENDNOTES

*M. P. Baumgartner, Theodore Caplow, Randall Collins, Mark Cooney, John Herrmann, John Griffiths, Calvin Morrill, Roberta Senechal de la Roche, and James Tucker commented on earlier drafts of this chapter.

1. An exception is Albert Einstein's "cosmic repulsion force" that increases with physical distance (and counteracts the attractive force of gravitation) — proposed to explain the stability of the universe and discredited by the discovery that the universe is expanding. But cosmic repulsion has again been proposed to explain the expansion of the universe (see Davies 1984:186–193).

2. Another difference is that physical repulsion operates between similar elements (such as positive or negative charges of electricity) whereas social repulsion operates more strongly between different elements (such as members of different tribes, ethnicities, or nations).

The French sociologist Celestín Bouglé uses a concept of social repulsion to describe the Indian caste system: "The force which animates the whole system of the Hindu world is a force of repulsion which keeps the various bodies separate and drives each one to retire within itself" (1908:22). Although he speaks of "reciprocal repulsion" (27) and "mutual repulsion" (41), Bouglé seems to regard this process partly as a hierarchical and asymmetrical opposition between the "pure" and "impure" elements of Indian society (Dumont 1966:43; see also 197).

3. This section reconceptualizes and extends an earlier analysis of third-party behavior by Black and Baumgartner (1983:especially 113–114).

4. Social inferiors only infrequently interfere in the conflicts of their superiors (Black and Baumgartner 1983:113). Children, for example, may seek to pacify their quarreling parents.

5. In colonial America, a simpler and more intimate society, judges unabashedly handled cases informally and seldom justified their decisions with legal doctrines (Boorstin 1958:199). In one case, for instance, a judge dismissed the importance of a contrary precedent — his own — by remarking that "every tub must stand on its own bottom" (201).

6. Formalism and other dimensions of moralism vary not only with the social location of third parties but more generally across a population. In American courts, for example, litigants of higher status appear to be more rule-oriented than those of lower status, who are more relationship-oriented and personal in their handling of conflict (see Conley and O'Barr 1990:Chapter 4). And American males appear to be more rule-oriented than females (see Gilligan 1982). See also the next section on "Unilateral Moralism."

7. Jerome Frank calls this "juries' prudence" in contrast to "jurisprudence" (1930: Chapter 16).

8. Exceptions arise when simple tribes mobilize for communal hunts, warfare, or other collective action (see, e.g., MacLeod 1937; Black 1976:89–90).

9. Among the Mundurucú, warfare is seemingly pursued for its own sake, as "an essential and unquestioned part of their way of life" (Murphy 1957:1025). It involves no acquisition of territory, defense of territory, vengeance, or any other discernible purpose of an instrumental nature (1026).

10. The solidarity of a group — its overall intimacy — may also increase the tendency of its members to treat outsiders as enemies. This would explain the extreme degree of moralism toward outsiders exhibited by close-knit tribes such as those mentioned above, and its relative absence among less solidary and more fluid tribes of hunter-gatherers such as the Chenchu

of India (Fürer-Haimendorf 1943, 1967:Chapter 1), the Mbuti Pygmies of Zaire (Turnbull 1961, 1965), and the Hadza of Tanzania (Woodburn 1979). It would also explain what M. P. Baumgartner calls the "moral minimalism" of modern suburbia, which she similarly attributes (with different reasoning) to its "culture of weak ties" (1988:90–92).

On the other hand, conflict with outsiders tends to increase the solidarity of a group (Simmel 1908a:Chapter 3; Coser 1956:Chapter 5). The solidarity of a group and moralistic behavior toward outsiders may therefore be mutually reinforcing. We might also speculate that the same tendencies apply to the cultural homogeneity of a group: More homogeneous groups engage in a greater amount of moralistic behavior toward outsiders, while conflict with outsiders itself increases cultural homogeneity (see Simmel 1908a:91–94, 97–98).

11. This classification is interchangeable with the dimensions of third-party behavior discussed earlier. Distant superiors thus behave more formalistically, decisively, coercively, and punitively — whether acting unilaterally or as third parties. And third parties become colder and harder as their social remoteness and superiority increase.

12. It appears, however, that European werewolves were less often lynched than sentenced by courts to be burned at the stake (Oates 1989). The same applied to witches (see, e.g., Macfarlane 1970; Midelfort 1972).

13. Chimpanzees make enemies in much the same pattern as humans. A group will attack a lone member of a neighboring group, biting him severely and possibly castrating or killing him (see de Waal 1989:69–78).

14. It is impossible to know how often American slaves were executed by their owners. The financial loss would have been substantial, but the legal risk was almost nil (see, e.g., Schwarz 1988:52). In North Carolina, for example, the killing of a slave by a white could not be prosecuted as murder until 1774 (Spindel 1989:48).

15. But subordinates may employ violence or deprivation against themselves — such as suicide, self-mutilation, or fasting — to protest the behavior of their superiors (Baumgartner 1984a:317–318, 328–331).

16. Inferiors may also recruit elites to sponsor or prosecute their grievances (Baumgartner 1984a:316–320).

17. In addition to social distance, the elevation of conflict in social space may influence the character of moralistic behavior. Like earthly temperatures, it appears to be colder at higher levels. Social elites thus favor relatively impersonal forms of conflict, whereas those at the bottom of society are inclined to more "hot-blooded" forms. Compare, for instance, the duelling of the planter class to the brawling of the laboring class in the rural South of nineteenth-century America (see Stowe 1979; Williams 1980; Gorn 1985). Or compare adults to children (see Baumgartner 1992b).

Elites also more readily resort to litigation (see Black 1976:Chapters 2–6).

APPENDIX:

A STRATEGY OF
PURE SOCIOLOGY*

Science is the study of variation. Variation is also known as behavior — as in the behavior of matter in physics, of molecules and compounds in chemistry, of plants and animals in biology, and of persons in psychology. Moreover, in its pure form, each branch of science is a study of a particular kind of variation in its own terms. Pure physics ignores chemical and biological variation, for instance, as does pure psychology. Accordingly, sociology is the study of the behavior of social life, and pure sociology is the study of this behavior without regard to biological, psychological, or other variation (compare Ward 1903).

The following pages outline a strategy of pure sociology. The strategy first appeared in a study of law (Black 1976), but it can be applied to other phenomena as well. It takes for granted that social life of every kind is, in principle, measurable as a quantitative variable. It also takes for granted the importance of formulations that predict and explain as much variation as possible, as simply as possible. It does not, however, include a number of assumptions and implications about people as such, and about society as such, now found in social science. It has no concept of human nature, for example. It neither assumes nor implies that people are rational, goal-directed, pleasure-seeking, or pain-avoiding. It has nothing to say about how people experience themselves, their freedom of choice, or the causes of their actions. It does not assume or imply that social life is a system with needs and functions (compare, e.g., Radcliffe-Brown 1935), that it rests on a consensus or tends toward equilibrium (compare, e.g., Parsons 1951), or that conflict, coercion, or change inheres in it (compare, e.g., Dahrendorf 1959:157–165; 1968). It does not assume or imply that society as a whole, or any segment of society, ultimately benefits from any kind of social life. It predicts and explains the behavior of social life, and that is all.

SOCIAL SPACE

A major scientific strategy is to predict behavior with characteristics of the setting in which it occurs. When behavior is successfully deduced from a general proposition, this may be understood as explanation (see, e.g., Braithwaite 1953; Hempel 1965; Homans 1967: Chapter 1). Behavior can be predicted and explained with every aspect of its environment, that is, with its location and direction in space, whether physical, biological, or psychological, past or present. The distance of a falling object from the earth predicts and explains its velocity, for example; temperature and pressure predict and explain the volume of a gas; conditions for reproduction predict and explain the population of a species; and the training of a child predicts and explains his or her personality as an adult. This strategy has been followed in the study of social life as well, but for the most part implicitly if not unconsciously, without its own program, imagery, concepts, and questions.

Social life is a reality in its own right, a multidimensional space with locations, directions, and distances defined by human interaction itself. Social space includes vertical, horizontal, symbolic, corporate, and normative dimensions. Each differs from one setting to another, from an encounter between two persons to a family or organization, from a workplace to a neighborhood, community, or society. And each predicts and explains the behavior of social life.

Vertical Space

A vertical dimension of social space is present when there is an uneven distribution of wealth, or social stratification. Behavior of any kind may be described by its vertical location, whether higher or lower in such a distribution. Is there more crime higher up or lower, for instance, or more religion, friendship, or sport? A social phenomenon may also have a vertical direction, moving downward from a higher to a lower elevation or upward from a lower to a higher elevation. A crime may be upward or downward, for example, as may a gift, vote, request, or complaint. The difference in wealth itself, or vertical distance, varies as well. Whether higher or lower in a distribution of wealth, or downward or upward in its direction, a crime may span a greater or lesser distance in vertical space. The vertical dimension of social space also has other variable features, such as the shape of a distribution of wealth, its origin, degree of segmentation, range, stability, and age.

Horizontal Space

The horizontal dimension of social space arises from the distribution of people in relation to each other, or social morphology. It includes any division of labor, or differentiation, and also the pattern by which people participate in social life by working, raising children, or simply by conversing with their neighbors. Every activity is a circle of participation, with people closer or further from the center, and accordingly every social phenomenon has a radial location. It may likewise have a radial direction, moving centripetally or centrifugally, inward or outward from the center, as when a marginal person complains about someone more integrated, or vice versa. The difference in integration, or radial distance, varies as well. Another feature of horizontal space is the structure of intimacy — the relational distance among and between everyone — measured by the degree to which they participate in each other's lives, including the scope of their interaction, its frequency, duration, and their linkages in a wider network.

Symbolic Space

The symbolic dimension of social space refers to the expressive aspect of social life, or culture, whether aesthetic, intellectual, or moral. It includes arts, ideas, values, ideologies, religions, languages, and ceremonies. The quantity of culture is unevenly distributed, and social life varies with its location and direction in this distribution, and with the cultural distance that might be involved. Culture is also more or less conventional, measured by its relative frequency. Again a direction and distance might be involved — from more to less conventionality or from less to more — as when a member of the cultural mainstream victimizes or votes for an ethnic, or vice versa. Still another feature of symbolic space is its content, apart from its quantity or frequency. A difference in the content of culture is another kind of cultural distance. A Hindu is thus more distant from a Protestant or Catholic than is either of the latter from each other. There may also be an aesthetic, intellectual, or linguistic distance, even a culinary or musical distance, every expression of culture closer or further from the next.

Corporate Space

The corporate dimension of social space is the capacity for collective action, or organization. The quantity of organization varies across social settings — some centralized to a point of autocracy, others democratic; some dominated by groups, others by individuals on their own. And social life may have a direction from more to less organization or from less to more. A group might help or injure an individual, for instance, and vice versa, and the more organized the group, the more organizational distance this involves. Corporate space takes diverse forms — groups within groups, overlapping memberships, alliances between one group and another — and the population of groups expands and contracts.

Normative Space

Yet another dimension of social space results from the operation of social control, any process that defines and responds to deviant behavior. The quantity of social control varies across settings of all kinds — many conflicts, complaints, and punishments in some, few in others — and social life varies accordingly. And different varieties of social control — such as law, psychotherapy, and vengeance — have different styles: penal, compensatory, therapeutic, or conciliatory. In addition, the capacity for social control — authority — is unevenly distributed in hierarchies. A social phenomenon may therefore be described by its location and direction in hierarchical space. Normative space also bends backward in time and includes the respectability of individuals and groups: the degree to which they have been subject to social control in the past. Some have long records of more or less serious forms of deviant behavior; others have reputations entirely unblemished. Behavior is distributed unevenly in this space of respectability.

A Note on Status

The location of a person or group in social space, seen in relation to others, is a status (see Parsons 1951:25). People have a status in vertical space measured by their wealth, a radial status measured by their participation in social life, a normative status measured by the social control to which they have been subject, and so on. One person might have more vertical but less radial or normative status than another, for example, more cultural or organizational status, or some other combination. Moreover, all these together may be combined and compared, so that one individual or group may have, overall, more or less social status than another (see, e.g.,

Baumgartner 1978). Strictly speaking, a biological characteristic such as age, sex, or race is not a social status, since it is not itself a location in social space. Even so, biological characteristics sometimes correspond to one or more social locations and may serve as crude indicators of social status for practical purposes.

THE BEHAVIOR OF SOCIAL LIFE

Pure sociology predicts and explains the behavior of social life with its location and direction in social space. A tradition of social theory corresponds to each dimension of social space, and the importance of each has long been established in sociology and related fields such as anthropology and political science. The strategy of pure sociology outlined here incorporates all of these traditions, keeping what is valuable in each, discarding their peculiarities, and showing how they contribute to a single body of theory.

At least since Tocqueville (1840) and Marx and Engels (1846), for example, social variation has been understood with its location and direction in vertical space. Since Spencer (1876), Durkheim (1893), and Simmel (1908b), the horizontal dimension of social space has been given prominence, whether the division of labor, patterns of social participation, or the structure of intimacy. Among others, Hegel (1821) and Sorokin (1937) emphasized the symbolic dimension, Michels (1911) and Weber (1922) the corporate dimension, and Ross (1901) and Sumner (1906) the normative dimension. Self-consciously or not, much recent theory follows these traditions by seeking to predict and explain social variation with one or more aspects of a single dimension of social space, such as networks of interaction (Bott 1957; Mitchell 1969), the distribution of authority (Dahrendorf 1959), or the structure of group life (Swanson 1971; Smith 1974). Other theory includes variables from any and all these traditions, taking the world as it is and working up from the facts (e.g., Glaser and Strauss 1967; Stinchcombe 1968). Eclecticism is a tradition of its own.

Sociology and related fields polarize between these extremes of one-dimensional theory and eclectic theory, the former often elegant, simple, and general but weak in its ability to predict and explain variation, the latter often powerful but arbitrary in design, complicated, and narrow. Our strategy of pure sociology — with its multidimensional model of social space — is intended to transcend these extremes and to have the best of both. Consider a few examples.

The Behavior of Law

Pure sociology asks how law varies with its location and direction in social space (see generally Black 1976). Law is governmental social control (Black 1972:1096), whether an arrest, a lawsuit, a judgment on behalf of a plaintiff, a punishment, or an award of compensation. It includes litigation and adjudication of every kind. Moreover, law is a quantitative variable measurable everywhere, from a single case to the evolution of society over the centuries. We can describe every setting in the language of social space, and predict and explain the quantity of law accordingly.

We can specify how law varies with its location and direction in vertical space, for instance, whether it increases or decreases with the wealth of the parties, and whether it is greater in an upward than a downward direction, from less to more wealth or from more to less. In fact, the quantity of law apparently increases with its vertical elevation. This means that a dispute between wealthy people is more likely to result in litigation than a dispute between poor people (see, e.g., Mayhew and Reiss 1969). It also means that a wealthy person injuring someone equally wealthy is more serious than a poor person injuring someone equally poor: A conviction is more likely, for example, as is a severe punishment (e.g., Johnson 1941; Myrdal 1944:550–555). If the injury is accidental, a wealthier victim is likely to be awarded more compensation. In every way, law defines the well-being of wealthier people as more important. Downward law is also greater than upward law. This means that if one party is wealthier, he or she has an advantage at every stage of the legal process. A poor person offending a wealthier person is more serious than an offense in the opposite direction (e.g., Johnson 1941; Garfinkel 1949). And the greater the difference in wealth, the more downward law increases and upward law decreases. Law therefore varies directly with the wealth of the victim and inversely with the wealth of the offender. Lastly, law varies directly with stratification itself: Societies and communities with more inequality of wealth have more law as well (see Engels 1884:Chapter 9; Fried 1967).

The style of law is similarly predictable. Downward law is more penal than upward law, for instance, and the conciliatory style decreases as stratification increases. Law varies with its location and direction along every dimension of social space — vertical, horizontal, symbolic, corporate, and normative. It varies directly with status of every kind. It is greater from more to less status than from less to more, increasing with social distance in the former, decreasing in the latter. Its relationship to cultural and relational distance is curvilinear: The least law occurs at the extremes (e.g., Black 1970:740–741; 1971:1097–1098). It varies directly with organization (e.g., Wittfogel 1957:Chapters 3–7; Bergesen 1977). It varies with the quantity of culture, the division of labor, and other social control. This strategy also applies to social control of other kinds, such as morality, the treatment of mental illness, and the accusation of witchcraft.

Since social control defines deviant behavior, the theory of social control paradoxically predicts and explains the rate of deviant behavior as well. Since crime is conduct that is subject to criminal law, for example, the location and direction of criminal law generates the rate of crime itself (see Kitsuse and Cicourel 1963; Black 1970). The theory of law therefore implies the same facts as the theory of crime. For instance, deprivation theory predicts that a poor person is more likely than a wealthier person to commit a crime (e.g., Bonger 1916:Part 2, Book 2, Chapters 1–2; Merton 1938), and the facts support this prediction (see, e.g., Sutherland and Cressey 1960:189–193). But the theory of law predicts the same facts: Law varies inversely with the wealth of the offender. The same applies to the facts predicted by other theories of deviant behavior, such as marginality theory (e.g., Hirschi 1969), subcultural theory (e.g., Miller 1958), and labeling theory (e.g., Lemert 1967). The theory of law predicts the same facts as every successful theory of deviant behavior, but explains them with a completely different logic.

The Behavior of Medicine

Just as social control defines and responds to deviant behavior, medicine defines and responds to illness, injury, and related problems (compare Parsons 1958; Freidson 1970:Chapters 10, 12). It defines who needs care and treatment and how much is needed in each case. It is found in every society and is possible in every setting, whether a family, a friendship, or among strangers. It may be folklore practiced by anyone, or the responsibility of an expert such as a shaman or physician.

Medicine is a quantitative variable. Its magnitude depends on whether a particular condition is defined as a problem and, if so, how much attention is provided — diagnostic, therapeutic, or convalescent. In a modern society, for instance, a person may receive more or less professional attention; from a specialist or only a general practitioner; as an emergency or not; with or without drugs, surgery, or other techniques; in or out of a hospital; with or without intensive care; for a longer or a shorter period of time. The greater the attention in each case — whether by admission to a hospital or other medical setting, application of the latest techniques, by physicians, nurses, or anyone else — the greater is the quantity of medicine. And medicine varies with its location and direction in social space. It varies across and within societies and communities, up and down the distribution of wealth, across networks of interaction, from one subculture to another. No expense is spared for some; others are ignored.

Medicine varies directly with the status of the patient, for example, with his or her wealth, integration, education, and respectability (see, e.g., Duff and Hollingshead 1968:Chapters 7–9, 11; Richardson 1969; Bice, Eichhorn, and Fox 1972; McKinlay 1975; Roth 1975). But it varies inversely with the relational and cultural distance between the patient and whoever might provide help (see Freidson 1970:Chapter 13). In addition, professional medicine varies inversely with folk medicine. This applies not only to the evolution of medicine over the centuries, but also from one case to another. The more care and treatment a person receives at home, for instance, the less likely is a visit to a physician. Those who live alone, the unmarried and widowed, are therefore more likely to see a physician. Similarly, where women care for men more than men care for women, women are more likely to seek professional help (see, e.g., Andersen and Anderson 1967:Chapter 2).

Those who receive more help are also more likely to ask for it in the first place. Accordingly, just as people of higher status are more likely to receive medical care, so they are more likely to define themselves as sick or injured. Their associates are more likely to urge them to see a professional, and they are more likely to follow this advice (see, e.g., McKinlay 1975). People of higher status seek and receive more preventive medicine such as physical examinations and immunizations (e.g., Moody and Gray 1972; Coburn and Pope 1974), and more cosmetic medicine such as plastic surgery and dentistry for the sake of appearance (e.g., Koos 1954:Chapter 8). And they have higher standards of public health (see Simmons 1958:Chapter 4). The same formulations predict and explain all of this.

It might seem that medicine varies not only with its location and direction in social space but also with who needs it — who is sick or injured, and how seriously. But who needs help is an evaluation, not a question of fact (compare, e.g., Mechanic 1968:141–142). Just as science can tell us only who is subject to social control, not who deserves to be, so it can tell us only who is defined and treated as sick or injured, not who ought to be. Who needs medicine is a question for medicine itself, not science.

The Behavior of Ideas

An idea is a statement about the nature of reality. It is a statement of fact, of what is the case, and not of value or emotion. It may appear in any setting, whether religious, scientific, political, or sociable. It may be recognized as true or false, important or not. Every idea thus has a life of its own, with more or less success.

An idea is a quantitative variable, its magnitude a matter of its contribution to knowledge — its truth and importance — measured by how people define and respond to it. The reception of an idea may be informal, as in a round of applause or the nodding of a head, or more formal, as in the acceptance of a manuscript for publication, its citation in an article or book, or an honorific award bestowed on its author. People may relate to an idea as true but unimportant, as may occur at a party or other sociable gathering (compare Simmel 1908b:112–113), or even significant but false, as may occur in a book review or other publication in the scientific literature. In any setting, then, the success of an idea is measured by the recognition it receives. Ideas also vary in their content, by whether they are theoretical or practical, for example, or supernatural, metaphysical, or empirical (see Comte 1830:1–8).

Pure sociology predicts and explains the behavior of ideas with their location and direction in social space. It is possible, for instance, to predict and explain the success of an idea with the social location of its source and audience: A downward idea (that moves from more to less status) is more likely to succeed than an upward idea (that moves from less to more status). The greater the status difference between the source and the audience, the greater is this variation. Accordingly, the success of an idea varies directly with the status of its source and inversely with the status of its audience. The higher the status of a scientist, for example, the more likely are his or her ideas to be recognized and rewarded. If two scientists co-author a paper or make the same discovery at the same time, the one with more status prior to the event is more likely to receive credit for it (Merton 1968). And the higher the status of a scientist, the more likely is publication, citation, and other recognition of his or her work (see, e.g., Crane 1967; Allison and Stewart 1974; compare Cole and Cole 1973). Scientists may therefore have difficulty winning recognition in their early years, even while they do the work for which they are later celebrated (see, e.g., Manniche and Falk 1957). But the chances of a younger scientist improve when a more eminent colleague steps forth as his or her sponsor. This raises the social elevation of the work. Sponsorship is itself a form of recognition, however, predictable from such variables as the relational distance between those involved and the degree to which the younger scientist is otherwise well-connected, conventional, and respectable.

These tendencies appear not only in science but everywhere that people make statements about the nature of reality. Among the members of a jury, for instance, those of higher status have more influence on the verdict (Strodtbeck, James, and Hawkins 1957). In a factory, even one formally run by the workers, white-collar employees enjoy more credibility (e.g., Obradović 1972). In politics, an organized faction is more likely to win acceptance of its programs and proposals (e.g., Gamson 1975:Chapter 7). In conversation, an adult's remarks are taken as more important than a child's, a man's as more important than a woman's, a white's as more important than a black's (see, e.g., West and Zimmerman 1977). Everywhere, people of higher status are defined as more intelligent, and whatever they say is recognized as more useful and interesting. Over time, ideas rise and fall with the status of their proponents (see Mannheim 1927), and in every epoch the ruling ideas are the ideas of the ruling class (Marx and Engels 1846:39).

The success of an idea also varies inversely with the relational distance between its source and audience. The more intimate people are, the more valuable they find each other's ideas. In science, for instance, the recognition of ideas is concentrated within networks of acquaintances, or "invisible colleges" (see Price 1963:Chapter 3; Crane 1972; Kadushin 1976). In medicine, physicians are more likely to adopt new drugs when they are recommended by friends or colleagues (Coleman, Katz, and Menzel 1966:Chapters 6–9). Among the public at large, ideas of all kinds follow a "two-step flow," from informal leaders to their intimates, such as relatives, friends, and neighbors (Katz and Lazarsfeld 1955). Relational distance explains why students prefer seminars — both the teachers and subject matter — to larger classes such as lectures, and why teachers give better grades to smaller classes and to students they know more intimately. New ideas are more successful in small groups (see Mead 1964:Chapter 8). And the longer people know each other, the more they share a view of the world and agree about everything (see, e.g., Berger and Kellner 1964). Conversely, people renounce old beliefs as their old relationships come apart and, especially when unattached and adrift, embrace new beliefs as they find new relationships (see Lofland and Stark 1965).

It might be added that the importance of an idea — including its truth — is not a matter of fact. Its importance is only knowable, sociologically, by its reception. For example, the importance of a scientific idea can only be evaluated by the participants. To claim otherwise — or even to endorse the consensus of the scientists — is to participate in the scientific evaluation itself. Thus, from an observer's standpoint, how well a scientific theory orders facts is not an empirical question and cannot explain the success of the theory (compare, e.g., Kuhn 1970). Nor can the quality of their work explain the careers of scientists (compare Cole and Cole 1973). Nowhere can the truth of an idea sociologically explain its success. Like the seriousness of deviant behavior or the need for medicine, a contribution to knowledge is a question of value, not fact. The same applies to the beauty of art.

The Behavior of Art

Art is a creation defined as beautiful and worthy of appreciation. It might include music, dance, literature, painting, sculpture, photography, architecture, furniture or other interior decoration, clothing or other body adornment, or the preparation and presentation of food. People may do anything more or less artistically. But this is a matter of taste, not fact (compare, e.g., Shils 1960; Jaeger and Selznick 1964; Adorno 1968).

It is possible to measure the degree to which people define and respond to any creation as artistic — beautiful and worthy of appreciation (see Gray 1966). In this sense, art is a quantitative variable. The degree of appreciation might range from a word of praise to acquisition, private display, or even display in a museum. If acquired, its price is a measure of appreciation as well. If a performance, attendance might be more or less costly for the audience, and the performers might receive more or less compensation. Although neither the essence of art nor its importance is a matter of fact, the artistic success of any creation can thus be measured in quantitative terms. And this varies with its location and direction in social space.

For example, the success of art varies directly with the status of its patrons. This means that, in a modern society, the work appreciated by wealthier and more educated people is more likely to be recognized as genuine art, and the best of its genre. It is more likely to be exhibited in museums, staged in concert halls, studied in universities, and praised in the mass media. It is more likely to be classified as fine art rather than popular art, high culture rather than mass culture or low culture (e.g., Gans 1974), and superior or refined culture rather than mediocre or brutal culture (Shils 1960; see also Shils 1957). The literature, music, and movies appreciated by people of higher status are defined as more serious, their food as *haute cuisine*, their clothing as *haute couture*. In everything, their taste is considered better.

Among themselves, however, the people of each social location commonly have their own taste. In modern America, for instance, taste varies not only between social classes but also between ethnicities, generations, genders, and other groups and aggregates. It may therefore seem that questions of aesthetics are different from, say, questions of science, where there is more consensus about what is important. It may seem that the quality of scientific work is more obvious. But this is only because people from so many different locations in social space participate in the evaluation of art, whereas in science this is not the case. What is a good book or movie is a question addressed by practically everyone, not merely by a small number of similar people such as those who evaluate the work in a specialized branch of science. In every field of endeavor, the degree of consensus varies inversely with the range of social locations involved in the process of evaluation. The degree of consensus also varies inversely with the relational and cultural distance among and between those involved. This is why the people of a simple tribe or village agree so much about everything, and about beauty as much as truth. The same applies to the many enclaves and subcultures of a modern society, such as families, friendship circles, colleagues, and cliques. Disagreements do not arise because art or anything else is inherently difficult to evaluate, but because of the social structure of evaluation itself.

Pure sociology also predicts and explains the form and content of art. It is possible to predict and explain the varieties of art found across societies (see, e.g., Kroeber 1944:Chapters 5–9, 11; Gray 1972) and across the settings of a single society (see, e.g., Ridgeway 1976). Some people have more music or more visual or literary art, and the particular expressions of each vary as well. In the case of music, for example, the lyrics, rhythm, harmony, and instrumentation vary directly in their complexity with the stratification of a society (Lomax 1968). In dance, the number of body parts employed varies directly with social stratification as well (Lomax, Bartenieff, and Paulay 1968). We can likewise understand aesthetic variation across history. Thus, as simple societies become more complex, so does their music, dance, and design. But in some respects modern art resembles the art of the earliest and simplest societies. Some of modern painting and sculpture is reminiscent of tribal art, for instance, even prehistoric drawings on the walls of caves (see Giedion 1956; McLuhan and Parker 1968:197, 209). Much of modern and tribal art is, for example, similarly abstract. Perhaps this is because modern societies are evolving toward a social structure with characteristics partially resembling the simplest societies in human history (see Black 1976:Chapter 7; see also McLuhan 1964; Douglas 1973:Chapter 4). In any event, art is orderly and subject to pure sociology.

CONCLUSION

Pure sociology is the study of social variation in its own terms. It predicts and explains the behavior of social life with its location and direction in the multidimensional space of human interaction, including vertical, horizontal, symbolic, corporate, and normative space. Moreover, it does so without regard to individuals as such. We can understand deviant behavior as the distribution of social control, for example, the use of health services as the distribution of medicine, intellectual and aesthetic achievement as the distribution of ideas and art. We can understand the attainment and loss of social status as the distribution of various locations in social space. What has always been seen as the behavior of persons may thus be seen as the behavior of social life itself (compare, e.g., Winch 1958; Homans 1964). Every kind of social life is a quantitative variable, with greater or lesser amounts from one social location or direction to another. Every kind is a matter of degree, like heat or sound or light.

Our strategy of pure sociology is a synthesis of earlier traditions, designed to be as elegant, simple, and general as each, and as powerful as all together. It also has its own conception of social reality and its own logic. But it is forever ready to change, to include dimensions of social space now unseen, new locations and directions, undiscovered principles, unknown implications. It has possibilities without end.

ENDNOTE

*Reprinted with permission (and minor revision) from pages 149–168 in *Theoretical Perspectives in Sociology*, edited by Scott G. McNall. New York: St. Martin's Press, 1979.

This essay was originally presented at the annual meeting of the American Sociological Association, San Francisco, California, September, 1978. For commenting on an earlier draft, I thank M. P. Baumgartner, Herbert L. Costner, George Farkas, Allan Horwitz, Arthur G. Lindsay, Scott G. McNall, W. Russell Neuman, and Frank Romo.

References

Abbott, Jack Henry
    1981   *In the Belly of the Beast: Letters from Prison*. New York: Vintage Books, 1982.
Abel, Richard L.
    1974   "A comparative theory of dispute institutions in society." *Law and Society Review* 8: 217–347.
    1979   "Western courts in non-Western settings: patterns of court use in colonial and neo-colonial Africa." Pages 167–200 in *The Imposition of Law*, edited by Sandra B. Burman and Barbara E. Harrell-Bond. New York: Academic Press.
Addiss, Penny
    1980   "The life history complaint case of Martha and George Rose: 'honoring the warranty.'" Pages 171–189 in *No Access to Law: Alternatives to the American Judicial System*, edited by Laura Nader. New York: Academic Press.
Adorno, Theodor W.
    1968   *Introduction to the Sociology of Music*. New York: Seabury Press, 1976 (second edition; first edition, 1962).
Allen, John
    1977   *Assault with a Deadly Weapon: The Autobiography of a Street Criminal*, edited by Dianne Hall Kelly and Philip Heymann. New York: McGraw-Hill.
Allison, Paul D., and John A. Stewart
    1974   "Productivity differences among scientists: evidence for accumulative advantage." *American Sociological Review* 39: 596–606.
Alschuler, Albert W.
    1968   "The prosecutor's role in plea bargaining." *University of Chicago Law Review* 36: 50–112.
    1979   "Plea bargaining and its history." *Law and Society Review* 13: 211-245.

Andenaes, Johannes
    1966   "The general preventive effects of punishment." *University of Pennsylvania Law Review* 114: 949–983.

Andersen, Ronald, and Odin W. Anderson
    1967   *A Decade of Health Services: Social Survey Trends in Use and Expenditure*. Chicago: University of Chicago Press.

Andrew, Donna T.
    1980   "The code of honour and its critics: the opposition to duelling in England, 1700–1850." *Social History* 5: 409–434.

Arendt, Hannah
    1958   *The Origins of Totalitarianism*. Cleveland: World Publishing Company (second edition; first edition, 1951).
    1969   *On Violence*. New York: Harcourt, Brace & World.

Aubert, Vilhelm (editor)
    1969   *Sociology of Law: Selected Readings*. Baltimore: Penguin Books.

Australian Law Reform Commission
    1980   *Aboriginal Customary Law — Recognition?* Discussion Paper 17. Sydney: Law Reform Commission.

Axelrod, Robert
    1984   *The Evolution of Cooperation*. New York: Basic Books.

Ayers, Edward L.
    1984   *Vengeance and Justice: Crime and Punishment in the 19th-Century American South*. New York: Oxford University Press.

Ayoub, Victor F.
    1965   "Conflict resolution and social reorganization in a Lebanese village." *Human Organization* 24: 11–17.

Bailey, F. G.
    1969   *Strategems and Spoils: A Social Anthropology of Politics*. New York: Schocken.

Balbus, Isaac D.
    1973   *The Dialectics of Legal Repression: Black Rebels before the American Criminal Courts*. New York: Russell Sage Foundation.

Baldick, Robert
    1965   *The Duel: A History of Duelling*. London: Chapman & Hall.

Balikci, Asen
    1970   *The Netsilik Eskimo*. Garden City: Natural History Press.

Bard, Morton, and Joseph Zacker
    1976   *The Police and Interpersonal Conflict: Third-Party Intervention Approaches*. Washington, D. C.: Police Foundation.

Barry, Donald D., and Harold J. Berman
    1968   "The Soviet legal profession." *Harvard Law Review* 82: 1–41.

Bar-Tal, Daniel
    1976   *Prosocial Behavior: Theory and Research*. Washington, D.C.: Hemisphere.

Barth, Fredrik
    1959   *Political Leadership among Swat Pathans*. London: Athlone Press.

Barton, Roy Franklin
    1919   *Ifugao Law*. Berkeley: University of California Press, 1969.

Bateson, Gregory
    1958   *Naven: A Survey of the Problems Suggested by a Composite Picture of the Culture of a New Guinea Tribe Drawn from Three Points of View*. Stanford: Stanford University Press (second edition; first edition, 1936).

Baumgartner, M. P.

1978 "Law and social status in colonial New Haven, 1639–1665." Pages 153–178 in *Research in Law and Sociology: An Annual Compilation of Research*, Vol. 1, edited by Rita J. Simon. Greenwich: JAI Press.

1981 Social Control in a Surburban Town: An Ethnographic Study. Unpublished doctoral dissertation, Department of Sociology, Yale University.

1984a "Social control from below." Pages 303–345 in *Toward a General Theory of Social Control*, Volume 1: *Fundamentals*, edited by Donald Black. Orlando: Academic Press.

1984b "Social control in suburbia." Pages 79–103 in *Toward a General Theory of Social Control*, Volume 2: *Selected Problems*, edited by Donald Black. Orlando: Academic Press.

1985 "Law and the middle class: evidence from a suburban town." *Law and Human Behavior* 9: 3–24.

1988 *The Moral Order of a Suburb*. New York: Oxford University Press.

1992a "Violent networks: the origins and management of domestic conflict." 209–231 in *Violence and Aggression: The Social Interactionist Perspective*, edited by Richard B. Felson and James Tedeschi. Washington, D.C.: American Psychological Association.

1992b "War and peace in early childhood." Pages 1–38 in *Virginia Review of Sociology*, Volume 1: *Law and Conflict Management*, edited by James Tucker. Greenwich: JAI Press.

Baxter, P. T. W.

1972 "Absence makes the heart grow fonder: some suggestions why witchcraft accusations are rare among East African pastoralists." Pages 163–191 in *The Allocation of Responsibility*, edited by Max Gluckman. Manchester: Manchester University Press.

Beattie, J. H. M.

1971 " 'Cutting kinship' in Bunyoro." *Ethnology* 10: 211–214.

Becker, Howard S.

1963 *Outsiders: Studies in the Sociology of Deviance*. New York: Free Press.

Beidelman, T. O.

1966 "Intertribal tensions in some local government courts in colonial Tanganyika: I." *Journal of African Law* 10: 118–130.

1967 "Intertribal tensions in some local government courts in colonial Tanganyika: II." *Journal of African Law* 11: 27–45.

Berger, Peter, Brigitte Berger, and Hansfried Kellner

1973 *The Homeless Mind: Modernization and Consciousness*. New York: Random House.

Berger, Peter, and Hansfried Kellner

1964 "Marriage and the construction of reality: an exercise in the microsociology of knowledge." *Diogenes* 46: 1–25.

Berger, Raoul

1940a "From hostage to contract: part 1." *Illinois Law Review* 35: 154–174.

1940b "From hostage to contract: part 2." *Illinois Law Review* 35: 281–292.

Bergesen, Albert

1977 "Political witch-hunts: the sacred and the subversive in cross-national perspective." *American Sociological Review* 42: 220–233.

1984 "Social control and corporate organization: a Durkheimian perspective." Pages 141–170 in *Toward a General Theory of Social Control*, Volume 2: *Selected Problems*, edited by Donald Black. Orlando: Academic Press.

Berman, Harold J.
1978 "The background of the Western legal tradition in the folklaw of the peoples of Europe." *University of Chicago Law Review* 45: 553–597.

Berman, Jesse
1969 "The Cuban popular tribunals." *Columbia Law Review* 69: 1318–1354.

Bice, Thomas W., Robert L. Eichhorn, and Peter D. Fox
1972 "Socioeconomic status and use of physician services: a reconsideration." *Medical Care* 10: 261–271.

Biderman, Albert D.
1967 "Surveys of population samples for estimating crime incidence." *The Annals of the American Academy of Political and Social Science* 374: 16–33.

Bittner, Egon
1967 "The police on skid-row: a study of peace keeping." *American Sociological Review* 32: 699–715.

1967 "Police discretion in emergency apprehension of mentally ill persons." *Social Problems* 14: 278–292.

Black, Donald
1970 "Production of crime rates." *American Sociological Review* 35: 733–748.

1971 "The social organization of arrest." *Stanford Law Review* 23: 1087–1111.

1972 "The boundaries of legal sociology." *Yale Law Journal* 81: 1086–1100.

1973 "The mobilization of law." *Journal of Legal Studies* 2: 125–149.

1976 *The Behavior of Law.* New York: Academic Press.

1979a "A note on the measurement of law." *Informationsbrief für Rechtssoziologie*, Sonderheft 2: 92–106 (reprinted in *The Manners and Customs of the Police*, by Donald Black. New York: Academic Press, 1980).

1979b "A strategy of pure sociology." Pages 149–168 in *Theoretical Perspectives in Sociology*, edited by Scott G. McNall. New York: St. Martin's Press (*reprinted as Appendix to the present volume*).

1980 *The Manners and Customs of the Police.* New York: Academic Press.

1983 "Crime as social control." *American Sociological Review* 48: 34–45. Longer version: Pages 1–27 in *Toward a General Theory of Social Control*, Volume 2: *Selected Problems*, edited by Donald Black. Orlando: Academic Press, 1984 (*reprinted as Chapter 2 of the present volume*).

1984a "Jurocracy in America." *The Tocqueville Review — La Revue Tocqueville* 6: 273–281.

1984b "Social control as a dependent variable." Pages 1–36 in *Toward a General Theory of Social Control*, Volume 1: *Fundamentals*, edited by Donald Black. Orlando: Academic Press (*reprinted as Chapter 1 of the present volume*).

(editor)
1984c *Toward a General Theory of Social Control.* Volume 1: *Fundamentals*; Volume 2: *Selected Problems.* Orlando: Academic Press.

1987a "Compensation and the social structure of misfortune." *Law and Society Review* 21: 563–584 (*reprinted as Chapter 3 of the present volume*).

1987b "A note on the sociology of Islamic law." Pages 47–62 in *Perspectives on Islamic Law, Justice and Society*, edited by R. S. Khare. Charlottesville: Center for Advanced Studies, University of Virginia.

1989 *Sociological Justice.* New York: Oxford University Press.

1990 "The elementary forms of conflict management." Pages 43–69 in *New Directions in the Study of Justice, Law, and Social Control*, prepared by the School of Justice Studies, Arizona State University. New York: Plenum Press (*reprinted as Chapter 5 of the present volume*).

1992 "Social control of the self." Pages 39–49 in *Virginia Review of Sociology*, Volume 1: *Law and Conflict Management*, edited by James Tucker. Greenwich: JAI Press (*reprinted as Chapter 4 of the present volume*).

Black, Donald, and M. P. Baumgartner

1980 "On self-help in modern society." Pages 193–208 in *The Manners and Customs of the Police*, by Donald Black. New York: Academic Press.

1983 "Toward a theory of the third party." Pages 84–114 in *Empirical Theories about Courts*, edited by Keith O. Boyum and Lynn Mather. New York: Longman (*reprinted as Chapter 6 of the present volume*).

Black, Donald, and Maureen Mileski (editors)

1973 *The Social Organization of Law*. New York: Academic Press.

Black, Robert A.

1967 "Hopi grievance chants: a mechanism of social control." Pages 54–67 in *Studies in Southwestern Ethnolinguistics: Meaning and History in the Languages of the American Southwest*, edited by Dell H. Hymes and William E. Bittle. The Hague: Mouton.

Black-Michaud, Jacob

1975 *Cohesive Force: Feud in the Mediterranean and the Middle East*. Oxford: Basil Blackwell.

Blassingame, John W.

1979 *The Slave Community: Plantation Life in the Antebellum South*. New York: Oxford University Press (revised and enlarged edition; first edition, 1972).

Bloch, Maurice

1939 *Feudal Society*. Volume 1: *The Growth of Ties of Dependence*. Chicago: University of Chicago Press, 1964.

1940 *Feudal Society*. Volume 2: *Social Classes and Political Organization*. Chicago: University of Chicago Press, 1964.

Block, Richard

1974 "Why notify the police: the victim's decision to notify the police of an assault." *Criminology* 11: 555–569.

Blok, Anton

1974 *The Mafia of a Sicilian Village, 1860–1960: A Study of Violent Peasant Entrepreneurs*. New York: Harper & Row.

Boehm, Christopher

1984 *Blood Revenge: The Enactment and Management of Conflict in Montenegro and Other Tribal Societies*. Philadelphia: University of Pennsylvania Press, 1987.

Bohannan, Paul

1957 *Justice and Judgment among the Tiv*. London: Oxford University Press.

1960 "Patterns of murder and suicide." Pages 230–266 in *African Homicide and Suicide*, edited by Paul Bohannan. Princeton: Princeton University Press.

(editor)

1967 *Law and Warfare: Studies in the Anthropology of Conflict*. Garden City: Natural History Press.

Bolton, Ralph

1970 "Rates and ramifications of violence: notes on Qolla homicide." Paper presented at the International Congress of Americanists, Lima, Peru, August, 1970.

1973 "Aggression and hypoglycemia among the Qolla: a study in psychobiological anthropology." *Ethnology* 12: 227–257.

1974 "To kill a thief: a Kallawaya sorcery session in the Lake Titicaca region of Peru." *Anthropos* 69: 191–215.

Bolton, Ralph, and Charlene Bolton
    1973   "Domestic quarrels among the Qolla." Paper presented at the annual meeting
           of the American Anthropological Association, New Orleans, Louisiana, Octo-
           ber, 1973 (published in Spanish as *Conflictos en la Familia Andina*. Cuzco: Centro
           de Estudios Andinos, 1975).

Bonger, William Adrian
    1916   *Criminality and Economic Conditions*. Boston: Little, Brown.

Boorstin, Daniel J.
    1958   *The Americans: The Colonial Experience*. New York: Random House.

Boswell, John
    1980   *Christianity, Social Tolerance, and Homosexuality: Gay People in Western Europe from
           the Beginning of the Christian Era to the Fourteenth Century*. Chicago: University of
           Chicago Press.

Botein, Stephen
    1981   "The legal profession in colonial North America." Pages 129–146 in *Lawyers in
           Early Modern Europe and America*, edited by Wilfrid Prest. New York: Holmes &
           Meier.

Bott, Elizabeth
    1957   *Family and Social Network: Roles, Norms, and External Relationships in Ordinary
           Urban Families*. London: Tavistock.

Bouglé, Celestín
    1908   *Essays on the Caste System*. Cambridge: Cambridge University Press, 1971.

Boulding, Kenneth E.
    1953   *The Organizational Revolution: A Study of the Ethics of Economic Organization*. New
           York: Harper.
    1964   "A pure theory of conflict applied to organizations." Pages 41–49 in *The Frontiers
           of Management*, edited by George Fisk. New York: Harper & Row.

Bourdieu, Pierre
    1966   "The sentiment of honour in Kabyle society." Pages 191–241 in *Honour and Shame:
           The Values of Mediterranean Society*, edited by J. G. Peristiany. Chicago: University
           of Chicago Press.

Bowers, William J., and Glenn L. Pierce
    1980   "Arbitrariness and discrimination under post-*Furman* capital statutes." *Crime
           and Delinquency* 26: 563–635.

Brain, Robert
    1970   "Child-witches." Pages 161–179 in *Witchcraft Confessions and Accusations*, edited
           by Mary Douglas. London: Tavistock.

Braithwaite, Richard Bevan
    1953   *Scientific Explanation: A Study of the Function of Theory, Probability and Law in
           Science*. New York: Harper & Row, 1960.

Brögger, Jan
    1968   "Conflict resolution and the role of the bandit in peasant society." *Anthropologi-
           cal Quarterly* 41: 228–240.

Brown, Claude
    1965   *Manchild in the Promised Land*. New York: American Library, 1966.

Brown, Paula
    1964   "Enemies and affines." *Ethnology* 3: 335–356.

Bryan, James H., and Mary Ann Test
    1967   "Models and helping: naturalistic studies in aiding behavior." *Journal of Person-
           ality and Social Psychology* 6: 400–407.

Buckle, Suzann R. Thomas, and Leonard G. Buckle
    1977   *Bargaining for Justice: Case Disposition and Reform in the Criminal Courts.* New York: Praeger.

Byock, Jesse L.
    1982   *Feud in the Icelandic Saga.* Berkeley: University of California Press.

Campbell, J. K.
    1964   *Honour, Family and Patronage: A Study of Institutions and Moral Values in a Greek Mountain Community.* Oxford: Clarendon Press.

Caplow, Theodore
    1968   *Two against One: Coalitions in Triads.* Englewood Cliffs: Prentice-Hall.

Capra, Fritjof
    1976   *The Tao of Physics.* New York: Bantam, 1977.

Carlin, Jerome E.
    1962   *Lawyers on Their Own: A Study of Individual Practitioners in Chicago.* New Brunswick: Rutgers University Press.

Carniero, Robert L.
    1970   "A theory of the origin of the state." *Science* 169: 733–738.

Chagnon, Napoleon A.
    1977   *Yanomamö: The Fierce People.* New York: Holt, Rinehart & Winston (second edition; first edition, 1968).

Chalidze, Valery
    1977   *Criminal Russia: Essays on Crime in the Soviet Union.* New York: Random House.

Chambliss, William J.
    1967   "Types of deviance and the effectiveness of legal sanctions." *Wisconsin Law Review* 1967: 703–719.

Chanock, Martin
    1985   *Law, Custom and Social Order: The Colonial Experience in Malawi and Zambia.* Cambridge: Cambridge University Press.

Ch'en, Paul Heng-chao
    1979   *Chinese Legal Tradition under the Mongols: The Code of 1291 as Reconstructed.* Princeton: Princeton University Press.

Chevigny, Paul
    1969   *Police Power: Police Abuses in New York City.* New York: Vintage Press.

Christie, Nils
    1977   "Conflicts as property." *British Journal of Criminology* 17: 1–15.

Chroust, Anton-Hermann
    1954a   "The legal profession in ancient Athens." *Notre Dame Lawyer* 29: 339–389.
    1954b   "The legal profession in ancient Republican Rome." *Notre Dame Lawyer* 30: 97–148.

Clark, Alexander L., and Jack P. Gibbs
    1965   "Social control: a reformulation." *Social Problems* 12: 398–415.

Cleaver, Eldridge
    1968   *Soul on Ice.* New York: Dell.

Cloward, Richard A., and Lloyd E. Ohlin
    1960   *Delinquency and Opportunity: A Theory of Delinquent Gangs.* New York: Free Press.

Coburn, David, and Clyde R. Pope
    1974   "Socioeconomic status and preventive health behavior." *Journal of Health and Social Behavior* 15: 67–78.

Codere, Helen
    1950   *Fighting with Property: A Study of Kwakiutl Potlatching and Warfare, 1792–1930.* Seattle: University of Washington Press.

Cohen, Albert K.
    1955   *Delinquent Boys: The Culture of the Gang*. New York: Free Press.
    1966   *Deviance and Control*. Englewood Cliffs: Prentice-Hall.
    1976   "Prison violence: a sociological perspective." Pages 3–22 in *Prison Violence*, edited by Albert K. Cohen, George F. Cole, and Robert G. Bailey. Lexington: D.C. Heath.

Cohen, Eugene
    1972   "Who stole the rabbits? Crime, dispute, and social control in an Italian village." *Anthropological Quarterly* 45: 1–14.

Cohn, Bernard S.
    1965   "Anthropological notes on disputes and law in India." Pages 82–122 in *The Ethnography of Law*, edited by Laura Nader. Published as supplement to *American Anthropologist* 67: (December).

Cohn, Norman
    1975   *Europe's Inner Demons: An Enquiry Inspired by the Great Witch-Hunt*. New York: Basic Books.

Cole, Jonathan R., and Stephen Cole
    1973   *Social Stratification in Science*. Chicago: University of Chicago Press.

Coleman, James S.
    1982   *The Asymmetric Society*. Syracuse: Syracuse University Press.

Coleman, James S., Elihu Katz, and Herbert Menzel
    1966   *Medical Innovation: A Diffusion Study*. Indianapolis: Bobbs-Merrill.

Collier, Jane Fishburne
    1973   *Law and Social Change in Zinacantan*. Stanford: Stanford University Press.

Collins, Randall
    1974   "Three faces of cruelty: towards a comparative sociology of violence." *Theory and Society* 1: 415–440.

Colson, Elizabeth
    1953   "Social control and vengeance in Plateau Tonga society." *Africa* 23: 199–212.
    1969   "Spirit possession among the Tonga of Zambia." Pages 69–103 in *Spirit Mediumship and Society in Africa*, edited by John Beattie and John Middleton. New York: Africana Publishing Corporation.

Comte, Auguste
    1830   *Introduction to Positive Philosophy*. Indianapolis: Bobbs-Merrill, 1970.

Conley, John M., and William M. O'Barr
    1990   *Rules versus Relationships: The Ethnography of Legal Discourse*. Chicago: University of Chicago Press.

Cooley, Charles Horton
    1902   *Human Nature and the Social Order*. New York: Schocken Books, 1964.

Cooney, Mark
    1988   The Social Control of Homicide: A Cross-Cultural Study. Unpublished doctoral dissertation, Harvard Law School.
    1991a Law, Morality, and Conscience: The Social Control of Homicide in Modern America. Unpublished doctoral dissertation, Department of Sociology, University of Virginia.
    1991b "The social production of evidence." Paper presented at the joint annual meeting of the Law and Society Association and the International Sociological Association Research Committee on the Sociology of Law, University of Amsterdam, The Netherlands, June, 1991.

Coser, Lewis
    1956   *The Functions of Social Conflict*. New York: Free Press.

Counts, Dorothy Ayers
1980 "Fighting back is not the way: suicide and the women of Kaliai." *American Ethnologist* 7: 332–351.

Crane, Diana
1967 "The gatekeepers of science: some factors affecting the selection of articles for scientific journals." *The American Sociologist* 2: 195–201.
1972 *Invisible Colleges: Diffusion of Knowledge in Scientific Communities*. Chicago: University of Chicago Press.

Cressey, Donald R.
1953 *Other People's Money: A Study in the Social Psychology of Embezzlement*. Glencoe: Free Press.

Cumming, Elaine, Ian Cumming, and Laura Edell
1965 "Policeman as philosopher, guide and friend." *Social Problems* 12: 276–286.

Curran, Barbara A.
1977 *The Legal Needs of the Public: The Final Report of a National Survey*. Chicago: American Bar Foundation.
1986 "American lawyers in the 1980s: a profession in transition." *Law and Society Review* 20: 19–52.

Currie, Elliott P.
1968 "Crimes without criminals: witchcraft and its control in Renaissance Europe." *Law and Society Review* 3: 7–32.

Dahrendorf, Ralf
1959 *Class and Class Conflict in Industrial Society*. Stanford: Stanford University Press (revised edition; first edition, 1957).
1968 "In praise of Thrasymachus." Pages 129–150 in *Essays in the Theory of Society*, by Ralf Dahrendorf. Stanford: Stanford University Press.

Darley, John M.
1967 "The sharing of responsibility." Paper presented at the annual meeting of the American Psychological Association, Washington, D.C., September, 1967.

Davies, Paul
1984 *Superforce: The Search for a Grand Unified Theory of Nature*. New York: Simon & Schuster.

de Waal, Frans
1989 *Peacemaking among Primates*. Cambridge: Harvard University Press.

Diamond, A. S.
1935 *Primitive Law*. London: Longmans, Green.
1957 "An eye for an eye." *Iraq* 19: 151–155.

Dickens, Charles
1859 *Tale of Two Cities*. London: Chapman & Hall.

Dillon, Richard G.
1980 "Violent conflict in Metá society." *American Ethnologist* 7: 658–673.

Dore, Ronald P.
1978 *Shinohata: A Portrait of a Japanese Village*. New York: Pantheon Books.

Douglas, Jack D.
1967 *The Social Meanings of Suicide*. Princeton: Princeton University Press.

Douglas, Mary
1966 *Purity and Danger: An Analysis of Concepts of Pollution and Taboo*. London: Routledge & Kegan Paul.

1973 *Natural Symbols: Explorations in Cosmology*. New York: Vintage Books (revised edition; first edition, 1970).

Drew, Katherine Fischer
1973 "Introduction." Pages 1–37 in *The Lombard Laws*. Philadelphia: University of Pennsylvania Press.

Driver, Edwin D.
1961 "Interaction and criminal homicide in India." *Social Forces* 40: 153–158.

Duff, Raymond S., and August B. Hollingshead
1968 *Sickness and Society*. New York: Harper & Row.

Dumont, Louis
1970 *Homo Hierarchicus: The Caste System and Its Implications*. Chicago: University of Chicago Press (revised edition; first edition, 1966).

Durkheim, Emile
1893 *The Division of Labor in Society*. New York: Free Press, 1964.
1897 *Suicide: A Study in Sociology*. New York: Free Press, 1951.
1900 "Two laws of penal evolution." *University of Cincinnati Law Review* 38: 32–60 (translation published in 1969).

Eckhoff, Torstein
1966 "The mediator, the judge and the administrator in conflict-resolution." *Acta Sociologica* 10: 148–172.

Edgerton, Robert B.
1972 "Violence in East African tribal societies." Pages 159–170 in *Collective Violence*, edited by James F. Short, Jr., and Marvin E. Wolfgang. Chicago: Aldine Press.
1979 *Alone Together: Social Order on an Urban Beach*. Berkeley: University of California Press.

Edgerton, Robert B., and Francis P. Conant
1964 "*Kilapat*: the 'shaming party' among the Pokot of East Africa." *Southwestern Journal of Anthropology* 20: 404–418.

Eggleston, Elizabeth
1976 *Fear, Favour or Affection: Aborigines and the Criminal Law in Victoria, South Australia and Western Australia*. Canberra: Australian National University Press.

Eisenberg, Melvin A.
1976 "Private ordering through negotiation: dispute-settlement and rulemaking." *Harvard Law Review* 89: 637–681.

Ekvall, Robert B.
1954 "*Mi sTong*: the Tibetan custom of life indemnity." *Sociologus* 4: 136–145.
1964 "Peace and war among the Tibetan nomads." *American Anthropologist* 66: 1119–1148.
1968 *Fields on the Hoof: Nexus of Tibetan Nomadic Pastoralism*. New York: Holt, Rinehart & Winston.

Elias, Norbert
1939 *The Civilizing Process: The Development of Manners*. Volume 1. New York: Urizen Books, 1978.

Ellickson, Robert C.
1986 "Of Coase and cattle: dispute resolution among neighbors in Shasta County." *Stanford Law Review* 38: 623–687.

Ellsworth, Phoebe C., and Ellen J. Langer
1976 "Staring and approach: an interpretation of the stare as a non-specific activator." *Journal of Personality and Social Psychology* 33: 117–122.

Engel, David M.
1978   *Code and Custom in a Thai Provincial Court: The Interaction of Formal and Informal Systems of Justice*. Tucson: University of Arizona Press.
1984   "The oven bird's song: insiders, outsiders, and personal injuries in an American community." *Law and Society Review* 18: 551–582.

Engels, Friedrich
1884   *The Origin of the Family, Private Property and the State: In the Light of the Researches of Lewis H. Morgan*. New York: International Publishers, 1942.

Erikson, Kai T.
1962   "Notes on the sociology of deviance." *Social Problems* 9: 307–314.

Evans-Pritchard, E. E.
1937   *Witchcraft, Oracles and Magic among the Azande*. London: Oxford University Press.
1940   *The Nuer: A Description of the Modes of Livelihood and Political Institutions of a Nilotic People*. London: Oxford University Press.
1956   *Nuer Religion*. Oxford: Clarendon Press.

Fallers, Lloyd A.
1969   *Law without Precedent: Legal Ideas in Action in the Courts of Colonial Busoga*. Chicago: University of Chicago Press.

Fallers, Lloyd A., and Margaret C. Fallers
1960   "Homicide and suicide in Busoga." Pages 65–93 in *African Homicide and Suicide*, edited by Paul Bohannan. Princeton: Princeton University Press.

Faragher, John Mack
1979   *Women and Men on the Overland Trail*. New Haven: Yale University Press.

Farrell, Ronald A., and Victoria Lynn Swigert
1978   "Prior offense as a self-fulfilling prophecy." *Law and Society Review* 12: 437–453.

Fattah, Ezzat A.
1976   "The use of the victim as an agent of self-legitimization: toward a dynamic explanation of criminal behavior." *Victimology: An International Journal* 1: 29–53.

Feeley, Malcolm M.
1979   *The Process Is the Punishment: Handling Cases in a Lower Criminal Court*. New York: Russell Sage Foundation.

Feifer, George
1964   *Justice in Moscow*. New York: Simon & Schuster.

Felstiner, William L. F.
1974   "Influences of social organization on dispute processing." *Law and Society Review* 9: 63–94.

Firth, Raymond
1936   *We, the Tikopia: A Sociological Study of Kinship in Primitive Polynesia*. New York: American Book Company.

FitzGerald, Jeffrey M., David C. Hickman, and Richard L. Dickins
1980   "A preliminary discussion of the definitional phase of the dispute process." Paper presented at the annual meeting of the Law and Society Association, Madison, Wisconsin, June, 1980.

Fogel, Robert William, and Stanley L. Engerman
1974   *Time on the Cross: The Economics of American Negro Slavery*. Boston: Little, Brown.

Fortes, Meyer
1945   *The Dynamics of Clanship among the Tallensi: Being the First Part of an Analysis of the Social Structure of a Trans-Volta Tribe*. London: Oxford University Press.

Foucault, Michel
1975   *Discipline and Punish: The Birth of the Prison*. New York: Pantheon, 1977.

Frake, Charles O.
   1963   "Litigation in Lipay: a study in Subanun law." *Proceedings of the Ninth Pacific Science Congress* 3: 217–222.
   1980   "Kin and supporters among the Yakan." Pages 202–213 in *Language and Cultural Description: Essays by Charles O. Frake*, edited by Anwar S. Dil. Stanford: Stanford University Press.
Frank, Jerome
   1930   *Law and the Modern Mind*. New York: Brentano's.
Freidson, Eliot
   1970   *Profession of Medicine: A Study of the Sociology of Applied Knowledge*. New York: Harper & Row.
Fried, Jacob
   1953   "The relation of ideal norms to actual behavior in Tarahumara society." *Southwestern Journal of Anthropology* 9: 286–295.
Fried, Morton H.
   1967   *The Evolution of Political Society: An Essay in Political Anthropology*. New York: Random House.
Friedman, Lawrence M.
   1980   "The six million dollar man: litigation and rights consciousness in modern America." *Maryland Law Review* 39: 661–677.
Friedman, Lawrence M., and Stewart Macaulay (editors)
   1977   *Law and the Behavioral Sciences*. Indianapolis: Bobbs-Merrill (second edition; first edition, 1969).
Friedman, Lawrence M., and Robert V. Percival
   1976   "A tale of two courts: litigation in Alameda and San Benito Counties." *Law and Society Review* 10: 267–301.
Fuller, Lon L.
   1964   *The Morality of Law*. New Haven: Yale University Press.
   1971   "Human interaction and the law." Pages 171–217 in *The Rule of Law*, edited by Robert Paul Wolff. New York: Simon & Schuster.
   1978   "The forms and limits of adjudication." *Harvard Law Review* 92: 353–409.
Fürer-Haimendorf, Christoph von
   1943   *The Chenchus: Jungle Folk of the Deccan*. London: Macmillan.
   1967   *Morals and Merit: A Study of Values and Social Controls in South Asian Societies*. Chicago: University of Chicago Press.
Gaertner, Samuel, and Leonard Bickerman
   1971   "Effects of race on the elicitation of helping behavior: the wrong number technique." *Journal of Personality and Social Psychology* 20: 218–222.
Galanter, Marc
   1974   "Why the 'haves' come out ahead: speculations on the limits of legal change." *Law and Society Review* 9: 95–160.
   1981   "Justice in many rooms: courts, private ordering, and indigenous law." *Journal of Legal Pluralism* 19:1–47.
   1983   "Reading the landscape of disputes: what we know and don't know (and think we know) about our allegedly contentious and litigious society." *UCLA Law Review* 31: 4–71.
Galtung, Johan
   1965   "Institutionalized conflict resolution: a theoretical paradigm." *Journal of Peace Research* 2: 349–397.

Gamson, William A.
    1975   *The Strategy of Social Protest*. Homewood: Dorsey Press.
Gans, Herbert J.
    1974   *Popular Culture and High Culture: An Analysis and Evaluation of Taste*. New York: Basic Books.
Garfinkel, Harold
    1949   "Research note on inter- and intra-racial homicides." *Social Forces* 27: 369–381.
Garnsey, Peter
    1968   "Legal privilege in the Roman Empire." *Past and Present* 41: 3–24.
Getman, Julius G.
    1979   "Labor arbitration and dispute resolution." *Yale Law Journal* 88: 916–949.
Gibbs, Jack P.
    1981   *Norms, Deviance, and Social Control: Conceptual Matters*. New York: Elsevier.
Gibbs, James L., Jr.
    1962   "Poro values and courtroom procedures in a Kpelle chiefdom." *Southwestern Journal of Anthropology* 18: 341–350.
    1963   "The Kpelle moot: a therapeutic model for the informal settlement of disputes." *Africa* 33: 1–10.
Giddings, Jane
    1975   "Soviet legal consultation." *Review of Socialist Law* 1: 261–264, 268–269, 275–279.
Giedion, Sigfried
    1956   "Space conception in prehistoric art." *Explorations: Studies in Culture and Communication* 6: 38–55.
Gilligan, Carol
    1982   *In a Different Voice: Psychological Theory and Women's Development*. Cambridge: Harvard University Press.
Gillin, John
    1934   "Crime and punishment among the Barama River Carib of British Guiana." *American Anthropologist* 36: 331–344.
    1948   "Magical fright." *Psychiatry* 11: 387–400.
    1956   "The making of a witch doctor." *Psychiatry* 19: 131–136.
Ginnell, Laurence
    1924   *The Brehon Laws: A Legal Handbook*. Dublin: P. J. O'Callaghan (third edition; first edition, 1894).
Girard, René
    1987   "Generative scapegoating." Pages 73–105 in *Violent Origins: Ritual Killing and Cultural Formation*, edited by Robert G. Hamerton-Kelly. Stanford: Stanford University Press.
Given, James Buchanan
    1977   *Society and Homicide in Thirteenth-Century England*. Stanford: Stanford University Press.
Glaser, Barney G., and Anselm L. Strauss
    1967   *The Discovery of Grounded Theory: Strategies for Qualitative Research*. Chicago: Aldine.
Gleick, James
    1987   *Chaos: Making a New Science*. New York: Viking.
Gluckman, Max
    1956   *Custom and Conflict in Africa*. New York: Barnes & Nobel, 1969.
    1963   "Gossip and scandal." *Current Anthropology* 4: 307–316.

1965a *The Ideas in Barotse Jurisprudence*. New Haven: Yale University Press.

1965b *Politics, Law and Ritual in Tribal Society*. New York: New American Library.

1967 *The Judicial Process among the Barotse of Northern Rhodesia*. Manchester: Manchester University Press (second edition; first edition, 1955).

1972 "Moral crises: magical and secular solutions." Pages 1–50 in *The Allocation of Responsibility*, edited by Max Gluckman. Manchester: Manchester University Press.

Goffman, Erving

1961 *Asylums: Essays on the Social Situation of Mental Patients and Other Inmates*. Garden City: Anchor Books.

1969 "The insanity of place." Pages 335–390 in *Relations in Public: Microstudies of the Public Order*. New York: Basic Books, 1971.

Goldschmidt, Walter

1967 *Sebei Law*. Berkeley: University of California Press.

Goody, Jack

1957 "Fields of social control among the LoDagaba." *Journal of the Royal Anthropological Institute of Great Britain and Ireland* 87: 75–104.

Gorn, Elliott J.

1985 " 'Gouge and bite, pull hair and scratch': the social significance of fighting in the Southern backcountry." *American Historical Review* 90: 18–43.

Gould, Leroy C., Andrew L. Walker, Lansing E. Crane, and Charles W. Lidz

1974 *Connections: Notes from the Heroin World*. New Haven: Yale University Press.

Gouldner, Alvin W.

1960 "The norm of reciprocity: a preliminary statement." *American Sociological Review* 25: 161–178.

Grabosky, Peter

1984 "The variability of punishment." Pages 163–189 in *Toward a General Theory of Social Control*, Volume 1: *Fundamentals*, edited by Donald Black. Orlando: Academic Press.

Gray, Charles Edward

1966 "A measurement of creativity in Western civilization." *American Anthropologist* 68: 1384–1417.

1972 "Paradoxes in Western creativity." *American Anthropologist* 74: 676–688.

Gray, Robert F.

1969 "The Shetani cult among the Segeju of Tanzania." Pages 171–187 in *Spirit Mediumship and Society in Africa*, edited by John Beattie and John Middleton. New York: Africana Publishing Corporation.

Green, Thomas A.

1972 "Societal concepts of criminal liability for homicide in mediaeval England." *Speculum* 47: 669–694.

1976 "The jury and the English law of homicide, 1200–1600." *Michigan Law Review* 74: 413–499.

Greenberg, David F.

1977 "Delinquency and the age structure of society." *Contemporary Crisis: Crime, Law, Social Policy* 1: 189–223.

1988 *The Construction of Homosexuality*. Chicago: University of Chicago Press.

Greenberg, James B.

1989 *Blood Ties: Life and Violence in Rural Mexico*. Tucson: University of Arizona Press.

Greuel, Peter J.

1971 "The leopard-skin chief: an examination of political power among the Nuer." *American Anthropologist* 73: 1115–1120.

Griffiths, John
    1984   "The division of labor in social control." Pages 37–70 in *Toward a General Theory of Social Control*, Volume 1: *Fundamentals*, edited by Donald Black. Orlando: Academic Press.
    1986   "What do Dutch lawyers actually do in divorce cases?" *Law and Society Review* 20: 135–175.
Grönfors, Martti
    1986   "Social control and law in the Finnish gypsy community: blood feuding as a system of justice." *Journal of Legal Pluralism* 24: 101–125.
Gross, Jan T.
    1979   *Polish Society under German Occupation: The Generalgouvernement, 1939–1944.* Princeton: Princeton University Press.
    1984   "Social control under totalitarianism." Pages 59–77 in *Toward a General Theory of Social Control*, Volume 2: *Selected Problems*, edited by Donald Black. Orlando: Academic Press.
Gross, Samuel R., and Robert Mauro
    1984   "Patterns of death: an analysis of racial disparities in capital sentencing and homicide victimization." *Stanford Law Review* 37: 27–153.
Gulliver, P. H.
    1963   *Social Control in an African Society: A Study of the Arusha, Agricultural Masai of Northern Tanganyika.* Boston: Boston University Press.
    1969   "Dispute settlement without courts: The Ndendeuli of southern Tanzania." Pages 24–68 in *Law in Culture and Society*, edited by Laura Nader. Chicago: Aldine.
    1971   *Neighbours and Networks: The Idiom of Kinship in Social Action among the Ndendeuli of Tanzania.* Berkeley: University of California Press.
    1977   "On mediators." Pages 15–52 in *Social Anthropology and Law*, edited by Ian Hamnett. London: Academic Press.
    1979   *Disputes and Negotiations: A Cross-Cultural Perspective.* New York: Academic Press.
Hackler, James C., Kwai-yiu Ho, and Carol Urquhart-Ross
    1974   "The willingness to intervene: differing community characteristics." *Social Problems* 21: 328–344.
Haft-Picker, Cheryl
    1980   "Beyond the subculture of violence: an evolutionary and historical approach to social control." Pages 181–210 in *Crime and Deviance: A Comparative Perspective*, edited by Graeme R. Newman. Sage Annual Reviews of Studies in Deviance, Volume 4. Beverly Hills: Sage.
Hagan, John
    1982   "The corporate advantage: a study of the involvement of corporate and individual victims in a criminal justice system." *Social Forces* 60: 993–1022.
Hagan, John, and Ilene Nagel Bernstein
    1979   "The sentence bargaining of upperworld and underworld crime in ten federal district courts." *Law and Society Review* 13: 467–478.
Hagan, William T.
    1966   *Indian Police and Judges: Experiments in Acculturation and Control.* New Haven: Yale University Press.
Hanawalt, Barbara A.
    1979   *Crime and Conflict in English Communities, 1300–1348.* Cambridge: Harvard University Press.

Harner, Michael J.
1972 *The Jívaro: People of the Sacred Waterfalls*. Garden City: Anchor Books, 1973.
Harris, D. R.
1974 "Accident compensation in New Zealand: a comprehensive insurance system." *Modern Law Review* 37: 361–376.
Hart, H. L. A.
1961 *The Concept of Law*. Oxford: Clarendon Press.
Hart, Henry M., Jr., and Albert M. Sacks
1958 The Legal Process: Basic Problems in the Making and Application of Law. Cambridge: Harvard Law School (tentative edition).
Hasluck, Margaret
1954 *The Unwritten Law in Albania*. Cambridge: Cambridge University Press.
Hastie, Reid, Steven D. Penrod, and Nancy Pennington
1983 *Inside the Jury*. Cambridge: Harvard University Press.
Hay, Douglas, Peter Linebaugh, John G. Rule, E. P. Thompson, and Cal Winslow
1975 *Albion's Fatal Tree: Crime and Society in Eighteenth-Century England*. New York: Pantheon.
Hegel, Georg Wilhelm Friedrich
1821 *Hegel's Philosophy of Right*. London: Oxford University Press, 1952.
Hempel, Carl G.
1965 "Aspects of scientific explanation." Pages 331–496 in *Aspects of Scientific Explanation and Other Essays in the Philosophy of Science*, by Carl G. Hempel. New York: Free Press.
Henry, Andrew F., and James F. Short, Jr.
1954 *Suicide and Homicide: Some Economic, Sociological and Psychological Aspects of Aggression*. Glencoe: Free Press.
Hepworth, Mike, and Bryan S. Turner
1982 *Confession: Studies in Deviance and Religion*. London: Routledge and Kegan Paul.
Herrmann, John
1992 "Gossip in science: a study of social control and reputation." Paper presented at the annual meeting of the American Sociological Association, Pittsburgh, Pennsylvania, August, 1992.
Hiatt, L. R.
1965 *Kinship and Conflict: A Study of an Aboriginal Community in Northern Arnhem Land*. Canberra: Australian National University Press.
Hirschi, Travis
1969 *Causes of Delinquency*. Berkeley: University of California Press.
Hirschman, Albert O.
1970 *Exit, Voice, and Loyalty: Responses to Decline in Firms, Organizations, and States*. Cambridge: Harvard University Press.
Hobbes, Thomas
1651 *Leviathan: Or the Matter, Forme and Power of a Commonwealth Ecclesiasticall and Civil*. New York: Macmillan, 1962.
Hobhouse, L. T.
1906 *Morals in Evolution: A Study in Comparative Ethics*. New York: Henry Holt.
Hobsbawm, Eric
1959 *Primitive Rebels: Studies in Archaic Forms of Social Movement in the 19th and 20th Centuries*. New York: W. W. Norton (originally published as *Social Bandits and Primitive Rebels*).
1969 *Bandits*. New York: Dell, 1971.

Hoch, Steven L.
    1986   *Serfdom and Social Control in Russia: Petrovskoe, a Village in Tambov*. Chicago: University of Chicago Press.
Hoebel, E. Adamson
    1940   *The Political Organization and Law-Ways of the Comanche Indians*. Memoirs of the American Anthropological Association, Number 54. Menasha: American Anthropological Association.
    1954   *The Law of Primitive Man: A Study in Comparative Legal Dynamics*. Cambridge: Harvard University Press.
Hoffmann, Stanley
    1968   "International law and the control of force." Pages 34–66 in *The Relevance of International Law*, edited by Karl Deutsch and Stanley Hoffmann. Garden City: Anchor Books, 1971.
Hofstadter, Douglas R.
    1979   *Gödel, Escher, Bach: An Eternal Golden Braid*. New York: Vintage Books, 1980.
Hogbin, H. Ian
    1934   *Law and Order in Polynesia: A Study of Primitive Legal Institutions*. New York: Harcourt.
Hollingshead, August B.
    1941   "The concept of social control." *American Sociological Review* 6:217–224.
Holmstrom, Lynda Lytle, and Ann Wolbert Burgess
    1978   *The Victim of Rape: Institutional Reactions*. New Brunswick: Transaction Books, 1983.
Homans, George C.
    1950   *The Human Group*. New York: Harcourt, Brace.
    1964   "Bringing men back in." *American Sociological Review* 29: 809–818.
    1967   *The Nature of Social Science*. New York: Harcourt, Brace & World.
Horowitz, Ruth
    1983   *Honor and the American Dream: Culture and Identity in a Chicano Community*. New Brunswick: Rutgers University Press.
Horowitz, Ruth, and Gary Schwartz
    1974   "Honor, normative ambiguity and gang violence." *American Sociological Review* 39: 238–251.
Horwitz, Allan V.
    1982   *The Social Control of Mental Illness*. New York: Academic Press.
    1984   "Therapy and social solidarity." Pages 211–250 in *Toward a General Theory of Social Control*, Volume 1: *Fundamentals*, edited by Donald Black. Orlando: Academic Press.
    1990   *The Logic of Social Control*. New York: Plenum Press.
Horwitz, Morton J.
    1977   *The Transformation of American Law, 1780–1860*. Cambridge: Harvard University Press.
Howell, P. P.
    1954   *A Manual of Nuer Law: Being an Account of Customary Law, Its Evolution and Development in the Courts Established by the Sudan Government*. London: Oxford University Press.
Hunt, Eva, and Robert Hunt
    1969   "The role of courts in rural Mexico." Pages 109–139 in *Peasants in the Modern World*, edited by Philip K. Bock. Albuquerque: University of New Mexico Press.

Iga, Mamoru
    1986   *The Thorn in the Chrysanthemum: Suicide and Economic Success in Modern Japan.* Berkeley: University of California Press.

Jaeger, Gertrude, and Philip Selznick
    1964   "A normative theory of culture." *American Sociological Review* 29: 653–669.

James, Fleming, Jr.
    1970   "Analysis of the origin and development of the negligence actions." In *The Origin and Development of the Negligence Action.* Washington, D.C.: U.S. Department of Transportation.

Jeffreys, M. D. W.
    1952   "Samsonic suicide or suicide of revenge among Africans." *African Studies* 11: 118–122.

Johnson, G. B.
    1941   "The Negro and crime." *The Annals of the American Academy of Political and Social Science* 271: 93–104.

Jones, Schuyler
    1974   *Men of Influence in Nuristan: A Study of Social Control and Dispute Settlement in Waigal Valley, Afghanistan.* New York: Academic Press.

Kadushin, Charles
    1976   "Networks and circles in the production of culture." *American Behavioral Scientist* 19: 769–784.

Kagan, Richard L.
    1981   *Lawsuits and Litigants in Castile, 1500–1700.* Chapel Hill: University of North Carolina Press.

Kalven, Harry, Jr., and Hans Zeisel
    1966   *The American Jury.* Boston: Little, Brown.

Karsten, Rafael
    1923   *Blood Revenge, War, and Victory Feasts among the Jívaro Indians of Eastern Ecuador.* Smithsonian Institution Bureau of American Ethnology, Bulletin Number 79. Washington, D.C.: U.S. Government Printing Office.

Katz, Elihu, and Paul F. Lazarsfeld
    1955   *Personal Influence: The Part Played by People in the Flow of Mass Communications.* Glencoe: Free Press.

Kawashima, Takeyoshi
    1963   "Dispute resolution in contemporary Japan." Pages 41–72 in *Law in Japan: The Legal Order in a Changing Society,* edited by Arthur T. von Mehren. Cambridge: Harvard University Press.

Kelly, J. M.
    1966   *Roman Litigation.* Oxford: Clarendon Press.

Kiefer, Thomas M.
    1972   *The Tausug: Violence and Law in a Philippine Moslem Society.* New York: Holt, Rinehart & Winston.

Kitsuse, John I.
    1962   "Societal reaction to deviant behavior: problems of theory and method." *Social Problems* 9: 247–256.

Kitsuse, John I., and Aaron V. Cicourel
    1963   "A note on the uses of official statistics." *Social Problems* 11: 131–139.

Knauft, Bruce M.
    1985   *Good Company and Violence: Sorcery and Social Action in a Lowland New Guinea Society.* Berkeley: University of California Press.

1987a "Reconsidering violence in simple human societies: homicide among the Gebusi of New Guinea." *Current Anthropology* 28: 457–500.

1987b "Violence in the simplest human societies: comparison among great ape, simple, and not-so-simple pre-state human populations." Paper presented at the annual meeting of the American Political Science Association, Chicago, Illinois, September, 1987.

1990 "Melanesian warfare." *Oceania* 60: 250–311.

Köbben, André J. F.
1969 "Law at the village level: the Cottica Djuka of Surinam." Pages 117–140 in *Law in Culture and Society*, edited by Laura Nader. Chicago: Aldine.

Koch, Klaus-Friedrich
1974 *War and Peace in Jalémó: The Management of Conflict in Highland New Guinea.* Cambridge: Harvard University Press.

1979 "Introduction." Pages 1–16 in *Access to Justice*, Volume 4: *The Anthropological Perspective*, edited by Klaus-Friedrich Koch. Alphen aan den Rijn: Sijthoff & Noordhoff.

1984 "Liability and social structure." Pages 95–129 in *Toward a General Theory of Social Control*, Volume 1: *Fundamentals*, edited by Donald Black. Orlando: Academic Press.

Koch, Klaus-Friedrich, and John A. Sodergren (with the collaboration of Susan Campbell)
1976 "Political and psychological correlates of conflict management: a cross-cultural study." *Law and Society Review* 10: 443–466.

Kolchin, Peter
1987 *Unfree Labor: American Slavery and Russian Serfdom.* Cambridge: Harvard University Press.

Koos, Earl Lomon
1954 *The Health of Regionville: What the People Thought and Did about It.* New York: Hafner, 1967.

Kopytoff, Igor
1961 "Extension of conflict as a method of conflict resolution among the Suku of the Congo." *Journal of Conflict Resolution* 5: 61–69.

Kroeber, A. L.
1925 *Handbook of the Indians of California.* Volume 1. Washington, D.C.: U.S. Government Printing Office.

1926 "Law of the Yurok Indians." Pages 511–516 in *Proceedings of the 22nd International Congress of Americanists.* Volume 2. Rome: Instituto Christoforo Colombo.

1944 *Configurations of Culture Growth.* Berkeley: University of California Press.

Kuhn, Thomas S.
1970 *The Structure of Scientific Revolutions.* Chicago: University of Chicago Press (enlarged edition; first edition, 1962).

La Brecque, Mort
1987 "Fractal applications." *Mosaic* 17: 35–48.

La Fave, Wayne R., and Austin W. Scott, Jr.
1972 *Handbook on Criminal Law.* St. Paul: West.

La Fontaine, Jean
1960 "Homicide and suicide among the Gisu." Pages 94–129 in *African Homicide and Suicide*, edited by Paul Bohannan. Princeton: Princeton University Press.

La Free, Gary D.
1980 "Variables affecting guilty pleas and convictions in rape cases: toward a social theory of rape processing." *Social Forces* 58: 833–850.

Lamley, Harry J.
    1990   "Lineage feuding in southern Fujian and eastern Guangdong under Qing rule."
            Pages 27–64 in *Violence in China: Essays in Culture and Counterculture*, edited by
            Jonathan N. Lipman and Stevan Harrell. Albany: State University of New York
            Press.
Langness, L. L.
    1972   "Violence in the New Guinea highlands." Pages 171–185 in *Collective Violence*,
            edited by James F. Short, Jr., and Marvin E. Wolfgang. Chicago: Aldine-
            Atherton.
La Piere, Richard T.
    1954   *A Theory of Social Control*. New York: McGraw-Hill.
Lasswell, Harold D.
    1964   "Preface." Pages ix–xiii in *Moral Indignation and Middle Class Psychology: A Soci-
            ological Study*, by Svend Ranulf. New York: Schocken.
Lea, Henry Charles
    1892   *Superstition and Force: Essays on the Wager of Law — The Wager of Battle — The
            Ordeal — Torture*. Philadelphia: Lea Brothers (fourth edition; first edition, 1878).
Leacock, Eleanor
    1982   "Relations of production in band society." Pages 159–170 in *Politics and History
            in Band Societies*, edited by Eleanor Leacock and Richard Lee. Cambridge: Cam-
            bridge University Press.
Leacock, Eleanor, and Richard Lee (editors)
    1982   *Politics and History in Band Societies*. Cambridge: Cambridge University Press.
Le Bon, Gustave
    1895   *The Crowd: A Study of the Popular Mind*. New York: Viking Press, 1960.
Lee, Richard Borshay
    1979   *The !Kung San: Men, Women and Work in a Foraging Society*. Cambridge: Cam-
            bridge University Press.
Leibniz, Gottfried Wilhelm
    1728   "Monadology." Pages 251–272 in *Leibniz: Discourse on Metaphysics, Correspon-
            dence with Arnauld, and Monadology*, edited by Thomas J. McCormack. Chicago:
            Open Court Publishing Company, 1902 (posthumously published; completed
            1714).
Lemert, Edwin M.
    1964   "Social structure, social control, and deviation." Pages 57–97 in *Anomie and
            Deviant Behavior: A Discussion and Critique*, edited by Marshall B. Clinard. New
            York: Free Press.
    1967   "The concept of secondary deviation." Pages 40–64 in *Human Deviance, Social
            Problems, and Social Control*. Englewood Cliffs: Prentice-Hall.
Le Vine, Robert A.
    1959   "Gusii sex offenses: a study in social control." *American Anthropologist* 61:
            965–990.
Lewis, I. M.
    1959   "Clanship and contract in northern Somaliland." *Africa* 29: 274–293.
    1961   *A Pastoral Democracy: A Study of Pastoralism and Politics among the Northern Somali
            of the Horn of Africa*. London: Oxford University Press.
    1966.   "Spirit possession and deprivation cults." *Man* 1: 307–329.
Lewis, Mark Edward
    1990   *Sanctioned Violence in Early China*. Albany: State University of New York
            Press.

Lieberman, Jethro K.
 1981 *The Litigious Society*. New York: Basic Books.
Lintott, A. W.
 1968 *Violence in Republican Rome*. London: Oxford University Press.
Llewellyn, Karl N., and E. Adamson Hoebel
 1941 *The Cheyenne Way: Conflict and Case Law in Primitive Jurisprudence*. Norman: University of Oklahoma Press.
Lofland, John, and Rodney Stark
 1965 "Becoming a world-saver: a theory of conversion to a deviant perspective." *American Sociological Review* 30: 862–875.
Lomax, Alan
 1968 "Song as a measure of culture." Pages 117–169 in *Folk Song Style and Culture*, edited by Alan Lomax. Washington, D.C.: American Association for the Advancement of Science, Publication Number 88.
Lomax, Alan, Irmgard Bartenieff, and Forrestine Paulay
 1968 "Dance style and culture." Pages 222–247 in *Folk Song Style and Culture*, edited by Alan Lomax. Washington, D.C.: American Association for the Advancement of Science, Publication Number 88.
Lowie, Robert H.
 1935 *The Crow Indians*. New York: Farrar & Rinehart.
 1948 "Some aspects of political organization among the American aborigines." *Journal of the Royal Anthropological Institute of Great Britain and Ireland* 78: 11–24.
Lundman, Richard J.
 1979 "Organizational norms and police discretion: an observational study of police work with traffic law violators." *Criminology* 17: 159–171.
Lundsgaarde, Henry P.
 1977 *Murder in Space City: A Cultural Analysis of Houston Homicide Patterns*. New York: Oxford University Press.
Macaulay, Stewart
 1963 "Non-contractual relations in business: a preliminary study." *American Sociological Review* 28: 55–67.
 1979 "Lawyers and consumer protection laws." *Law and Society Review* 14: 115–171.
MacCormack, Geoffrey
 1976 "Procedures for the settlement of disputes in 'simple societies.' " *The Irish Jurist* 11 (New Series): 175–188.
Macfarlane, Alan
 1970 *Witchcraft in Tudor and Stuart England: A Regional and Comparative Study*. New York: Harper & Row.
MacLeod, William Christie
 1937 "Police and punishment among native Americans of the Plains." *Journal of the American Institute of Criminal Law and Criminology* 28: 181–201.
Maddock, Kenneth
 1977 "Two laws in one community." Pages 13–32 in *Aborigines and Change: Australia in the '70s*, edited by R. M. Berndt. Canberra: Australian Institute of Aboriginal Studies.
Maitland, Frederic William
 1881 "The laws of Wales: the kindred and the blood feud." Pages 202–229 in *The Collected Papers of Frederic William Maitland*, Volume 1, edited by H. A. L. Fisher. Cambridge: Cambridge University Press, 1911.
 1883 "The early history of malice aforethought." Pages 304–328 in *The Collected Papers*

of Frederic William Maitland, Volume 1, edited by H. A. L. Fisher. Cambridge: Cambridge University Press, 1911.

Malinowski, Bronislaw
> 1926 *Crime and Custom in Savage Society.* Paterson: Littlefield, Adams, 1962.

Malone, Wex S.
> 1970 "Ruminations on the role of fault in the history of torts." In *The Origin and Development of the Negligence Action.* Washington, D.C.: U.S. Department of Transportation.

Malott, Robert H.
> 1985 *America's Liability Explosion: Can We Afford the Cost?* Chicago: FMC Corporation.

Mann, Michael
> 1986 *The Sources of Social Power.* Volume 1: *A History of Power from the Beginning to A.D. 1760.* Cambridge: Cambridge University Press.

Mannheim, Karl
> 1927 "Conservative thought." Pages 74–164 in *Essays on Sociology and Social Psychology,* edited by Paul Kecskemeti. New York: Oxford University Press, 1953.
> 1940 *Man and Society in an Age of Reconstruction: Studies in Modern Social Structure.* New York: Harcourt, Brace & World (revised edition; first edition, 1935).

Manniche, E., and G. Falk
> 1957 "Age and the Nobel Prize." *Behavioral Science* 2: 301–307.

Marshall, Lorna
> 1961 "Sharing, talking, and giving: relief of social tensions among the !Kung Bushmen." *Africa* 31: 231–249.

Marx, Karl, and Friedrich Engels
> 1846 *The German Ideology.* New York: International Publishers, 1947.

Mather, Lynn
> 1979 *Plea Bargaining or Trial? The Process of Criminal Case Disposition.* Lexington: Lexington Books.

Mather, Lynn, and Barbara Yngvesson
> 1981 "Language, audience, and the transformation of disputes." *Law and Society Review* 15: 775–822.

Matza, David
> 1964 *Delinquency and Drift.* New York: Wiley.
> 1969 *Becoming Deviant.* Englewood Cliffs: Prentice-Hall.

Maybury-Lewis, David
> 1967 *Akwĕ-Shavante Society.* Oxford: Clarendon Press.

Mayhew, Leon, and Albert J. Reiss, Jr.
> 1969 "The social organization of legal contacts." *American Sociological Review* 34: 309–318.

Maynard, Douglas W.
> 1984 *Inside Plea Bargaining: The Language of Negotiation.* New York: Plenum Press.

McBarnet, Doreen J.
> 1981 *Conviction: Law, the State and the Construction of Justice.* London: Macmillan.

McGillis, Daniel, and Joan Mullen
> 1977 *Neighborhood Justice Centers: An Analysis of Potential Models.* Washington, D.C.: National Institute of Law Enforcement and Criminal Justice, Law Enforcement Assistance Administration, U.S. Department of Justice.

McGrath, Roger D.
> 1984 *Gunfighters, Highwaymen, and Vigilantes: Violence on the Frontier.* Berkeley: University of California Press.

McKinlay, John B.
1975 "The help-seeking behavior of the poor." Pages 224–273 in *Poverty and Health: A Sociological Analysis*, edited by John Kosa and Irving Kenneth Zola. Cambridge: Harvard University Press (revised edition; first edition, 1969).

McLuhan, Marshall
1964 *Understanding Media: The Extensions of Man*. New York: New American Library.

McLuhan, Marshall, and Harley Parker
1968 *Through the Vanishing Point: Space in Poetry and Painting*. New York: Harper & Row.

McNeill, John T., and Helena M. Gamer (editors)
1938 *Medieval Handbooks of Penance: A Translation of the Principal Libri Poenitentiales and Selections from Related Documents*. New York: Columbia University Press.

Mead, George Herbert
1934 *Mind, Self, and Society: From the Standpoint of a Social Behaviorist*. Chicago: University of Chicago Press.

Mead, Margaret
1964 *Continuities in Cultural Evolution*. New Haven: Yale University Press.

Mechanic, David
1968 *Medical Sociology: A Selective View*. New York: Free Press.

Meggitt, M. J.
1962 *Desert People: A Study of the Walbiri Aborigines of Central Australia*. Sydney: Angus and Robertson.

Mentschikoff, Soia
1961 "Commercial arbitration." *Columbia Law Review* 61: 846–869.

Merry, Sally Engle
1979 "Going to court: strategies of dispute management in an American urban neighborhood." *Law and Society Review* 13: 891–925.
1981 *Urban Danger: Life in a Neighborhood of Strangers*. Philadelphia: Temple University Press.
1982 "The social organization of mediation in nonindustrial societies: implications for informal community justice in America." Pages 27–45 in *The Politics of Informal Justice*, Volume 2: *Comparative Studies*, edited by Richard L. Abel. New York: Academic Press.
1984 "Rethinking gossip and scandal." Pages 271–302 in *Toward a General Theory of Social Control*, Volume 1: *Fundamentals*, edited by Donald Black. Orlando: Academic Press.

Merton, Robert K.
1938 "Social structure and anomie." *American Sociological Review* 3: 672–682.
1968 "The Matthew effect in science." *Science* 159: 55–63.

Michels, Robert
1911 *Political Parties: A Sociological Study of the Oligarchical Tendencies of Modern Democracy*. New York: Collier Books, 1962.

Middleton, John
1965 *The Lugbara of Uganda*. New York: Holt, Rinehart & Winston.

Middleton, John, and David Tait (editors)
1958 *Tribes without Rulers: Studies in African Segmentary Systems*. New York: Humanities Press, 1970.

Midelfort, H. C. Erik
1972 *Witch Hunting in Southwestern Germany, 1562–1684: The Social and Intellectual Foundations*. Stanford: Stanford University Press.

Mileski, Maureen
  1971   "Courtroom encounters: an observation study of a lower criminal court." *Law and Society Review* 5: 473–538.
Miller, Walter B.
  1958   "Lower class culture as a generating milieu of gang delinquency." *Journal of Social Issues* 14: 5–19.
Mitchell, J. Clyde
  1969   "The concept and use of social networks." Pages 1–50 in *Social Networks in Urban Situations: Analyses of Personal Relationships in Central African Towns*, edited by J. Clyde Mitchell. Manchester: Manchester University Press.
Moody, Philip M., and Robert M. Gray
  1972   "Social class, social integration, and the use of preventive health services." Pages 250–261 in *Patients, Physicians and Illness: A Sourcebook in Behavioral Science and Health*, edited by E. Gartley Jaco. New York: Free Press (second edition; first edition, 1958).
Moore, Sally Falk
  1972   "Legal liability and evolutionary interpretation: some aspects of strict liability, self-help and collective responsibility." Pages 51–107 in *The Allocation of Responsibility*, edited by Max Gluckman. Manchester: Manchester University Press.
  1973   "Law and social change: the semi-autonomous social field as an appropriate subject of study." *Law and Society Review* 7: 719–746.
  1978   *Law as Process: An Anthropological Approach*. London: Routledge & Kegan Paul.
Morrill, Calvin
  1986   Conflict Management among Corporate Executives: A Comparative Study. Unpublished doctoral dissertation, Department of Sociology, Harvard University.
  1989   "The management of managers: disputing in an executive hierarchy." *Sociological Forum* 4: 387–407.
  1992   "Vengeance among executives." Pages 51–76 in *Virginia Review of Sociology*, Volume 1: *Law and Conflict Management*, edited by James Tucker. Greenwich: JAI Press.
Muir, William Ker, Jr.
  1977   *Police: Streetcorner Politicians*. Chicago: University of Chicago Press.
Mullin, Gerald W.
  1972   *Flight and Rebellion: Slave Resistance in Eighteenth-Century Virginia*. New York: Oxford University Press.
Murphy, Robert F.
  1957   "Intergroup hostility and social cohesion." *American Anthropologist* 59: 1018–1035.
  1960   *Headhunter's Heritage: Social and Economic Change among the Mundurucú Indians*. Berkeley: University of California Press.
Myrdal, Gunnar (with the assistance of Richard Sterner and Arnold Rose)
  1944   *An American Dilemma: The Negro Problem and Modern Democracy*. New York: Harper.
Nader, Laura
  1965   "Choices in legal procedure: Shia Moslem and Mexican Zapotec." *American Anthropologist* 67: 394–399.
  (editor)
  1965   *The Ethnography of Law*. Supplement to *American Anthropologist* 67 (December).
  1969   "Styles of court procedure: to make the balance." Pages 69–91 in *Law in Culture and Society*, edited by Laura Nader. Chicago: Aldine.

Nader, Laura, and Elaine Combs-Schilling
    1976   "Restitution in cross-cultural perspective." Pages 27–44 in *Restitution in Criminal Justice*, edited by Joseph Hudson and Burt Galaway. Lexington: D.C. Heath.
Nader, Laura, and Harry F. Todd, Jr. (editors)
    1978   *The Disputing Process — Law in Ten Societies*. New York: Columbia University Press.
Nash, June
    1967   "Death as a way of life: the increasing resort to homicide in a Maya Indian community." *American Anthropologist* 69: 445–470.
Newman, Donald J.
    1956   "Pleading guilty for consideration: a study of bargain justice." *Journal of Criminal Law, Criminology and Police Science* 46: 780–790.
    1966   *Conviction: The Determination of Guilt or Innocence without Trial*. Boston: Little, Brown.
Oakes, James
    1982   *The Ruling Race: A History of American Slaveholders*. New York: Random House.
Oates, Caroline
    1989   "Metamorphosis and lycanthropy in Franche-Comté, 1521–1643." Pages 304–363 in *Zone 3: Fragments for a History of the Human Body*, Part 1, edited by Michel Feher (with Ramona Naddaff and Nadia Tazi). New York: Urzone.
Oberg, Kalervo
    1934   "Crime and punishment in Tlingit society." *American Anthropologist* 36: 145–156.
Obradović, Josip
    1972   "Distribution of participation in the process of decision making on problems related to the economic activity of the company." Pages 137–164 in *Participation and Self-Management*, Volume 2, edited by Eugen Pusić. Zagreb: Institute for Social Research, University of Zagreb.
O'Connell, Jeffrey
    1975   *Ending Insult to Injury: No-Fault Insurance for Products and Services*. Urbana: University of Illinois Press.
Otterbein, Keith F., and Charlotte Swanson Otterbein
    1965   "An eye for an eye, a tooth for a tooth: a cross-cultural study of feuding." *American Anthropologist* 67: 1470–1482.
Owens, Leslie Howard
    1976   *This Species of Property: Slave Life and Culture in the Old South*. New York: Oxford University Press.
Padgett, John F.
    1985   "The emergent organization of plea bargaining." *American Journal of Sociology* 90: 753–800.
Park, Robert E., and Ernest W. Burgess
    1921   *Introduction to the Science of Sociology*. Chicago: University of Chicago Press, 1969 (abridged edition).
Parnas, Raymond I.
    1967   "The police response to the domestic disturbance." *Wisconsin Law Review* 1967: 914–960.
Parsons, Talcott
    1951   *The Social System*. New York: Free Press.
    1958   "Definitions of health and illness in the light of American values and social structure." Pages 165–187 in *Patients, Physicians and Illness: Sourcebook in Behavioral Science and Medicine*, edited by E. Gartly Jaco. Glencoe: Free Press.

Patterson, Orlando
    1982   *Slavery and Social Death: A Comparative Study*. Cambridge: Harvard University Press.

Peristiany, J. G. (editor)
    1966   *Honour and Shame: The Values of Mediterranean Society*. Chicago: University of Chicago Press.

Perry, J. A. G.
    1977   "Law codes and brokerage in a Lesotho village." Pages 189–228 in *Social Anthropology and Law*, edited by Ian Hamnett. London: Academic Press.

Peters, Edward
    1985   *Torture*. New York: Basil Blackwell.

Peters, Emrys L.
    1967   "Some structural aspects of the feud among the camel-herding Bedouin of Cyrenaica." *Africa* 37: 261–282.
    1972   "Aspects of the control of moral ambiguities: a comparative analysis of two culturally disparate modes of social control." Pages 109–162 in *The Allocation of Responsibility*, edited by Max Gluckman. Manchester: Manchester University Press.
    1975   "Foreword." Pages ix–xxvii in *Cohesive Force: Feud in the Mediterranean and the Middle East*, by Jacob Black-Michaud. New York: St. Martin's Press.

Petersilia, Joan
    1983   *Racial Disparities in the Criminal Justice System*. Santa Monica: Rand Corporation.

Piaget, Jean (with the assistance of seven collaborators)
    1932   *The Moral Judgment of the Child*. New York: Free Press, 1965.

Pike, Luke Owen
    1873   *A History of Crime in England: Illustrating the Changes of the Laws in the Progress of Civilisation*. Volume 1: *From the Roman Invasion to the Accession of Henry VII*. London: Smith, Elder.
    1876   *A History of Crime in England: Illustrating the Changes of the Laws in the Progress of Civilisation*. Volume 2: *From the Accession of Henry VII to the Present Time*. London: Smith, Elder.

Piliavin, Irving M., Judith Rodin, and Jane Allyn Piliavin
    1969   "Good Samaritanism: an underground phenomenon?" *Journal of Personality and Social Psychology* 13: 289–299.

Pitt-Rivers, Julian
    1966   "Honour and social status." Pages 19–77 in *Honour and Shame: The Values of Mediterranean Society*, edited by J. G. Peristiany. Chicago: University of Chicago Press.

Pollock, Frederick, and Frederic William Maitland
    1898   *The History of English Law: Before the Time of Edward I*. Two volumes. Cambridge: Cambridge University Press, 1968 (second edition; first edition, 1895).

Posner, Richard A.
    1980   "A theory of primitive society with special reference to law." *Journal of Law and Economics* 23: 1–53.

Pospisil, Leopold
    1958   *Kapauku Papuans and Their Law*. Yale University Publications in Anthropology, Number 54. New Haven: Yale University Press.

Pound, Roscoe
    1921   *The Spirit of the Common Law*. Boston: Marshall Jones.
    1953   *The Lawyer from Antiquity to Modern Times: With Particular Reference to the Develop-*

ment of Bar Associations in the United States. St. Paul: West Publishing Company.

Price, Derek J. de Solla

    1963   *Little Science, Big Science*. New York: Columbia University Press.

Price, Richard

    1973   "Avenging spirits and the structure of Saramaka lineages." *Bydragen Tot de Taal-, Land-, en Volkenkunde* 129: 86–107.

Radcliffe-Brown, A. R.

    1935   "On the concept of function in social science." Pages 178–187 in *Structure and Function in Primitive Society: Essays and Addresses*. New York: Free Press, 1965.

    1952   "Taboo." Pages 133–152 in *Structure and Function in Primitive Society: Essays and Addresses*. New York: Free Press (originally presented as the Frazer Lecture in 1939).

Raper, Arthur F.

    1933   *The Tragedy of Lynching*. Chapel Hill: University of North Carolina Press.

Rattray, R. S.

    1927   *Religion and Art in Ashanti*. New York: AMS Press, 1979.

Reay, Marie

    1974   "Changing conventions of dispute settlement in the Minj area." Pages 198–239 in *Contention and Dispute: Aspects of Law and Social Control in Melanesia*, edited by A. L. Epstein. Canberra: Australian National University Press.

Rees, Alwyn D.

    1950   *Life in a Welsh Countryside: A Social Study of Llanfihangel yng Ngwynfa*. Cardiff: University of Wales Press.

Reid, John Phillip

    1970   *A Law of Blood: The Primitive Law of the Cherokee Nation*. New York: New York University Press.

    1980   *Law for the Elephant: Property and Social Behavior on the Overland Trail*. San Marino: Huntington Library.

Reiss, Albert J., Jr.

    1967   "Measurement of the nature and amount of crime." Pages 1–183 in *Studies in Crime and Law Enforcement in Major Metropolitan Areas*. Volume 1. A Report to the President's Commission on Law Enforcement and Administration of Justice. Washington, D.C.: U.S. Government Printing Office.

    1968   "Police brutality — answers to key questions." *Trans-action* 5: 10–19.

    1985   "The control of organizational life." Pages 294–308 in *Perspectives in Criminal Law: Essays in Honour of John Ll. J. Edwards*, edited by Anthony N. Doob and Edward L. Greenspan. Aurora: Canada Law Book.

Reuter, Peter

    1984   "Social control in illegal markets." Pages 29–58 in *Toward a General Theory of Social Control*, Volume 2: *Selected Problems*, edited by Donald Black. Orlando: Academic Press.

Riasanovsky, Valentin A.

    1938   *Customary Law of the Nomadic Tribes of Siberia*. Bloomington: Indiana University Press, 1965.

Richardson, William C.

    1969   "Poverty, illness, and the use of health services in the United States." *Hospitals* 43: 34–40.

Rickett, W. Allyn

    1971   "Voluntary surrender and confession in Chinese law: the problem of continuity." *Journal of Asian Studies* 30: 797–814.

Ridgeway, Cecilia L.
　　1976　"Affective interaction as a determinant of musical involvement." *Sociological Quarterly* 17: 414–428.

Rieder, Jonathan
　　1984　"The social organization of vengeance." Pages 131–162 in *Toward a General Theory of Social Control*, Volume 1: *Fundamentals*, edited by Donald Black. Orlando: Academic Press.
　　1985　*Canarsie: The Jews and Italians of Brooklyn against Liberalism.* Cambridge: Harvard University Press.

Roberts, Simon
　　1979　*Order and Dispute: An Introduction to Legal Anthropology.* New York: Penguin Books.

Roberts, W. Lewis
　　1922　"The unwritten law." *Kentucky Law Journal* 10: 45–52.

Robins, Cynthia
　　1988　"Suicide in cross-cultural perspective: a structuralist approach." Paper presented at a symposium entitled "Do Not Go Gentle: Cross-Cultural Perspectives on Homicide and Suicide," Department of Anthropology, University of Virginia, Charlottesville, Virginia, April, 1988.

Rohrl, Vivian J.
　　1984　"Compensation in cross-cultural perspective." Pages 191–210 in *Toward a General Theory of Social Control*, Volume 1: *Fundamentals*, edited by Donald Black. Orlando: Academic Press.

Romanucci-Ross, Lola
　　1986　*Conflict, Violence, and Morality in a Mexican Village.* Chicago: University of Chicago Press (second edition; first edition, 1973).

Rosaldo, Renato
　　1980　*Ilongot Headhunting, 1883–1974: A Study in Society and History.* Stanford: Stanford University Press.

Rosen, Lawrence
　　1984　*Bargaining for Reality: The Construction of Social Relations in a Muslim Community.* Chicago: University of Chicago Press.

Ross, Edward Alsworth
　　1901　*Social Control: A Survey of the Foundations of Order.* New York: Macmillan.

Ross, H. Laurence
　　1970　*Settled Out of Court: The Social Process of Insurance Claims Adjustments.* Chicago: Aldine.

Roth, Julius A.
　　1975　"The treatment of the sick." Pages 274–302 in *Poverty and Health: A Sociological Analysis*, edited by John Kosa and Irving Kenneth Zola. Cambridge: Harvard University Press (revised edition; first edition, 1969).

Rothenberger, John E.
　　1978　"The social dynamics of dispute settlement in a Sunni Muslim village in Lebanon." Pages 152–180 in *The Disputing Process — Law in Ten Societies*, edited by Laura Nader and Harry F. Todd, Jr. New York: Columbia University Press.

Rubinstein, Jonathan
　　1973　*City Police.* New York: Farrar, Straus & Giroux.

Rudé, George
　　1964　*The Crowd in History: A Study of Popular Disturbances in France and England, 1730–1848.* New York: John Wiley.

Ruffini, Julio L.
  1978   "Disputing over livestock in Sardinia." Pages 209–246 in *The Disputing Process —
          Law in Ten Societies*, edited by Laura Nader and Harry F. Todd, Jr. New York:
          Columbia University Press.

Sahlins, Marshall D.
  1958   *Social Stratification in Polynesia*. Seattle: University of Washington Press.
  1965   "On the sociology of primitive exchange." Pages 139–236 in *The Relevance of
          Models for Social Anthropology*, edited by Michael Banton. London: Tavistock.

Samaha, Joel
  1974   *Law and Order in Historical Perspective: The Case of Elizabethan Essex*. New York:
          Academic Press.

Sander, Frank E. A.
  1976   "Varieties of dispute processing." *Federal Rules Decisions* 70: 111–133.

Sanders, William B., and Howard C. Daudistel (editors)
  1976   *The Criminal Justice Process: A Reader*. New York: Praeger.

Saunders, Iwan B. (editor)
  1979   *The Future of Personal Injury Compensation*. Toronto: Butterworth.

Scheff, Thomas J.
  1966   *Being Mentally Ill: A Sociological Theory*. Chicago: Aldine Press.

Scheffler, Harold W.
  1964   "The social consequences of peace on Choiseul Island." *Ethnology* 3: 398–403.

Schneider, Jane
  1971   "Of vigilance and virgins: honor, shame and access to resources in Mediterra-
          nean societies." *Ethnology* 10: 1–24.

Schulman, Mark A.
  1979   *A Survey of Spousal Violence against Women in Kentucky*. Washington, D.C.: U.S.
          Department of Justice.

Schwartz, Richard D., and James C. Miller
  1964   "Legal evolution and societal complexity." *American Journal of Sociology* 70: 159–
          169.

Schwartz, Richard D., and Jerome H. Skolnick
  1962   "Two studies of legal stigma." *Social Problems* 10: 133–142.

Schwarz, Philip J.
  1988   *Twice Condemned: Slaves and the Criminal Courts of Virginia, 1705–1865*. Baton
          Rouge: Louisiana State University Press.

Scott, James C.
  1985   *Weapons of the Weak: Everyday Forms of Peasant Resistance*. New Haven: Yale
          University Press.

Scott, Robert A.
  1976   "Deviance, sanctions, and social integration in small-scale societies." *Social
          Forces* 54: 604–620.

Senechal de la Roche, Roberta
  1990   *The Sociogenesis of a Race Riot: Springfield, Illinois, in 1908*. Urbana: University of
          Illinois Press.
  1996   "Collective violence as social control." *Sociological Forum* 11: 97–128.

Service, Elman R.
  1971   *Primitive Social Organization: An Evolutionary Perspective*. New York: Random
          House (second edition; first edition, 1962).

Shapiro, Martin
    1975   "Courts." Pages 321–371 in *Handbook of Political Science*. Volume 5: *Governmental Institutions and Processes*, edited by Fred I. Greenstein and Nelson W. Polsby. Reading: Addison-Wesley.
    1980   *Courts: A Comparative and Political Analysis*. Chicago: University of Chicago Press.

Shils, Edward
    1957   "Daydreams and nightmares: reflections on the criticism of mass culture." *Sewanee Review* 65: 586–608.
    1960   "Mass society and its culture." *Daedalus* 89: 288–314.

Simmel, Georg
    1908a "Conflict." Pages 11–123 in *Conflict and The Web of Group-Affiliations*. New York: Free Press, 1955.
    1908b *The Sociology of Georg Simmel*, edited by Kurt H. Wolff. New York: Free Press, 1960.

Simmons, Ozzie G.
    1958   *Social Status and Public Health*. New York: Social Science Research Council, Pamphlet 13.

Skolnick, Jerome H.
    1966   *Justice without Trial: Law Enforcement in Democratic Society*. New York: John Wiley.
    1967   "Social control in the adversary system." *Journal of Conflict Resolution* 11: 52–70.

Smigel, Erwin O.
    1964   *The Wall Street Lawyer: Professional Organization Man?* Bloomington: Indiana University Press.

Smith, M. G.
    1974   *Corporations and Society*. London: Gerald Duckworth.

Snyder, Francis G.
    1981   *Capitalism and Legal Change: An African Transformation*. New York: Academic Press.

Solzhenitsyn, Aleksandr I.
    1973   *The Gulag Archipelago, 1918–1956: An Experiment in Literary Investigation*. Volumes 1–2. New York: Harper & Row.

Sorokin, Pitirim A.
    1937   *Social and Cultural Dynamics*. New York: American Book Company.

Spencer, Herbert
    1876   *The Principles of Sociology*. Volume 1. London: Williams & Norgate.

Spindel, Donna J.
    1989   *Crime and Society in North Carolina, 1663–1776*. Baton Rouge: Louisiana State University Press.

Spitzer, Steven
    1975   "Punishment and social organization: a study of Durkheim's theory of penal evolution." *Law and Society Review* 9: 613–635.

Spradley, James P.
    1970   *You Owe Yourself a Drunk: An Ethnography of Urban Nomads*. Boston: Little, Brown.

Stanko, Elizabeth Anne
    1982   "The impact of victim assessment on prosecutors' screening decisions: the case of the New York County District Attorney's Office." *Law and Society Review* 16: 225–239.

Stauder, Jack
1972 "Anarchy and ecology: political society among the Majangir." *Southwestern Journal of Anthropology* 28: 153–168.

Ste. Croix, G.E.M. de
1963 "Why were the early Christians persecuted?" *Past and Present* 26: 6–38.

Steele, Eric A.
1975 "Fraud, dispute, and the consumer: responding to consumer complaints." *University of Pennsylvania Law Review* 123: 1107–1186.

Stinchcombe, Arthur L.
1964 *Rebellion in a High School.* Chicago: Quadrangle Books, 1969.
1968 *Constructing Social Theories.* New York: Harcourt, Brace & World.

Stowe, Steven M.
1979 "The 'touchiness' of the gentleman planter: the sense of esteem and continuity in the ante-bellum South." *Psychohistory Review* 8: 6–15.

Strodtbeck, Fred L., Rita M. James, and Charles Hawkins
1957 "Social status in jury deliberations." *American Sociological Review* 22: 713–719.

Sumner, William Graham
1906 *Folkways: A Study of the Sociological Importance of Usages, Manners, Customs, Mores, and Morals.* New York: New American Library, 1960.

Sutherland, Edwin H., and Donald R. Cressey
1960 *Principles of Criminology.* Philadelphia: J. P. Lippincott (sixth edition; first edition, 1924).

Swanson, Guy E.
1971 "An organizational analysis of collectivities." *American Sociological Review* 36: 607–624.

Sweet, Louise E.
1965 "Camel raiding of North Arabian Bedouin: a mechanism of ecological adaptation." *American Anthropologist* 67: 1132–1150.

Sykes, Gresham M., and David Matza
1957 "Techniques of neutralization: a theory of delinquency." *American Sociological Review* 22: 664–670.

Tanner, R. E. S.
1966 "Cattle theft in Musoma, 1958–9." *Tanzania Notes and Records* 65: 31–42.

Tatai, Kichinosuke
1983 "Japan." Pages 12–45 in *Suicide in Asia and the Near East,* edited by Lee A. Headley. Berkeley: University of California Press.

Taylor, Michael
1982 *Community, Anarchy and Liberty.* Cambridge: Cambridge University Press.

Taylor, William B.
1979 *Drinking, Homicide and Rebellion in Colonial Mexican Villages.* Stanford: Stanford University Press.

Tentler, Thomas N.
1977 *Sin and Confession on the Eve of the Reformation.* Princeton: Princeton University Press.

Thoden van Velzen, H. U. E., and W. van Wetering
1960 "Residence, power groups and intra-societal aggression: an enquiry into the conditions leading to peacefulness within non-stratified societies." *International Archives of Ethnography* 49 (Part 2): 169–200.

Thoits, Peggy A.
1985 "Self-labeling processes in mental illness: the role of emotional deviance." *American Journal of Sociology* 91: 221–249.

Thomas, Keith
  1970 "The relevance of social anthropology to the historical study of English witchcraft." Pages 47–79 in *Witchcraft Confessions and Accusations*, edited by Mary Douglas. London: Tavistock.
  1971 *Religion and the Decline of Magic*. New York: Charles Scribner's Sons.
Thomas-Buckle, Suzann R., and Leonard G. Buckle
  1982 "Doing unto others: disputes and dispute processing in an urban American neighborhood." Pages 78–90 in *Neighborhood Justice: Assessment of an Emerging Idea*, edited by Roman Tomasic and Malcolm M. Feeley. New York: Longman.
Thompson, E. P.
  1975 "The crime of anonymity." Pages 255–344 in *Albion's Fatal Tree: Crime and Society in Eighteenth-Century England*, by Douglas Hay, Peter Linebaugh, John G. Rule, E. P. Thompson, and Cal Winslow. New York: Pantheon.
Thompson, Hunter S.
  1966 *Hell's Angels: A Strange and Terrible Saga*. New York: Random House.
Timerman, Jacobo
  1981 *Prisoner without a Name, Cell without a Number*. New York: Vintage Books, 1982.
Tocqueville, Alexis de
  1840 *Democracy in America*. Volume 2. Garden City: Anchor Books, 1969.
Torcia, Charles E.
  1979 *Wharton's Criminal Law*. Volume 2. Rochester: Lawyers Co-operative (fourteenth edition; first edition, 1846).
Toulmin, Stephen
  1982 "Equity and principles." *Osgoode Hall Law Journal* 20: 1–17.
Trubek, David M., Joel B. Grossman, William L. F. Felstiner, Herbert M. Kritzer, and Austin Sarat
  1983 Civil Litigation Research Project: Final Report. Part A. Madison: University of Wisconsin Law School.
Tucker, James
  1989 "Employee theft as social control." *Deviant Behavior* 10: 319–334.
  1993 "Everyday forms of employee resistance." *Sociological Forum* 8: 25–45.
Tumin, Melvin M.
  1952 *Caste in a Peasant Society: A Case Study in the Dynamics of Caste*. Princeton: Princeton University Press.
Turnbull, Colin M.
  1961 *The Forest People*. New York: Simon & Schuster.
  1965 *Wayward Servants: The Two Worlds of the African Pygmies*. Garden City: Natural History Press.
Turner, Victor W.
  1957 *Schism and Continuity in an African Society: A Study of Ndembu Village Life*. Manchester: Manchester University Press.
Turney-High, Harry Holbert
  1971 *Primitive War: Its Practice and Concepts*. Columbia: University of South Carolina Press (second edition; first edition, 1949).
Vago, Steven
  1981 *Law and Society*. Englewood Cliffs: Prentice-Hall.
van den Steenhoven, Geert
  1956 Research Report on "Caribou Eskimo Law." Ottawa: Canadian Department of Northern Affairs and National Resources.

1962   Leadership and Law among the Eskimos of the Keewatin District, Northwest Territories. Doctoral dissertation, Faculty of Law, University of Leiden.

van der Sprenkel, Sybille
1962   *Legal Institutions in Manchu China: A Sociological Analysis*. New York: Humanities Press.

Veith, Ilza
1965   *Hysteria: The History of a Disease*. Chicago: University of Chicago Press.

Vera Institute of Justice
1977   *Felony Arrests: Their Prosecution and Disposition in New York City's Courts*. New York: Vera Institute of Justice.

Wagatsuma, Hiroshi, and Arthur Rosett
1986   "The implications of apology: law and culture in Japan and the United States." *Law and Society Review* 20: 461–498.

Wallace, Samuel E.
1965   *Skid Row as a Way of Life*. Totowa: Bedminster Press.

Waller, Altina L.
1988   *Feud: Hatfields, McCoys, and Social Change in Appalachia, 1860–1900*. Chapel Hill: University of North Carolina Press.

Wanner, Craig
1974   "The public ordering of private relations. Part one: initiating civil cases in urban trial courts." *Law and Society Review* 8: 421–440.
1975   "The public ordering of private relations. Part two: winning civil court cases." *Law and Society Review* 9: 293–306.

Ward, Lester F.
1903   *Pure Sociology: A Treatise on the Origin and Spontaneous Development of Society*. New York: Macmillan.

Warner, W. Lloyd
1958   *A Black Civilization: A Social Study of an Australian Tribe*. New York: Harper (revised edition; first edition, 1937).

Weber, Max
1919   "Politics as a vocation." Pages 77–128 in *From Max Weber: Essays in Sociology*, edited by Hans Gerth and C. Wright Mills. New York: Oxford University Press, 1958.
1922   *The Theory of Social and Economic Organization*, edited by Talcott Parsons. New York: Free Press, 1964.
1925   *Max Weber on Law in Economy and Society*, edited by Max Rheinstein. Cambridge: Harvard University Press, 1954 (second edition; first edition, 1922).

Werthman, Carl
1969   "Delinquency and moral character." Pages 613–632 in *Delinquency, Crime, and Social Process*, edited by Donald R. Cressey and David A. Ward. New York: Harper & Row.

West, Candace, and Don H. Zimmerman
1977   "Women's place in everyday talk: reflections on parent–child interaction." *Social Problems* 24: 521–529.

Westermeyer, Joseph J.
1973   "Assassination in Laos: its psychosocial dimensions." *Archives of General Psychiatry* 28: 740–743.

Whiting, Beatrice Blyth
1950   *Paiute Sorcery*. New York: Viking Fund Publications in Anthropology, Number 15.

Whitrow, G. J. (editor)
    1967   *Einstein: The Man and His Achievement*. New York: Dover, 1973.
Wiedemann, Thomas
    1981   *Greek and Roman Slavery*. Baltimore: Johns Hopkins University Press.
Williams, Jack K.
    1980   *Dueling in the Old South: Vignettes of Social History*. College Station: Texas A&M University Press.
Williams, Linda S.
    1984   "The classic rape: when do victims report?" *Social Problems* 31: 459–467.
Willis, R. G.
    1970   "Instant millennium: the sociology of African witch-cleansing cults." Pages 129–139 in *Witchcraft Confessions and Accusations*, edited by Mary Douglas. London: Tavistock.
Wilson, Edward O.
    1971   *The Insect Societies*. Cambridge: Harvard University Press.
Winans, Edgar V., and Robert B. Edgerton
    1964   "Hehe magical justice." *American Anthropologist* 66: 745–764.
Winch, Peter
    1958   *The Idea of a Social Science and Its Relation to Philosophy*. London: Routledge & Kegan Paul.
Wiseman, Jacqueline P.
    1970   *Stations of the Lost: The Treatment of Skid Row Alcoholics*. Englewood Cliffs: Prentice-Hall.
Wispe, Laren G., and Harold B. Freshley
    1971   "Race, sex, and sympathetic helping behavior: the broken bag caper." *Journal of Personality and Social Psychology* 17: 59–65.
Wittfogel, Karl A.
    1957   *Oriental Despotism: A Comparative Study of Total Power*. New Haven: Yale University Press.
Witty, Cathie J.
    1980   *Mediation and Society: Conflict Management in Lebanon*. New York: Academic Press.
Wolfgang, Marvin E.
    1958   *Patterns in Criminal Homicide*. New York: Wiley, 1966.
Wolfgang, Marvin E., and Franco Ferracuti
    1966   *The Subculture of Violence: Towards an Integrated Theory in Criminology*. London: Tavistock, 1967.
Woodburn, James
    1979   "Minimal politics: the political organization of the Hadza of North Tanzania." Pages 244–266 in *Politics in Leadership: A Comparative Perspective*, edited by William A. Shack and Perry S. Cohen. Oxford: Clarendon Press.
Wyatt-Brown, Bertram
    1982   *Southern Honor: Ethics and Behavior in the Old South*. New York: Oxford University Press.
Yablonsky, Lewis
    1962   *The Violent Gang*. New York: Macmillan.
Yngvesson, Barbara
    1976   "Responses to grievance behavior: extended cases in a fishing community." *American Ethnologist* 3: 353–373.

Zimring, Franklin E.

    1971   *Perspectives on Deterrence*. Washington, D.C.: Center for Studies of Crime and Delinquency, National Institute of Mental Health.

Author Index

Complete references appear on the pages listed in italics. Endnotes are indicated by n.

Subject Index

Endnotes are indicated by n.

Intimacy, *see* Relational distance
Investigators, 99
Invisible colleges, 167
Irish, ancient, 19, 113; *see also* Celtic societies
Islamic law, 50, 143n.21
Italy, 44n.15

J

Jalé, 30, 49, 50, 53, 58, 75, 103, 115, 137
Japan, 21, 102–103, 110, 127
Jews, social control among, 94n.33
Jívaro Indians, 75
Judges, 5, 10, 13, 15, 17, 18, 42n.2, 51, 65, 66,
   67, 69, 85, 86, 87, 91, 92, 96, 97, 100, 110,
   112, 114–115, 118, 121, 123–124, 139,
   139–140, 141, 141n.3, 145, 146, 147, 156n.5
Juries, 38, 39, 44–45n.17, 67, 115, 124, 146,
   147, 148, 156n.7, 166

K

Kabyles, 17, 52, 92n.5
Kapauku, 101
Kenya, 38, 104, 130
Kidnapping, 151
Kirghiz, 30
Kpelle, 114
Kwakiutl Indians, 56

L

Labeling theory of crime, 24–25n.19, 164
Labor-management conflict, 6, 7, 34, 37, 51,
   57, 61
Landlord-tenant conflict, 7, 46n.24
Latin America, 103, 120, 151; *see also*
   individual countries and tribes
Law, 1–3, 4, 9, 10–11, 19, 21n.2, 21n.3, 21n.4,
   22n.6, 25n.20, 25n.21, 26n.27, 27, 31,
   36, 37, 45n.20, 52, 100, 115, 146, 148, 161,
   163–164
   and culture, 10–11, 146, 163
   and organizations, 10, 63–64n.19, 163–164
   and other social control, 11, 73n.8, 164
   quantity of, 9, 72n.7, 163
   and relational distance, 3, 10, 20, 67, 70,
      71, 72n.5, 146, 163
   and self-help, 38–39, 40–41, 44n.13,
      45n.20, 45n.21
   and social stratification, 2–3, 10, 20,
      25n.21, 67, 68–70, 71, 127, 143n.25,
      146, 163, 164

styles of, 163–164
Lawsuits and litigation, 1, 22n.8, 39, 51, 67,
   69, 83, 84, 84–85, 96, 97, 100, 102, 118,
   124, 127, 141, 143n.23
Lawyers, 1, 22n.8, 39, 51, 67, 69, 83, 84,
   84–85, 96, 97, 100, 102, 118, 124, 127,
   141, 143n.23
Lebanon, 15, 30
Lesotho, 100
Liability, 23n.12, 28, 49–51, 55–57
   collective, 28, 35–36, 44n.12, 56, 59, 60,
      85, 96, 106, 129
   and organization, 57, 58–60, 63n.15
   and relational distance, 56, 63n.14
   and social distance, 56–57
   and social stratification, 56, 63n.12
Liberia, 114
Libya, 48, 104; *see also* Bedouin
Litigation, *see* Lawsuits and litigation
Lozi, 114–115
Lugbara, 49, 53, 54
Lynching, 5, 38–39, 151–152, 153, 157n.12

M

Mafia, 75; *see also* Organized crime
Majangir, 130
Marginality theory of crime, 164
Markets, social control in, 80, 81, 82, 90, 91
Marriage, social control in, 3, 6, 12–13,
   21n.4, 29, 32, 39, 45n.19, 48, 54, 78, 85,
   92n.7, 104, 111, 130, 137, 138, 142n.13,
   153, 156n.4
Maya Indians, 28
Mbuti Pygmies, 8, 18, 26n.32, 30, 86, 109,
   156–157n.10
Mediation, 4, 6, 11, 16, 18, 22n.8, 26n.32, 48,
   74, 85, 86, 87, 89, 96, 112, 122, 123, 139
Mediators, 5, 10, 15, 17, 18, 26n.31, 67,
   85–86, 87, 96, 97, 110–112, 114, 135, 137,
   139, 141n.3, 145, 148
Medical malpractice, 11, 54
Medicine, 164–165, 167, 170
Mental hospitals, 22n.8, 42n.1, 121
Mental illness, 7, 10, 23–24n.17, 24–25n.19,
   25n.21, 48, 120, 164
Mesopotamia, 149
Metá, 45n.20
Mexico, 28, 35, 94n.29, 114, 143n.18, 145,
   146–147, 147, 148, 149
Migration, as social control, 79